Disregarded

Transforming the School and Workplace
through Deep Respect and Courage

Jack H. Bender

InnerWork Publications
Zeeland, Michigan

Copyright © 2007 by InnerWork Publications, 9182 Bluff Lake St., Zeeland, MI 49464. All rights reserved. No part of this publication may be reproduced, stored in a retrieval system, or transmitted, in any form or by any means, electronic, mechanical, photocopying, recording, or otherwise, without the prior written permission of the publisher. All rights reserved.

Permissions guidelines at www.Inner–Work.com.

Credits on pages 288-289

To contact InnerWork, visit www.Inner–Work.com or call 1-888-523-6337.

Discounts on bulk quantities of InnerWork books are available to organizations. For information, contact InnerWork Publications directly.

Acid-free paper is used throughout this work.

Bender, Jack H.
Disregarded: Transforming the School and Workplace through Deep Respect and Courage

ISBN: 978-0-9778272-7-5

Library of Congress Control Number: 2007926346

Suggested Dewey Decimal Classification:
658.314 5   General management
            Interpersonal relations
            With superiors, equals and subordinates

Contents

In Appreciation vi

Introduction xii

Chapter 1- The Journey Begins 1

Chapter 2- On Retreat 17

Chapter 3- Staying in Touch 34

Chapter 4- Winter, Death, Dormancy, Renewal 45

Chapter 5- Ambushed 58

Chapter 6- Spanning the Chasm 77

Chapter 7- Know Thyself 95

Chapter 8- From Scarcity to Abundance 110

Chapter 9- Chili, Served Hot 129

Chapter 10- Hanging by a Thread 151

Chapter 11- The Last Straw 169

Chapter 12- Minuteman 186

Chapter 13- Pendle Hill: Community 203

Chapter 14- But Seek the Welfare of the City 220

Chapter 15- Deep Respect and Courage 236

Chapter 16- Come Unity 248

Notes 264

Bibliography 275

About the Author 287

To the people of Pine County

and,

most especially, to my family.

In Appreciation

Special thanks go to Lisa Brownell Pierce. In the earliest stages, she was instrumental in helping me stay the course. Thanks also to Tom Nugent for his encouragement and Susan Harring for technical support.

I wish to acknowledge the large contribution that numerous authors have made toward my deeper understanding of inner work and organizations. Many of those authors are listed in the bibliography. The works of Chris Argyris, Peter Block, Arie De Geus, Barry Johnson, Elizabeth O'Connor, Barry Oshry, Parker J. Palmer, Susan Rosenholtz, Margaret Wheatley as well as Marvin Weisbord have been particularly valuable.

Adventurous readers of the first draft included Joe, Randy and Mary Lou Bender, Frank and Jenny Russell and Pat Cassell, now all eligible for the Purple Heart. Your support is deeply appreciated. I'm also grateful for the advice of the readers of later drafts: Rev. Michael Anton, Rev. Julie M. Cowie, Mel Hund, Doris Jarrell, Jim Metzger, Mickey Olivanti, Parker J. Palmer, Joy Ponce, Al Ridderbos, Marvin Weisbord, Tracy Whales, Mary Youngs and the folks at UAW Region 1D Headquarters. The care you demonstrated is an inspiration to me.

Those who have generously approved the inclusion of their words are: Sister Sue Tracy, Marianne Houston, Rick Serafini and Quakers June Etta Chanard, Donna Daniel, Kate W. Garland, Tom Jenik, Bobbi Kelly and Nancy Morgan. Bobbi Kelly graciously arranged the interviews at Pendle Hill. Karen Oshry of Power and Systems, Inc. not only read the draft on my experience of the business simulation described herein (created by husband Barry Oshry), but also arranged for my participation in it. Other important contributors have asked that their names be disguised in the text. It must say something about our institutions when telling the truth urges anonymity.

I owe much to Marvin Weisbord and Sandra Janoff of Future Search Network for great books, training, mentoring and support. As a colleague has remarked, "There is something about a future search…" Marvin's response to the draft has helped sustain my efforts. Ferne Kuhn, principal in the Kuhn Group, offered her wisdom and support as mentor and co-facilitator of the future search conference described in Chapter 11.

My gratitude for the work of the Fetzer Institute should be easily apparent, but I will formally say thank you here. Dave Sluyter and Mickey Olivanti are warm and dedicated people who are shining stars for the institute.

My deepest appreciation goes to Parker J. Palmer whose writing, retreat program framework and personal contact have greatly influenced my life. Always gracious and generous, Palmer has allowed great latitude to quote from his writings and describe his retreat work in detail.

Regardless of time elapsed since our last retreat or distance, I remain in community with my colleagues who were part of the pilot group for the Courage to Teach program: Maggie Adams, Mark Bond, Lauri Bowersox, Margaret Ells, Rich Fowler, Linda Hamel, Eli Hayward, Marianne Houston, Kathie Kennedy, Mike Perry, Linda Powell, Toni Rostami, Rick Serafini, Marcia Weller, Cherie McCloughan and Jerry Thompson.

While I have renamed characters and places in much of the book, I feel compelled to thank countless contemporaries who have given so much of themselves to their work and supported me as colleague and friend. Taken in its totality, this book is a tangible wish and prayer for their well being and success.

My wife, Cindy, has supported me throughout this project. She was most often first to see the text and, consequently, suffered the most. Her willingness to stand with me has been a vital part of the process. Our marriage and family remain the great joy in my life.

Names, Places and Chronology

The names of the school district, city and county have been changed as well as those working in the county. Some others have asked that their names be disguised. Very few events are out of chronological order, but are accurate in all other aspects.

Disregarded

Transforming the School and Workplace
through Deep Respect and Courage

Jack H. Bender

Introduction

The catalyst of the story is Michigan's Public Act 25, which gave my colleagues and I a significant voice in the workplace. Along with a few others, I signed on as a member of our school improvement team. In this role, my tenuous dance with power and peers began.

Later, two major influences pulled at me from opposite directions. When I joined the pilot of The Courage to Teach[1] retreat program, I sought my true identity while my colleagues and I formed a community of support. (Sharing this experience alone would be valuable to others.) However, it wasn't long after my new boss arrived that he assumed the role of Terminator. Our staff splintered, careers were in jeopardy, and I felt the pain of disconnection like never before. I was experiencing a breakup in one setting while becoming a part of a community in another. Those parallel, but opposite experiences created a voluminous gap. From that void came important questions, some of which were:

Why do groups split apart?
How can group members hold together?
How do we contribute to group cohesiveness or breakdowns?
Can personal growth and self-knowledge transform organizations?

I became a seeker. The end result of study and reflection was a greater sense of peace, a deeper understanding of myself and others, and an increased capacity for community.

I am confident that within these pages there is something of value for you. The simplicity of the settings is an excellent way for you to examine the complex subjects of human nature, personal growth, change and organizational development. You may delight in the not so logical behaviors of groups and group members. The description of the retreats may intrigue you. It's likely that the array of concepts herein will prove useful. You may become interested in the twists and turns of a person struggling to grow. If you relate to these tales, you might feel that you're not alone in your paradoxical experiences of organizational life.

While I hope you find the narrative compelling as a story, what is most important is grasping the larger picture. What I've learned about personal growth and community can have a positive impact on our journey to transform organizations into places worthy of their people's talent, creativity and commitment. Those places where people feel heard, respected and valued.

Although attempting to bring about world peace through the internal transformation of individuals is difficult, it is the only way.[1]

> H. H. the Dalai Lama

Chapter 1 – The Journey Begins

*It is we ourselves who must change
in order for the world to change.*

Larry stands sideways in the doorway, one foot in the room and the other in the hallway. If he enters, he'll not only have to share power with us, he will add one more responsibility to his overburdened schedule. If he heads down the hall, he'll take himself out of the ballgame and, perhaps, even destroy the bridge between us.

I'm torn, too. One part of me wants my boss to join our meeting, and the other hopes he'll leave, so we can get back to business. I look down and notice that I'm rapidly drumming my fingers on the desk.

Larry leans forward on the doorjamb and waits for an opening to speak.

We are in Sue Hardy's classroom, a circle of teachers at our first meeting of the newly mandated school improvement team for our building. I find myself wondering what brought people here. I know that when I heard the term "school improvement team" I felt energized. Decisions affecting the classroom are made too far from it. Perhaps they feel the same. Even after a long day, this is where I most want to be.

I'm also here because it's the law. Our Michigan State Legislature passed Public Act 25, which stipulates that each school must turn in an annual report, mandates that a core curriculum be established, and requires school accreditation in six areas. Sue is the chairperson of the team and she is describing our responsibilities. She refers to PA 25 as the "Quality Act" while she distributes a

Disregarded

summary around our circle. Scanning the document, I see that it contains a carrot and a stick. If we satisfy the new requirements, our district gets more money per pupil. Fail, and we will receive less than our existing entitlement. Hmm.

I focus on the mandate for the establishment of a building-level school improvement team—that's us—and the long list of our responsibilities. For me, the chance to participate outweighs the large amount of work ahead.

Larry makes an upward gesture with his head. "No sweat," he says, "I'll handle it. I'll write the annual report and sign your names. It'll be less work for you."

I bristle and lean forward. "No, we aren't going to do that." His suggestion is preposterous. It's not the forgery that bothers me; blocking my involvement is unacceptable.

Larry's face remains unchanged. "I'll write the report and sign your names. It'll be less work for you."

I see that he doesn't understand our right and need to be involved. "No, we aren't going to do that," I say again. "If our names have to go on the report, we must write the report."

Sue's tone is more diplomatic. "Larry, we must have a part in this. I'll be happy to stop by your office tomorrow morning and talk with you."

He makes one more attempt to sway us while Sue remains pleasant, but firm.

The oak floor sighs in relief as Larry chooses to leave. A school principal can't stand long in one place, there's too much to do. His furrowed brow shows that he's more confused than offended, not understanding where we're coming from.

Sylvia quickly slides out of a student desk and follows Larry down the hallway, her whole body telegraphing tension. In so doing she takes herself off the team, at least for today. Time and again I have watched people choose between loyalties to colleagues and power. I wonder, must it always be this way?

Those of us left in Room 207 exhale and shift our positions in the student desks. We look around the circle at one another as if to say, is our resolve strong enough for all this turbulence?

This new law is about a fresh beginning. It legalizes that we have a stake in our workplace and our resistance to Larry's suggestion is a claim of ownership for our work. Staking our claim felt as new and awkward as a child's first step.

In the past, superintendents have been all powerful and their principals have been messengers, stuck in the middle. With the new mandates that call for employee involvement, we could be entering an era of collaboration and shifting responsibility. As I think about that, I can see that Larry's and my ambivalence come from this new possibility. The rules that negate the old power arrangement cause us to feel unsure of where to begin. I can't help but ask myself, "Will this team backslide into business as usual or choose adventure?"

Sue summarizes what we've covered, bringing closure to the meeting. She suggests ways that we can prepare for our next one, and then we adjourn.

Footsteps echo off dreary plaster walls, large ceiling pipes and student lockers as we go our separate ways. I climb the steel-edged steps polished brilliant silver from decades of use. My steps send familiar, gritty whooshes up the stairwell. I've been making these same sounds since high school, for I teach in my hometown of Crawford.

As I walk back to my classroom, I try to simplify what we've read and discussed. I interpret the role of this committee as one of leadership and I feel a responsibility to be worthy of that task. I don't want to contribute from an ignorant perspective; students and teachers deserve better. I decide to read and learn as much as I can while two questions surface. What does excellent leadership look like? What makes organizations great?

I would not know for years that our first meeting was a subtle warning of the drama to come. I missed the signs. I failed to appreciate Larry's struggle with an archetypal dilemma of leaders—to work above or work with followers. I had no inkling that someone to follow him would not only seek to work above some of us, but to destroy us as well. To him PA 25 and our leadership would represent candles to be snuffed.

In that meeting were the classic dilemmas of followers—the struggle to find meaning, the decision to honor or surrender one's own power and the choice to split or hang with others.

All this I missed.

Disregarded

Encountering Deming

I act on Sue's advice and join the Association for Supervision and Curriculum Development. From them I receive *Schools of Quality: An Introduction to Total Quality Management in Education* by John Jay Bonstingl. Words and phrases like *synergy, total quality management, paradigm, Pareto Chart, assignable causes, secondary customer* and *kaizen* jump from the pages. Reading slowly, to capture every morsel, I realize that I'm in unfamiliar territory.

Bonstingl challenges the long-held belief that workers are interchangeable and replaceable cogs in a machine; also the notion that work is to be simple, thoughtless and repetitious.

> Unfortunately, most organizations—including businesses and schools all around the world—still function…with hierarchical, top-down authoritarian power structures based upon compliance, control, and command; little true empowerment of front-line workers to create, monitor, and control their own work processes; little real participation by workers in the governance of the organization; and more attention paid to end products than to the processes essential to increased productivity.[1]

We are currently operating with rules that no longer work.

The words "empowerment," "participation," "governance" and "process" look to me like key words of this new, collaborative era. Concentrating on quality processes will more likely result in quality products.

I use the bibliography to go deeper and read *The Deming Management Method* by Mary Walton. When I apply the text to my own situation, I see that Deming would view students and parents as customers, and the customer is king. Don't just satisfy customers, he urges, attempt to thrill them. Having worked with unpredictable eighth graders, I think this will be the ultimate challenge. I could tell Deming a thing or two about "wild variance" and "unfathomable causes."

Chapter 1

W. Edwards Deming says our current workplaces have been "degrading to the human spirit" and that workers are capable of self-direction. Deming exhibits great sympathy for the worker and unloads both barrels at management. He shocks leaders into new understandings. Workers are not in charge of the system in which they work, management is. It is the system, not worker skills and effort, that influences how an employee performs. It's management's responsibility to change the system.

Leaders are often surprised at the level of dedication and caring that emerges among workers when new management practices are put into effect. Asking the worker for suggestions pays off with a landslide of improvements, shattering manager beliefs about low worker potential.

Those at the top must be committed change agents. Deming will not work with a company that hasn't demonstrated support from the highest levels of the organization. He declines an invitation to work with a Detroit automaker until another invitation comes from the very top.

It now appears that our central administration and school improvement team are the change agents. I believe that our team's challenge will be to awaken the sleeping giant in our building—our staff. I see dedicated teaching and a level of commitment that makes me proud to be a part of this school. The teachers here take ownership of their work. What I don't see is the belief that workers should be involved with systemic issues. That idea is revolutionary.

I'm aware that three quarters of a century of top-down management can't be undone in a day. Workers have long been taught to be powerless. As one Ford employee and Deming advocate explains, "Part of a bureaucratic system...is shifting the blame. You're taught to be helpless in a bureaucratic system...You really don't realize or believe in your own power because you've been told so often it's not there. It's really hard in a bureaucracy. People that want to change feel there's so little they have control over directly."[2]

I certainly see this in my school. Teachers will have to develop some faith that their input will be welcome and valued. Too many teachers believe that they are powerless to change the system, but thinking you're powerless is nonsense. Our organizations are human-made and humans can change them. It is those who think themselves powerless who give the system its mechanical persona and entrenched characteristics. I'm more aware than ever that we are not separate from the system; we *are* the system.

Widening Our Circle

A few months have passed since we first met and the almost weekly meetings have resulted in a good bit of clarity for what we must do. Sue Hardy is consistent in her efforts to recruit other teachers, but only a half dozen of us are regulars. She circulates the minutes to every member of the staff and publishes future meeting dates. Before each meeting, Sue uses the PA to invite all staff to attend. From all this effort, no one joins us. Privately, I'm not too displeased. The way I see it, the smaller the group, the faster we can go. When we do add a new member, we must bring that person up to speed and this slows us down. But I begin to struggle with the spirit of inclusion embedded in PA 25. In our need to find our way, we have yet to welcome any parents. They probably don't know that Public Act 25 even exists and they've rarely been encouraged to become meaningfully active in school affairs. I know that including parents will slow us down, but I have a deepening sense that inclusion is not only a legal mandate, it's only fair. I decide to attend PTO meetings.

Approaching the PTO

The faces of parents register surprise as I walk into the library. I'll admit that I feel somewhat foreign in their midst. Some parents look curious while others show concern. They're used to PTO meetings where only parents and the principal are present. The presence of teachers is pretty rare. In defense of my colleagues, so much of life after the last bell rings is still devoted to work; we have to protect what little time remains.

I know about half of the people gathered. It's clear that many of these parents are capable of substantial work, but past practice has placed them at the fringes of the school. The way things are, significant contributions would be considered meddling. Consequently, meeting topics stay in the safe zone. "Can we come up with $35 for special materials in Mrs. Smith's classroom?" "On what game night should we host a bake sale?"

Linda Meyer is current PTO president. She moves through the agenda easily, encouraging participation. I know that she has a degree in early childhood education and has teaching experience. She has also given presentations on child development in the community. To her right is Lea Chay who makes respectful but challenging comments. I believe her veiled sarcasm reveals that she wants to do substantial work with this group. After a half hour on old business, we move to new business and Linda offers me a chance to speak. I give a brief overview of PA 25 and then ask if anyone would be interested in "doing more than baking cookies." It's as if the waters part. The energy shifts as smiles erupt, but the room is dead quiet. I guess that minds are searching for buried hopes and dreams.

"What does that look like?" Lea Chay breaks the silence. "What do you want to accomplish?" I catch her skeptical stare as I say that the school improvement team is in its infancy, but there are a lot of ideas being tossed around. I mention a mission statement, career day, a new logo and motto, painting the hallways, a new schedule and curriculum, team structure, better school/home communication and parent representation on the school improvement team.

I can feel the release of a bonding force. We're being seized by possibility. I'm delighted to find that these parents also seek meaningful involvement. I promise to return next month and, with that, Linda adjourns.

As I walk to the van, another question comes to mind. What positive results have come from parent involvement in schools? It isn't long before my search uncovers mixed findings. Coincidentally, I come across a book, *Beyond the Bake Sale*. Author Anne Henderson states that much of the research about parental involvement and influence is inconclusive. A complex array of forces promotes student success. I learn that single parents can do as credible a job of supporting their children's schooling as do married couples. The key factor is quality time, not the amount of time or number of parents.

Useful Concepts

I read Joel Barker's *Future Edge*. He suggests that the future holds the greatest leverage because we are not constrained by real time. Forward thinking is vital.

I begin to understand my initial uncertainty as a member of the school improvement team. In a new era, everybody goes back to zero. The game board and the rules are fuzzy at best. But as understanding develops over time, the game board becomes clearer, as does a growing list of successful moves. Rules for success in a given space are called a paradigm. We all live and work in a variety of these "fields," each one having its own rules for success. There are spaces and conventions for chefs, auto glass repairers, dentists and parents. Scientist Thomas Kuhn introduced the concept of paradigms. Before him, no one saw or gave importance to them. Kuhn relates the earnest words of one person upon grasping a new paradigm—"The scales have fallen from my eyes."[3]

Why do new paradigms appear? The rules of any paradigm don't work for all situations, so unsolvable problems collect over time. Eventually, some of the problems have to be solved in order to move ahead. When someone creates new rules that solve some of those problems, a paradigm "shift" occurs. Countless shifts have occurred throughout history, but now people have begun to consciously look for the boundaries that constrain them and purposefully work to create a shift.

It's usually outsiders, new employees or organizational mavericks, who innovate and break new ground. These types of workers are the most likely to be naïve or unwilling to accept "This is how we do it around here." I begin to realize that I'm a maverick. I've been at my school for eighteen years. I know how we do it around here and most of the time I don't agree. Adult talents are being wasted day in and day out, including mine.

I learn that, "The higher one's position, the greater the risk. The better you are at your paradigm ... the more you have to lose by changing paradigms."[4] Are my administrators change agents? Of course, they can be. But I see one plausible explanation of gridlock—managers have the responsibility to change the system, but they have the most to lose in doing so.

Laying a New Foundation

Painstakingly our school improvement team develops a framework for change. My boss finds a few projects of ours that either match his available time or transform the status quo the least. He agrees to involve students to create a motto. A school-wide student contest yields—"An Environment for Excellence." My daughter Jenny is the winner.

The process of coming up with a logo is subtler and not as democratic. A friend of mine would call it "seepage." It starts from a handmade poster in my classroom. On it is a triangle. Over the top angle is a circle with the word "Student" inside. At the base angles, one circle contains "Parent" and the other "Teacher." Each side of the triangle has arrowheads at both ends—everybody connected, everybody interacting. I believe this image represents the heart of public education and give a rough drawing of it to Maud Evans and forget about it. An office aide with a great artistic eye, Maud must have experimented with it over the next few weeks. I first see the result of her work on official school stationery. Three artful triangles sit atop the letterhead without accompanying text. Without a contest, or a vote, this symbol has become our new school logo. I'm baffled by the process but pleased with the result. Months later I ask Tonya Greenfield, our art teacher, if she knows what the triangles stand for. She answers, "Student, parent and teacher working together." I have no idea how she knows.

Opening Our Doors

Enlivened by the school improvement process, our PTO picks Career Day as a project. There hasn't been one in years. Parents meet the challenge of scheduling 800 students into four morning sessions of their choice. From the community, chefs to funeral directors share their work experience and, as they have been asked to do, stress the schooling, training and preparation needed to enter their field. The presenters match the energy of the parents, some running back and forth from the parking lot a number of times to bring in tools and materials of their trade. Parents are everywhere, helping students find their sessions and reconstructing lost schedules. More than a bake sale indeed.

A Strange Feeling

There's much to be excited about, as career day is another accomplishment for our team, but I find myself looking over my shoulder. Seemingly without cause, I'm anxious. I feel like everybody knows a secret except me. It's as if there's a dark cloud over the horizon, just out of view, the kind that ominously lumbers in and sneers at you with its green underbelly. The threatening cloud reeks of expectation and you know you are in for something different. Sometimes the massive fist passes over and pounds the next county, other times it sends you to the storm cellar. All I can do is wait and see what comes my way…

Painting Day

It's early Saturday morning and my brother, sister-in-law and I are at school before the others. Soon teachers, parents and students will arrive to help paint the hallways. On Friday night, the three of us finished organizing the painting project and placed work assignment posters in the halls. I couldn't ask for better help. These two can get more done in a day than anyone else I know. They've checked with the fire marshal and have soaked colorful cloth banners in a fire retardant solution. We will hang the banners in the stairwells.

As workers appear, a young teacher walks in and drops a well-worn equipment belt to the floor. I remark that she looks very prepared and she replies that she and her husband used to paint houses for a livelihood. Judy has already proven herself to be wise beyond her years through comments she has made at our school improvement meetings. I feel the bond between us strengthen from our shared commitment and working side-by-side on this big project.

The painting goes well. The halls that were untouched for years are now bright and fresh. We'll add broad, horizontal stripes of color to the walls next weekend.

The three of us return on Sunday to do touch up work and

finish a few areas that had been left undone. The bathrooms get a fresh coat as well.

On Monday, I find a note in my box. I must stop in the central office and see Ed Frisk, Director of Non-Instructional Services. He oversees bus transportation, food service, custodians and maintenance. I head for his office during my planning period. Frisk's message is simple—I've been bad. By painting the halls and bathrooms, I've taken potential work away from other school employees. I'm told the painting must stop.

I walk out dazed. First of all, I don't know the identities of my accusers. Whoever they are, their fears are irrational. I hate to paint. If I were sent to Hell, I would be given a paintbrush on arrival. Second, the school hadn't been painted within anyone's memory. Third, the support people have more work than they can accomplish. Did maintenance really complain? It's all rather suspicious. I phone a fellow painter and relay what's happened. He believes the real issue is that we're making waves. All I know is that the meeting with Ed spoiled the sense of accomplishment that had developed during the weekend.

What We Want

A number of us want to make the transition from a junior high school to a middle school. One of the main features yet to be implemented is a team configuration for teachers and students. Instead of using a computer program to randomly place students into the master schedule, two to four teachers are placed on a team and given a group of students for the entire year. The literature reports many benefits from this arrangement. Teachers and students get to know each other well and students are less likely to slip through the cracks. Subjects can be integrated and reinforced by the teacher teams. Students and teachers become more accountable to each other in this arrangement.

The end of the year is pressing on us and I know that we will soon reach a time when a new schedule can't be implemented.

I stop our new principal, Ken Davis, on my way to lunch and ask him if he has a moment. He says he does and I begin. "Ken, are you really in charge of this building or does someone else call the shots?" "Are we really empowered as a school improvement

Disregarded

team or are we just so much window dressing?" "If we come up with a team schedule, can we move to that structure?"

Ken surprises me with his answers. He believes he has a free hand and assures me that the school improvement team has his support. On the issue of teams, he says he'll check on the schedule with central office, just to be sure.

I get a response from Ken the very next day. As classes are passing, he finds me at my door. He's checked with Gordon Thompson, our superintendent, and Thompson will support our efforts on one condition—it can't cost a dollar.

Creating a Team Schedule

Pat Knopp and Marilyn Keen, both math teachers, meet with me after school in the library. Pat is about my age and Marilyn is a young teacher. We're going to design a schedule that places students with teams of teachers. In uncharted waters, we glance at each other in anticipation, trading quick glances of optimism and support.

I discover that we not only have to design a schedule, we have to learn *how* to do it. We lack a common language for the task, but move beyond that hurdle by defining terms such as blocks, teams, levels and strands. We hover over untamed sheets of paper full of erasures and comments scribbled in the margins. The banter zings. The new schedule is a snake under the rug. If we push down a lump, it pops up somewhere else. If we focus too strenuously on one element, we forget about a constraint elsewhere. We can't think parts, we have to think whole.

Marilyn's husband Tom comes to the door. He's been wondering where Marilyn is. It's dinnertime. When will we be done? We don't know. Marilyn suggests leftover pizza and looks back at the schedule. Tom looks for more from her, but sees she has tuned back in to our work.

I suggest that we use a large chalkboard on casters, so we can better see. We wheel it into place and redo our work. Pops and snaps ring out as chalk hits the board.

The three of us are in the zone, but I can see that Pat and Marilyn are on a higher plane. There's something about this thinking that's bread and butter to math teachers. I understand their

Chapter 1

cross talk and offer suggestions they haven't considered, but I sense that my most important role is keeper of the faith. I say in many different ways that the answer is in the room. Just one more move on the chessboard and we'll have it.

Now Pat's husband is at the door. He's been worried because it's past dinnertime. Can Pat leave now, he asks. Pat says no, she can't leave, and she's not sure when she will. He too is dismissed with little ceremony and little information about what's happening that keeps her here.

We change class loads, shuffle team sizes and move teacher's names like a fast game of checkers. All of a sudden, everyone freezes. Three pairs of eyes dart around the board that displays a maze of information.

Everything fits!

Well, almost everything.

Half of a teaching assignment is dangling in the chalky air. Where the names have fallen, it's Gene Whitmore, math teacher. We joke that if Gene is willing to teach 3 sections of Spanish, we've got ourselves a schedule. We note that we made better schedules earlier, but each took many additional staff. This is the leanest version by far. Pat copies our work onto paper and we agree that we've reached a stopping point.

As I leave, I feel good all over from the satisfaction of having done this work. We are making substantial progress. Never before has a detailed team schedule been created for this building.

Asking for Permission

Sue Hardy asks Ken to arrange a meeting for us with the central office folk and our own counselors. Over the next three days, we double check our work and rehearse the presentation. Pat and I suggest to Marilyn that she should be the main presenter. She demonstrated the deepest and fastest understanding of our schedule.

It's finally meeting time. As I wheel the chalkboard from the library toward Marilyn's room, I say a little prayer that the meeting will go well. Pat arrives. Marilyn looks at the schedule on the board and then at us. She pushes up her glasses with one finger, takes a big breath and chuckles. Marilyn is as wired as I am.

Disregarded

Administrators and counselors enter in single file, sullen. I finally discover why I've been looking over my shoulder. The green-bellied cloud slams into the region, flashing its menacing claws. What I thought would be a request for understanding and support appears to be like the closing argument to a rogue jury. These people have not only lived the old order, they *are* the old order. Machiavelli's observation comes to mind—that innovators make enemies of those who benefited from the old order.

Marilyn is skillful in both her presentation and at answering questions. I can't help but tune out some of the proceedings while trying to understand the atmosphere in the room. What's going on here?

As our guests file out we experience a small victory when Ed Frisk, our former principal, says in an appreciative and complimentary tone that this schedule never crossed his mind.

Next day, there's a note in my mailbox. Ken wants to see me. His door is open and he's free. I step in. He goes from leaning back in his chair to sitting forward, elbows on his desk. "Jack, Gordon said no. The new schedule would cost more than one dollar. That was the deal."

"Surely," I say, "they're willing to work with us on this. We can't make such a huge change without expecting the need for some resources, some support. This schedule is no Cadillac. It's bare bones. We had other schedules, but they required many more resources."

Ken is smiling and pleasant. "We're in a crunch. I wish we could move forward, but the answer is no."

Just like so many times before, I feel completely let down and betrayed by this antiquated system. Just a little support, a little teamwork and something good could come from all the hard work. Instead, efforts just get flushed down the toilet. Balance sheet annihilates mission. I hate the legalism, the absence of compassion and understanding and decision-making before discussion.

I'm supposed to feel guilty. I broke the rules. I restructured for more than a buck. It's my fault that the deal fell through.

I don't buy it. We've created an opportunity for the taking.

Chapter 1

We're supposed to be on the same team and support each other. There is no inkling of support here.

What bothers me the most, about nearly all of these situations, is the missing word—sorry. Not a polite "get them off my back" apology, but a heartfelt one. Sorry, the one word that would mean there is some little thread of a relationship that exists between us, is a word entirely missing in the language of this place.

I pull myself together a bit and realize that not all is lost. At least I experienced some synergy working with Pat and Marilyn. At least we came up with something good. Ironically, Jan Hill, a crusty science teacher, had pressed the administration for a block schedule a dozen years earlier. She befriended me during her push for a new schedule, but I didn't know why. Then, when the diagnosis of her cancer became public knowledge, I assumed that she had picked me to carry her torch forward. Who would have guessed it would have taken us a dozen years to come this close. But now it would have to wait.

My scheduling experience with Marilyn and Pat has a vague likeness to a story told by author Peter Senge about a computer design team at Data General. While comparing compliance and worker commitment, he writes, "A group of people truly committed to a common vision is an awesome force. They can accomplish the seemingly impossible...Several months behind schedule...three engineers...came into the office one evening and...accomplished two to three months work. No one could explain how. These are not the feats of compliance."[5]

I don't know how we came up with the schedule, only that it had its beginning in our hearts.

Reflections

As I look back on that time, I can more clearly see that the decision to immerse myself in books was a fortunate choice. I benefited greatly from the vast experience of others. I discovered that the world will share its secrets with the hungry as well as provide a new pair of eyes with which to see.

However, I would eventually learn that my private study

could not be a substitute for the learning available only through encounters with co-workers. I was so energized that I was a blur of action, leaving little room for listening. It would be a long time before I would learn that those around me weren't just part of the landscape, they were my teachers.

I was looking for a quick fix for the system, unaware that an arduous personal journey of my own was required. I was quick to change the world, but slow to realize that it was me who needed to change as well. I observed the behaviors of colleagues without understanding their systemic roots.

I felt the sting of the painting stoppage and schedule rejection collide with the fresh look in the halls, a successful career day and progress at building a conceptual framework. But I wasn't discouraged for long. The potential for improvement remained so great for us that my optimism and energy level were pushed to new highs. We were a people at odds, but I found energy in the setbacks. Opposition only raised my determination.

I did learn that customers want to be involved and that they can make a big contribution. Parents made career day and the hall painting possible. Through inclusion, creative energy and talent were unleashed. In addition, the scheduling experience taught me that innovation is possible.

Without knowing, I had already begun a journey of growing intensity that would eventually offer profound discoveries. At its beginning, there were no signs that I would be forced to fight a protracted struggle with power. There were no warnings that my heart would have to break open in order for me to see more clearly. Only by wintering through this time would I learn invaluable truths about our lives together that I am now compelled to share.

During this time, a host of questions tossed about. How could we better work together? What were the secret ingredients that could propel us forward? What had our small committee really changed? Was the status quo firmly in place?

I barely understood that the administration wanted fresh-baked cookies. No more.

Chapter 2 – On Retreat

To have a profound experience is to be changed forever.

In the quiet of our bedroom I reread the letter:
Dear Mr. Bender:
Thank you for your thoughtful application to participate in the Fetzer Institute's pilot program "The Courage to Teach."
We are pleased to offer you a place in this program.

I put the letter on top of my clothes and zip shut the suitcase. As I walk down the stairs, I become aware of the heavy feeling of exhaustion. Even a good week with junior high students and computers puts a strain on my batteries.

I kiss my wife Cindy goodbye and place my bags in the rear compartment of the van. As I drive south toward the retreat center, I can't imagine what this weekend with strangers will be like. The asphalt is hard as steel with remnants of snow and ice on the centerline. Snaking around the shoreline of Gull Lake, my thoughts oscillate with each crook in the road. I steer left and feel excited over the opportunity to meet with other teachers. I angle right and sense concern about the unknown.

A bizarre circumstance puts me here. Months earlier, I had been using the phone in the teacher's lounge. While waiting for the other party to answer, I noticed a piece of paper sticking out at a rebellious angle from the neatly stacked collection of journals and brochures. I pulled the paper from the stack and saw that it was an invitation to a retreat sponsored by The Fetzer Institute of Kalamazoo and lead by author, speaker and master teacher Parker J. Palmer. It said,

> During this renewal weekend, we will not focus on the new teaching techniques or on the structural reform of the school system. Instead, we will focus on renewing that which is within our immediate reach—the inner life of a teacher. In large-group, small group, and solitary settings, we will explore "the heart of the teacher," making use of stories from our own journeys, reflections on classroom practice, and insights from various wisdom traditions. No one will be forced to share; there will simply be an open invitation to speak honestly about our lives, and to listen to each other (and ourselves) with compassion rather than judgment.

I had read Palmer's *To Know As We Are Known* and was impressed with his wisdom. The retreat looked like a special opportunity to learn more, but the deadline for registration was that very day. On the spot I called the Fetzer Institute and said that I'd just discovered the application and would send it immediately. Little did I know that this one action would draw me into eight intense retreat experiences spanning two and a half years. The program would provide life-altering inner work *and* an experience of community.

On the Premises

On arrival at the W. K. Kellogg Biological Station, site of the retreat, I park and then head to the lobby carrying my overpacked bags. Inside, I pass tight groups of people engaged in conversation. Many seem to already know each other. A woman confidently approaches, smiles and introduces herself as Mickey Olivanti. She appears to be in charge of registration. Her demeanor is warm and her dark eyes sparkle with energy. I'm immediately put at ease.

With nametag, room key, and folder I proceed outside toward the living quarters. The long side of the redbrick building faces westward toward the shoreline and it's built in the style of older motels. From the wooden walkway in front of my room, I can see the frozen lake through the bare trees.

Chapter 2

When I open the door, I'm transported back forty years by the decor and the smells. Round ceiling lights, brown speckled floor tiles and the enclosed smell of age conjure up images of towels and swimsuits on clothes lines, inner tubes leaning against trees, as well as the smell of bluegills in the frying pan.

I check to see that I have my folder and head for the dining room. From the end of the cafeteria line I choose a large table with one empty seat remaining. My colleagues and I begin to relax and open up as we eat. We are from Southwestern Michigan—South Haven, Kalamazoo, Grand Ledge, Grand Rapids, Paw Paw, Richland, Crawford and Mattawan. All grade levels and curricula of public education are represented. We look both ways to see if we're being watched, then sheepishly whisper across the table, admitting we're curious as to why we might have been chosen for this program.

Opening Remarks

After supper, we bus our trays and move to a large, carpeted conference room with a solarium on the south wall. Chairs are arranged in a circle at the north end with an easel integrated into the circle. Olivanti welcomes us and introduces Dave Sluyter. She explains that Sluyter is the program director for the retreat. His moves are fluid and he has an engaging smile. In turn, Sluyter introduces retreat leader Parker J. Palmer.

Palmer appears humbled as Sluyter presents his impressive credentials—author, master teacher, award winner, designer and leader of this retreat.

Palmer creates a large presence in the room. He must sing bass in the choir. He uses his deep voice to express his excitement at this new beginning. "This fall, the Fetzer Institute of Kalamazoo will complete a retreat center for rest and renewal—a place where people can deepen their spirituality. This weekend is a pilot event associated with the center and that intent."

I'm surprised by his frankness. "Teachers aren't getting enough support. Our institutions are riddled with pain and we are disconnected from our colleagues, our students and our own souls. The last thing we would ever do for teachers would be to support their inner souls. We must renew the inner life, the heart, because the best teaching comes from the heart." I'm being confronted with real concerns and an unusual willingness to discuss them.

I can relate to the contention that most workers need renewal. Power arrangements in the workplace frustrate our integrity, our own desires, our pride, our identity and a chance to make a difference. We are drained of energy from organizational forces that oppose who we are. One can get progressively more tired in tiny increments, day after day, until one slips into malaise—unaware. I decide that Palmer's message isn't meant for me, but immediately become uneasy. *Am I in need of renewal, too?*

I also believe the claim that most workers are disconnected from each other. Places of work are sharply divided horizontally and vertically. In my case, departments rarely talk. The divisions outlined in our organizational charts defeat us, as do the misunderstandings between us. The isolation invites projecting and shifting blame to others.

I begin to think about the disconnection in my daily work routine. In my situation, contact with colleagues is very limited. I'm the only computer teacher and I'm with students exclusively, except for lunch and the five minutes between classes. Passing a teacher in the hall is a moment of respite, but it's usually surface talk—I'm fine, they're fine. End of encounter. The organization of the workplace minimizes an exchange of thoughts and feelings about what matters most.

At this moment I realize that I'm waffling between cynicism and hope. *Is this weekend* really *going to be an experience of substance?*

Opening Wide

Palmer's questions soon give me a clue.

"Where is your gladness?" "Where is your suffering?" We are to ponder this in solitude for the next half-hour.

These questions are offered in a matter-of-fact manner, but how bold they are! I can sense that I'm being pulled open by these opposites. To consider joy and suffering is to consider the full spectrum of my work experience. For me, gladness is knowing students well, teamwork and excellence; sadness is working in a harsh culture—the loneliness, distortions and sanctions.

Eventually, we are asked to form groups of three. We are to listen to each other without interruption or critique. In my small group I share what I claim as my gladness and my suffering. Earlier in my career, I had the privilege of knowing students well. As a band director, I would start them on an instrument in fifth grade and see them daily in junior high and high school. I not only knew my students well, in the end, I knew their families. We worked hard together, adding to the cultural life of the community and helping make family life richer. I share that I am now teaching computers and students rotate in and out of my room rapidly. The comparison between knowing students for years and working with them for seven weeks is disheartening. This is my suffering.

The others share. Their joys center on warm relationships with students, the inspiration that comes from watching students grow and the satisfaction from seeing beautiful work materialize.

Their sadness comes from anxiety of strained relationships. I hear pain in the voice of one who speaks of increasing burdens with no additional support. Another is troubled by what she calls the brushfire mentality of leaders. They speak of supervisors who don't seem to know what is needed to help students learn.

Back in the larger circle we are asked to share with the whole group the important moments in our small groups. Palmer makes it clear that this is not a "share or die' situation. I see that the triad activity could help us make the transition from our private joys and sufferings to a large group discussion of them.

It hits me that we've just met and we are about to discuss our suffering. Can we overcome our vulnerability and speak freely? In this defining moment I look toward my neighbor just as she turns toward me. Our eyes meet and I think she's wondering the same thing. Fortunately, the first to speak bravely shares her suffering. The next does the same. Their courageous lead sets the example for the rest of us.

As the dialogue progresses, I observe that some of the retreatants have already been doing "the work." That work entails seeking experiences that help one grow and clarify self and world. There's also attention to healing. People offer to the center of the circle the names of books, quotes and pieces of wisdom. Jerry

Disregarded

Thompson recommends *Centering* by M.C. Richards and Kathie Kennedy shares the benefits of Outward Bound. I offer that *The Power of Myth* by Joseph Campbell is a wise guide.

Within the first few hours of the Courage to Teach Program, a number of things are already clear to me: I see that the Fetzer Institute is about quality work, I feel a deep desire to know these teachers well, and sense that new ways to live are being shaped.

In the Quiet

Following the night session, I walk back to my room and read the material in my packet. I'm drawn in by Palmer's paper on social movements. *Why is a paper on social movements included?* It says that significant change occurs when individuals act authentically, refusing to live divided lives. An example of such personal integrity is that of Rosa Parks. To know what America stands for and yet to sit in the back of the bus is to live a lie. There came a time in Rosa Park's life when this inner conflict was no longer bearable. On a particular day, the pain in her feet and heart were greater than any pain law enforcement could inflict. The collective resolve of others that echoed her example changed the landscape forever. I begin to realize how one of Palmer's opening questions fit into this context—Where is your suffering?

By the time I finish reading, it's after midnight. In the morning I have to wake three colleagues who didn't bring alarm clocks, so I set my alarm and place it out of reach. I hope that sleep will come quickly, but thoughts whirl about and won't land. Something's been ignited inside.

Morning Session

It has snowed during the night. In pajamas and galoshes, I clomp along the deck and knock on the doors of colleagues. They respond cheerfully, giving me a decisive boost. I realize that we are already starting to share small ways of living together.

After breakfast, Palmer begins with a question, "Amongst all the pressures, how can I nurture my heart, my courage?"

As I would come to understand, bold, compelling questions help activate our "inner teacher." I'd realize that answers for our lives reside within us, if we only make time to move inward and patiently listen. As shy as it is wise, our inner teacher hides when it encounters the violence born from overactive lives.

We'll use "The Woodcarver," a poem from Thomas Merton's *The Way of Chuang Tzu*, as tinder for discussion. The poem comes from the Taoist tradition. Palmer smiles broadly and then says that using Christian texts can result in fistfights. I think about Gandhi's claim—everyone knows that Christianity is about peace except Christians.

Jerry volunteers to read "The Woodcarver" and then does so with great care. His inflections breathe life into the poem and the rich swaths of silence add meaning.

The Woodcarver
Khing, the master carver, made a bell stand
Of precious wood. When it was finished,
All who saw it were astounded. They said it must be
The work of spirits.
The Prince of Lu said to the master carver:
"What is your secret?"

Khing replied: "I am only a workman:
I have no secret. There is only this:
When I began to think about the work you commanded
I guarded my spirit, did not expend it
On trifles, that were not to the point.
I fasted in order to set
My heart at rest.
After three days fasting,
I had forgotten praise or criticism.
After seven days
I had forgotten my body
With all its limbs.

"By this time all thought of your Highness
And of the court had faded away.
All that might distract me from the work
Had vanished.
I was collected in the single thought

Disregarded

Of the bell stand.
"Then I went to the forest
To see the trees in their own natural state.
When the right tree appeared before my eyes,
The bell stand also appeared in it, clearly, beyond doubt.
All I had to do was to put forth my hand
And begin.

"If I had not met this particular tree
There would have been
No bell stand at all.

"What happened?
My own collected thought
Encountered the hidden potential in the wood;
From this live encounter came the work
Which you ascribe to the spirits."[1]

    The woodcarver is *commanded* to create a work for the prince. We guess that the prince is not an easy fellow to work for; displeasing him can result in death. We surmise that the woodcarver knows that fear will distract him from his best work, so he chooses to transform the command into an *opportunity* to create. Fear, praise and blame are a wolf pack hungry for one's true identity. When the woodcarver casts off these shackles by preparing himself, his true nature creates a work of art. To create a work of art, there must first be "work behind the work."

Timeless Theme
    I think of Robert Pirsig's account of having his motorcycle repaired by current-day mechanics. In *Zen and the Art of Motorcycle Maintenance,* he describes worker attitudes vastly different from the woodcarver's.
    Pirsig enters a motorcycle repair shop and hears the radio blaring. Mechanics are clowning around "...trying not to have any thoughts about their work *on* the job."[2] Of course, Khing, the master carver, sets about to remove all distractions in order to work masterfully. He knows he must work twice. His first piece

of work is himself. Momentous work occurs even before Khing grips a tool and begins to carve.

The mechanics project the belief that they are separated from the motorcycle. "Here is the machine, isolated in time and space...It has no relationship to you, you have no relationship to it."³ Khing prepares for more than cutting and chiseling, he becomes receptive to a "live encounter." Khing knows the world reveals itself to those who are open. The tree actively reveals its potential to the woodcarver who is awake, approachable. *Together* the woodcarver and the tree create an inspiring work.

I think of other parallels between Khing and Pirsig, but begin to compare the woodcarver's life with my own. I realize that I am often overcome by distractions. Information overload and unrelenting change in technology cloud what's important in my teaching. Meaningless expectations strangle the seeds of my best work. Many above me assume they know best. I am told to do things a certain way and, try as I might, I cannot make sense of it. What is asked of me most often is thoughtless obedience. The saddest part of all is that I find it difficult to ward off these forces—I'm no woodcarver.

Yet, I know that my best work comes from my heart. My high ideals, my strong work ethic, my experience, my own passions, and my sense of who I am deeply influence my work. Khing knows who he is. Forgetting his limbs isn't really about forgetting himself. It's about being so centered that one isn't distorted or shackled by fear. My students and I can learn from Khing's example. To learn is to change and change can be frightening. I must demonstrate risk taking so my students are encouraged to do likewise.

Palmer looks around our circle and reminds us that we are not seeking one correct interpretation of the poem. Underlying each person's comment is each person's worldview. We are sharing how the world looks to us—our interpretations, our projections. He includes everyone. "Let's make sure we create a space for those who would like to share and haven't done so," he says. Our various temperaments are being accommodated. As the dialog continues, I realize I've let down my guard. No one here wants to score more points than someone else. No one has to win. On this cold and overcast Saturday, the warmth of acceptance seeps inward as I hear our perspectives being honored and protected in this most unusual atmosphere.

Walking to lunch, I think about our morning session. I'm struck by its pace. Time was redefined—it stood still. I was drawn into a timeless place by the large questions about life and vocation. Absent was the pressure to produce or cover the material, yet serious work had been done.

Ways of Transformation

Palmer begins the afternoon session with a smile and says that the woodcarver's intentionality contrasts sharply with his own method, which he calls "contemplation by catastrophe." We are often propelled into examining our lives, he explains, only when we find ourselves in the middle of some emergency. We can live our lives differently. We can consciously decide to live intentionally day after day.

The woodcarver displayed four transformations available to us as well. Palmer stands and points to a chart that displays five words:

1. *Motives.* These are the sources of our thoughts and behaviors. Doing something out of generosity is different from doing the same thing for the spotlight.

2. *Gifts.* What inborn talents do I possess that can be brought to my work?

3. *"The Other."* The tree was "the other" for the woodcarver. We constantly dance with others (be it a person, tool or idea) and we can choose to transform how we see and how we are with "the other."

4. *Results.* If ends consume us, the journey will be strained and distorted. If we only concentrate on the process, results may never materialize. The balance of process and results is important.

I survey each of the four transformations and then explore

them in more detail. *What about my motives?* Are my intentions based on commands from others or are they from my own choices? Commands are related to someone else's work and can foster resentment. Can I work without resentment by shaping directives into invitations? Turning a command into a choice fundamentally alters the experience of the work. When my heart reframes the task, the work becomes *my* work.

What about my gifts? Part of the spiritual journey is about reclaiming our talents and celebrating them, else we forget them, rendering them useless. Palmer reminds us of an all-too-familiar life cycle, "Is our life all about forgetting who we are and then at mid-life we must begin a process to reclaim who we used to be?" As I sit here surrounded by probing questions, I can't help but dive deeply. What is unique in me that the world needs? What part of me has been forgotten? I spend so much time willing things into being that I have not taken inventory of my gifts. My general philosophy is that failure is not an option. Perseverance will produce results—talent or not.

Much of our pain comes from being disconnected from ourselves. The pain is a message that shouldn't be ignored, one that says our true self and the life we are living are at odds. When we take time and study our lives, reconnection becomes possible.

I continue down the chart. What about "the other?" What about my relationships? The answer that bobs to the surface stings. Especially in work discussions, I am too puffed up to give much credence to the comments of others. I can cite the research while my colleagues say "In my opinion…." I've done my homework fastidiously. My ideas are over-ripe for implementation.

Palmer's voice interrupts my thoughts. "Non-living and living things have a nature of their own, an integrity. My life is to be a dance with 'the other.' What kind of relationship do I have with people, things, ideas, words and nature? What do I take from and bring to these relationships? Which relationships need work? Which need celebrating?"

Of course, I think to myself, most of my relationships are not combative. Great relationships with family and friends abound. I realize that it's the rapid-fire work environment that brings out the worst in me and also, it seems, in my colleagues. Something's wrong with the container. I've often thought that if some of my sparring partners at work were my neighbors, we'd get along just fine. Maybe we emphasize results so much that we've forgotten how to listen.

Choosing Growth

Palmer invites us to engage deeply. "Which one of these transformations do you want to reclaim and celebrate? Ask yourself: Which one of these transformations is needed in my life?" We take a break and then find quiet places to consider choosing a transformation.

I move to the solarium portion of the room. The large swath of filtered light helps combat the press of dull clouds. In the silence, I walk through each transformation again. Motives and gifts remain viable options. I bog down when I consider "the dance with 'the other.'" That's a tough one. To me, transforming relationships with "the other" would mean I would have to listen better and honor my colleague's opinions. I'd have to make room for them in my world.

Again, I recall that we get along well in social settings within the building. It's in committee meetings and staff meetings that things get tense. What factors are present or absent in social settings compared to task-oriented ones? What makes working together so difficult? I feel resistance swell. This transformation is either too close to home, something I don't want to own up to, or it looks impossible right now.

I consider "Results" without difficulty and realize it's decision time. I felt the largest surge of energy while considering "Gifts," so I commit to intentionally identifying and using them over the ensuing months.

Personal Metaphor

It's mid-afternoon and we move to the former W.K. Kellogg mansion, meeting in the living room. It looks like its splendor has been muted by years of heavy use. The carpet is worn and so are the arms of my chair. Everything is beige except for the people gathered here.

Chapter 2

We're asked to write a case study. Each of us is to think back in time and record a description of a moment when we felt authentic, a time when our gifts were present. We are to frame a metaphor for ourselves as well. What is our identity at work?

We're given a half-hour to think about and write our case study as well as discover a metaphor. We scatter about, some choosing to find places beyond the mansion, but I take a deep breath and release it. I'll stay put. Sinking fully into my chair, I close my eyes and invite anything to bubble up from the last two decades.

After the allotted time, we reconvene and Palmer asks that we form groups of three and then share our work. I look about the room and spot two teachers with whom I've yet to talk. Our eyes meet, we nod in confirmation and break into wide smiles.

The three of us go upstairs to a large room with a fireplace and windows that face the lake. This room is more to human scale than the living room and I imagine it in its prime with a hearty fire, perhaps a billiards table, and small groups of people talking and laughing.

Marianne characterizes herself as a lark when she is at her best. She describes flitting around the classroom like a bird, taking her smile and encouragement to every student in the room. She is joyous and full of energy. Her mood is contagious.

Rick soars at his best moments. He is a kite. He feels the sun and breeze on his face. He feels joy as he brings joy. At his best he is meeting his highest aspirations. He has broken the restraints of gravity and is flying as high as his expectations.

In this intimate sharing of identity comes a strong sense that these metaphors perfectly match their owners. The styles of these two are decidedly different, but I imagine that both teachers are effective. I can imagine how supportive Rick is in the classroom. His quiet, sensitive persona must be a source of reassurance for his students. Who Rick *is* is the key to his success. I can picture Marianne unleashing her student's energies by example. Those timid and shy are caught up in her energy—blossoming, willing to take flight. Who Marianne *is* is the key to her success.

Good work is more than using tools and techniques—it's

identity. I'm becoming more sensitive to the importance of discovering one's true self and using that identity in one's work.

On my best days I confirm students' gifts, help them see their goodness and their capabilities. My main message is "You're wonderful." I nurture motivation from within and encourage risk taking. "You can do it." My best days are when students transcend the too-small boundaries of who they think they are.

But my metaphor contrasts with the others. I feel it catch in my throat as I speak.

"I'm a rubber stamp."

I am struck by the mechanical nature of my metaphor compared to Rick's and Marianne's. While my rubber stamp has positive imprints for students such as, "You're creative," "You stay with it," "You give attention to details," "You work well with others," I am bothered by it. In this moment my metaphor becomes my teacher. A rubber stamp is stiff and hard. It's a non-living thing. Am I stiff and hard? Am I distorting my students with praise?

Had the space been unsafe, I would have become evasive and withdrawn and never shared. But with Rick and Marianne, it was safe to risk disclosure. But now I'm caught up in the unnerving contrast of my metaphor with theirs. Am I who I say I am? Am I happy with that?

Near the end of our night session I realize I'm out of gas. The well's gone dry. Back in my room, I choose a soothing CD to listen to. Even if my inner teacher doesn't need a break—I do. Parts of my experience are beyond words. The rest produces a mass of ideas that spin around in my head searching for a solid resting place.

Claiming What We've Learned

Sunday morning's schedule is full. Midway, we write letters to ourselves that help us capture our experiences and are told they will eventually be mailed back to us. A closing circle will allow each one of us to state what we want to celebrate and take with us. Palmer offers a reminder. In order to care for others, we need to take care of ourselves and, in order to do that, we need to be "counterculture." An invitation to go against the grain? Hmm. Society sees self-care as self-absorbing, selfish, so we're discouraged from doing it. We can overcome this cultural pressure by realizing that we engage in this work in order to serve others.

What do I celebrate?

What do I take with me?

As I write, I reflect on all that has happened this weekend. I acknowledge the large impact the retreat has had on me and that I'm still processing big questions.

I see that the culture established at this retreat is life giving. It is helping me discover a voice and a capacity to listen for extended periods of time. I am beginning to see how beautiful another person's soul can be if that soul is given an opportunity to appear.

While the work in triads is an end in itself, I know that it is also the means toward corporate dialog. Small groups are safe places for our shy souls to appear. Having found no enemy in the small group, the soul is more willing to risk speaking in the space of the larger group. I want to include this new understanding in my own teaching.

I remember Palmer's comment that speaking can invite a variety of problems such as intellectualization, monopolizing group time, and debate. But if each of us speaks simple statements into the center of the circle, something amazing happens. There, a corporate truth will slowly emerge. Often, no response to a comment is best. No one has to be set straight by another. As the truth of the community emerges, all can use it. Each person can compare his personal truth with the corporate truth that is taking shape. We can see for ourselves how close or far away our opinion lies from that of the group. We come away with validation or a challenge to rethink our views and those of others.

During this weekend I engaged fully because of the choices I was given. It is clear that group work, at its best, can be deeply meaningful for each individual if the leader is comfortable with complexity. Palmer did not establish a predetermined outcome, hence, he honored the sovereignty of each individual here.

I come away from this retreat knowing that I want to insure that my students have many opportunities to pick from, ones that are meaningful to them.

In this kind of work a leader must have faith in the process and find peace with results that vary in degree and kind. Students are the source of information as much as the teacher is. With less control, there must be more faith. Palmer's confidence tells me that he knows this process works and I now know it too.

Although the goal is individual growth, I now see that participants need the help of others. The non-judgmental listening not only offers the healing acceptance of others, it bolsters self-acceptance as well. It is through community that individuals are growing. Here, in order to do individual work, the goal must also be formation of community.

I'm discovering new ways of being with others. It is clear that the management of time is one key ingredient. Here, time is provided for real work to be done. Back home, competition seems to be the natural outcome from discussing issues in a short time period—a human response to a systemic issue.

I'm struck by the contrast between dialog here and discussions back at work. There are few rules at school that help honor a person's words. Here, all of us have been respected. Simple rules created a healthy container. I would never have thought that a few guidelines could make such a big difference in how people can work together—but they do.

The power of speech comes from its trajectory. What a revelation! I'm surprised that *where* we speak matters as much as *what* we say. At work, we aim at a specific target and fire our salvo across the room. I remember when Lamar Bates called me at home after a building staff meeting. What had I thought of the staff meeting? Had he been victimized? In his words, "I felt like a target had been painted on the back of my head." Here, we speak to the center of the circle. I wonder if the practices in this retreat are medicine for Lamar's and my workplace. I sense deep down that they are.

In the last half-hour, Sluyter and Olivanti ask for our advice about continuing. This weekend could be the start of a series of retreats for teachers. Our response to this retreat will sway the decision to host others or not. Eli Hayward speaks instantly, "Fetzer has created a monster that must be fed! Having now exposed us to so many benefits and possibilities, Fetzer can't stop now!" It's clear that Eli feels as I do. Colleagues flood the room with accolades. It's been an amazing weekend.

From the Depths
    I head home with a sense of elation. But as I drive, an irritating feeling slowly emerges. Why am I so uneasy? What's going on deep inside?
    I pull into the driveway and make fresh tracks on the wet snow from the morning. I enter the kitchen and hug my wife, but I'm terribly short with her. All I can muster is, "I'll tell you all about the weekend later."
    I have to be alone.
    I grab a shovel from the garage and begin clearing snow off the top of the drive. It's deep and heavy and I attack it with a vengeance.
    At the bottom of the driveway it happens. I stand up straight and stare down the street to see what's coming. But nothing moves there. Suddenly, I begin to cry. My suffering has surfaced. I'm grieving a loss I experienced ten years earlier. I'm opening a bag of tears that I have unknowingly been carrying.
    Due to extensive layoffs in our district ten years ago, I had tried for three years to single-handedly do the job of two band directors. With 350 band students in six buildings I had poured myself out until there was nothing left. Exhausted, I had left the field I loved.
    I had been in music since the fourth grade—twenty-two years full of individual challenges, glorious teamwork and high emotion. Band directing had been an energizing career, one full of heart. While the transfer to computer science was good in some ways, it was still a forced move. I had changed identities on other than my own terms. I mourned.
    Palmer is right. I am disconnected from myself.
    A chilling blast brings me back to the mound at my feet.
    Finally, the retreat is over.

Chapter 3 – Staying in Touch

Tell me thy company, and I'll tell thee what thou art.[1]
                                         Miguel de Cervantes

In July, five of us from the first retreat meet at the Kalamazoo Airport. The Fetzer Institute is paying our way to attend a conference in Vermont on the Spirituality of Education. From the response following the first retreat, Fetzer has decided to offer the balance of a two-year quarterly cycle of retreats. Our next one with Parker Palmer is slated for January and the Seasons Retreat Center will be completed by then. Going to Goddard College will help us stay connected with Palmer, who will be a facilitator at the conference.

Journey to the East
We fly over Lake Champlain and land in Burlington, then proceed southeast by rental van on Interstate 89. Vermont displays her best side for us. The interstate follows river-cut valleys, their sides crowded with maple, pine, birch, oak and willow. I often look at trees backwards, thinking that the crimson and gold colors of fall surge upward into the leaves. It takes the whack of the first cool morning to remember that the glorious hues are there all along. I am backward on the robins as well. I picture the north as their home and think that they head south in winter. But the reverse is true. Somewhere south is home, with its abundance of fruits and insects. Robins in my yard are tourists.

The dome of the state capitol building in Montpelier has more trees as its backdrop than any other capitol I've seen. The town is nestled among hills and looks smaller than my hometown of Crawford, but with a population of 9,000 it is actually 2,500 souls larger. I get the impression that these Vermont people love their trees and choose to live under their branches instead of felling them to farm or ranch.

Bonding While Traveling
Kathie Kennedy is in the right front seat and uses the AAA TripTik I ordered. She keeps us informed of our progress and matter-of-factly shares with me that life has much to do with repeated acts of letting go. Kathie is a language arts teacher from Mattawan High School and I guess from her straightforward manner that she holds students to high standards. If my guess is true, I know that position to be a lonely place. Too many with whom she comes in contact consistently urge her to make their lives safe and easy.

I'm driving. Kathie tells me to turn onto Highway 2 and that Plainfield and Goddard College are just a short distance away now. Goddard is a farm turned college. Some small miracles have taken place here such as the transformation of the horse barn into the food commons. Its flavor is more farm than school and, if that was the plan, it seems to me it was a good one.

We are able to catch the evening meal, but miss a candlelit ceremony before it—a Jewish blessing and breaking of bread. We enter the food commons just as the people that are gathered around the candles and bread move apart. I estimate we are fifty in number. The casual dress, aged beams of the barn and aromas put me at ease. We're told that attendees are from across the U.S. and Canada and even from Europe. The five of us sink into our chairs and toast the success of a safe journey by air and land. I feel a deep sense of gratitude for having arrived safley and for having great traveling companions.

After dinner we Michiganders move to a two-story wooden dorm and chat, before turning in for the night. Again, I'm the one with the alarm clock. Cheri McCloughan is in room 211 and asks to be awakened around 6:15 am. Cheri is from South Haven on the Lake Michigan shoreline and teaches high school language arts. She seems to be what I call a "free spirit." Her gestures are large and her posture is loose and relaxed. Her smile and presence are some sort of medicine for me. She talks about the men's movement and its literature. Robert Bly's *Iron John* would be a good read. Am I supposed to know about this? I chuckle to myself over the irony of a woman introducing me to the men's movement. Each retreat reveals an unfamiliar world to me—the structure of social movements, personal transformation, self-knowledge, living intentionally. *I* need an alarm clock.

John Bates is from Noble. He'd like to be awakened at 6:30. He tells me that I pass his house on the way to the Fetzer Institute. He says that the staff at his school has been meeting with a psychologist to heal wounds brought on by a principal who incited divisions among them, then left. They're asking themselves how to put things to rest. Over the din of the food commons I think I hear a snippet of a health issue that has shaped his life philosophy.

Rick Serafini speaks smoothly and quietly, each word selected so as not to offend. I can imagine how respectful and gentle he is with his young students at Parchment Central Elementary. He says his district borders Kalamazoo Public Schools to the north. Rick showed a keen interest in Vermont's greenery as we drove toward Goddard and enthusiastically described plantings in his own yard.

In the morning I wake the others. At breakfast we re-introduce ourselves to Parker Palmer, for surely he has met hundreds of people since seeing us six months ago. Now having read his book, *The Active Life,* I know that he travels for two straight weeks each month and then returns home to Madison, Wisconsin. Retreats, lectures and conferences with public schools, colleges, seminaries and corporations make up the bulk of his time away from Madison. Writing is the counterweight to his travels. His life and his schedule reflect an intentional balance between action and contemplation.

The Conference Begins
Palmer makes the opening remarks. "The message of all the great religious traditions is the same—Be not afraid." Afraid? It's

the last word I expected to hear and I'm too dumbfounded to form a response. Just like at the first retreat, Palmer implies that we are to take our task and ourselves seriously. We will not avoid serious issues as we so often do in our daily living. He adds, "Fear is the force that challenges and makes necessary our spirituality."

We read and discuss Mary Oliver's poem "The Summer Day." It is written in the voice of a child. I picture Mary Oliver as the speaker in the poem. Maybe she is about ten years old and has the wonderful unguardedness of children her age. She's standing in the middle of a field rich with grasses and insects, as open to her surroundings as to the questions she poses. What is she to do with her life? Oliver moves beyond fear to ask those big questions and displays a willingness to consider whatever might come. She displays a willingness to meet the world—palms skyward, looking, asking, reverent.

Oliver holds a grasshopper in her hand that is taking in its surroundings. With great care and skill, Palmer guides our discussion of the poem and we join Oliver in opening ourselves to the subject at hand—our ways of knowing and learning.

Through the poem, our discussion and my recollection of Palmer's *To Know As We Are Known*, I try to piece together what goes wrong with our knowing and learning so that we end up with a distorted sense of the world and our own identity. While this would seem of interest only to educators, it turns out that our ways of knowing and learning are important for everyone. They inform our workplaces and society at large, greatly influencing how we live. Many of us view learning as a strictly private matter, a solitary construction process confined to our heads. We do this in what we believe to be a vast field of *objects*. We believe the world to be "out there"—we are separate from the world. A different view is that we are part of the world, a world that interacts with us continually. We can learn from our encounters with other *subjects* in the world.

The notion of being separate from the world encourages competition over cooperation. If our schooling has instilled fierce individualism and competitiveness in our youth, then teaming at work will be foreign and difficult. When we believe that our worldview should win over those of others, each of us will wage war to make that worldview widespread. But, if we frame knowing and learning as communal acts, we will recognize that respect for and cooperation with others is required.

While we "seek knowledge" we must remember that the world seeks us as well. The world that looks and flings itself at us, like the grasshopper, invites us to learn by using more than just our will. More of our searching must be in the form of deep listening and seeing. When the grasshopper catapults out of the grass, Oliver is organic, connected, open, fully present and ready for the encounter.

Palmer offers, "If we sit in our cell, it will teach us everything." He's made reference to an Orthodox contemplative named St. Barsanuphius who lived in the 6th century and knew the fruits of solitude. Barsanuphius refused to speak, but we do know of him from his writing. He's the one who wrote, "Keep to your cell and your cell will teach you everything." *Knowledge coming from stillness. Hmm.* Barsanuphius was noted for more than his wisdom. He was famous for living long periods without food or water.

I think of other examples of deep learning or being changed by listening. Palmer writes that Goethe did not create *Faust*. *Faust* created Goethe. His statement struck hard and I would later search for validation. In her book *If You Want to Write*, Brenda Ueland says that, "[we should be] idle, limp and alone for much of the time, as lazy as men fishing on the levee…looking and thinking…letting ideas in."[2] Letting ideas in—there's that notion again. A Mel Brooks character advises, "Listen to your broccoli, and your broccoli will tell you how to eat it."[3] Anne Lamott describes a time when a section of her writing was problematic, "So I got very quiet … and waited for the characters to come to me with their lives and intentions."[4] She calls herself "the designated typist." If Lamott's fictional characters teach her, the living world around us can do as much or more.

During the break, I think of a learning experience I had where I could not draw on experience or training, for I had none. I had no choice but to be open. I remember making a visit to Hamm's Farm Market near Barrett to pick raspberries for the first time. The pleasant woman weighing my empty bucket sensed how green I was and told me to "wear a hat and pick low." I walked on the bleached straw spread thick between the rows until I reached the middle of the patch. There, I was surrounded by the constant hum of honeybees, telling me that they were full partners in a grand process. I pulled on a bright red berry, its stem pointing to the horizon. It wouldn't come. I tried another. Nothing. I discovered a bunch of dark berries ankle high, stems bent like the backs of old men. They fell into my hand. Another bunch willingly came as well. A wild fluttering startled me and I looked up to see an oatmeal-colored grasshopper staring at me from a serrated leaf. When a bird dined on a nearby neighbor of the grasshopper, I discovered part of the big-eyed insect's role in the web. I was receptive enough to have been taught by the faculty of the farm.

I'm slowly coming to understand that my new way of knowing only works if accompanied by a respect for "the other" and genuine humility. Palmer makes that clearer when he says, "'To understand' is to stand under." He prods a little. "Maybe we should ask ourselves, What shall I stand under? What am I willing to have over me?" An attendee points out that, "to understand is to love." It is most likely that our fears spawn a false pride that pushes us to stand over the world, when real learning requires that we stand under. Humility is essential for knowing.

It strikes me that Palmer is a master of his craft. He uses powerful yet simple images—"Be not afraid" and a walk in a field. He stirs discussion with bold questions and makes room for a wide range of responses. The array of concepts offered by the attendees is more than I bargain for. I find that much of it is too new and coming a little too fast. I'm Lucille Ball at the candy conveyor.

Developing a Regard for Others

Our conference group acknowledges with regret that we often see each other as empty. With that view, the role of the supervisor or teacher is to raise the lid on people's heads and pour in motivation and information. I'm working to change that picture in my head. We, and that includes my students, are full of gifts. Each one of us has a special contribution to make to the world from out of our unique, inborn capacities.

Proof of our own talents appears when we see talent in others. To see admirable traits in others is to know that we too possess them. In *A Guide for the Perplexed,* E.F. Schumacher writes, "…the understanding of the knower must be *adequate* to the thing to be known."[5] In other words, we can only recognize goodness if goodness is in us. Our ability to see talents in others means *we* are full of what we admire, not empty.

Seeing others as "full," "talented," changes everything. We're more apt to develop respectful relationships that "protect and border and salute each other"[6] as Rainer Maria Rilke writes. By increasing our respect for others, we validate their sacredness and they, in turn, validate ours. Martin Buber describes the ultimate, respectful relationship between two subjects as "I-Thou." An "I-It" world contains objects to be "used" by us—hardly respectful. An "I-Thou" world is full of priceless subjects to be "met."[7]

Another wakeup call

Part of the rich experience of the conference is meeting the participants. During a break, Kathie and Rick find me tucked in an alcove and sit down. While we exchange remarks about the diverse background of participants, a man sits down next to us. He introduces himself as David and says he's from California. David easily joins in the conversation. Oliver's poem was just what he needed. He shares that the conference is a helpful reminder of how hectic his life is. While impressed with how much he accomplishes each day, it bothers him that the pace feels like violence to his soul. When caught up in action, David explains, he isn't present in the moment. He's now being as faithful as he can to his New Year's resolution—doing one thing at a time. When he dices onions, he dices onions. When he bathes, he bathes. I'm blown away. I'm dissatisfied with my lack of intentionality compared to David's resolve. He's a woodcarver. He not only has his work, he's working on himself. David's a wakeup call, an example that helps me strengthen my commitment toward a more intentional life.

Chapter 3

Why These *Three Words?*

In the free time following lunch, I can't shake the impact of "Be not afraid," now a relentless termite gnawing at my foundation. One doesn't say "afraid" in polite company, yet, these are Palmer's first words of the conference. I know he's straightforward, all business. In some way, "Be not afraid" is his main message. What's my response? What do I need to learn?

Separation surfaced as an important theme in one session and I make a connection between fear and separation. I guess I do keep at arms length the things I fear most—the unknown, dark truths about myself and people that would make claims on my life. Maybe what "Be not afraid" means is that I must open up to the truths and relationships seeking me and risk being changed by them. I now more fully realize that separation has been a solution for my fears, but a very poor one at that. I've used separation as protection, but my strategy has blocked my understanding and my growth.

Isolation, Separation, Chicken, Egg

In a small group session on the sun-drenched lawn, a teary-eyed young man expresses his deep gratitude for having found community. Back in Scandinavia, he and his fellow teachers are "lone cowboys." Amazing! An American term in Scandinavian culture! Not only that, the distance is a shocker. It took a flight across the Atlantic to find caring, listening and acceptance. I can only conclude that disconnection in the workplace is everywhere. Palmer's proclamation at our first retreat about our separation from each other continues to ring true.

After the first retreat, armed with a new sensitivity to our aloneness, I found a stunning description of our isolation, now supported by global evidence. In *Improving Schools from Within*, Roland Barth writes that we act like children in a sandbox who engage in solitary play, ignoring those close at hand. University professors, like teachers at other levels, are described as "a group of isolated individuals connected by a common heating system and parking lot."[8]

Disregarded

Spirit

On Saturday night an open invitation is extended to anyone interested in participating in a Sunday morning nondenominational service. It is to be a "spiritual celebration." There won't be a main speaker. We are encouraged to bring stories, poems, songs, and dances, anything that can contribute to the celebration. I'd like to contribute, so I find an empty bench under a maple tree and write about an incident while on a family vacation to Yellowstone National Park.

As I finish, the sun sinks behind the trees and I return to my room. Stillness spreads over campus, but the whirlwind inside refuses to subside. I'm real stirred up—Be Not Afraid, ways of knowing, an intentional life, authenticity, separation...

In the filtered light of dusk that makes its way into my room, it comes to me that I'm seriously hooked—Fetzer can't throw me back. I can think of many factors that have influenced my growing commitment to the retreat program. First, my application was accepted and that made me feel welcome. Second, everyone at the first retreat expressed great care for each other. The program is not only of the highest quality, it is a program that has heart. Third, anything that will uncover a ten-year-old wound, my transfer from music, has to be taken seriously. In addition, I've found that my retreat colleagues are an interesting lot. Maybe exciting and inspiring are better words. Finally, going in and down is unspeakably appealing. Some need in me is being satisfied.

Sunday Celebration

Sitting in a large circle, we share with each other. One participant reads a touching account about his thoughts and feelings as he stood at his kitchen window watching another man embrace and kiss his daughter. How was he to deal with a man who had won his daughter's heart? Now what was his relationship with his daughter? Next, we learn and then dance a Mid-Eastern dance of celebration.

The piece I'll offer to the group deals with breaking out of our thoughtless dependency on leaders and becoming fully involved. Sometimes the spirit goes out of our spirituality and we plod along without thought or commitment. Father Vega, my priest back home, told a story that highlights the mechanical way in which a congregation can mumble through the liturgy. During mass, the priest offers a blessing to the congregation and, at the conclusion of the blessing, the congregation responds by saying "And also with you." Father Vega recounts that during a mass at another parish, he tapped what he had thought to be a dead microphone and muttered, "There is something wrong with this mike." The congregation responded, "And also with you."

As I read my offering, laughter erupts at the first line.

Birthday Miracle
Believe it or not, I found God in church!
While on vacation, my family and I attended services in a little western church. The day we worshipped, the parish had decided to give their priest the day off—his only day off of the year and his 80th birthday.
As the mass progressed, a disaster took shape. The usually confident, automatic responses of the congregation became embarrassed, hesitant mumbles. Gone were the reassuring cues of the priest, our pipeline to God. It was a situation that called for emergency measures—
we prayed.
Silently, but intensely we began to root for the lay leaders as if mass was the championship game and they our home team. We even used body English, leaning forward, stretching on tiptoe to help pull the words from them.
Then it happened.
The powerful presence of the Holy Spirit filled the church. It could be felt everywhere. Eyes sparkled and voices grew strong. The sounds of the final hymn soared.
We left the church renewed and to be greeted by the fresh scent of pine and the sight of sunshine on snow-covered peaks. God fills spaces and voids.
God understands our groans.
God helps us to marvel at all of creation—
mountains, miracles, body English, and birthdays.

Maybe our religious leaders could help us best rekindle spirit by going hunting, fishing or playing golf—forcing us to bring our whole selves to worship. Lord knows they need the time off.

Rediscovering Solitude

On the last day of the conference I get up early and head to the farmhouse. Its casual atmosphere is created from old wood floors and wainscot. We've been invited to meditate together here before breakfast. I'm very excited to renew meditation, a practice I had dropped when my children, Jenny and Joe, were young. I hadn't felt it was fair to my wife Cindy to go off and serenely practice meditation while she was taking care of meals and the children. The anticipation of a meditation high is intoxicating. Spirituality running through the veins is as powerful as any drug.

I'm the first to arrive. I find the softest looking chair out of the many stuffed chairs and couches spread throughout the room. With eyes closed, I'm unaware that many others are entering. My mantra moves over me like a gentle ocean breeze. Suddenly, a thunderclap rattles the windows and gives me a terrible jolt. No, I'm wrong. It's my stomach. The wild growling grows from a rumbling steam engine to a screaming dragster. Afraid of robbing everyone of their practice because of my booming appetite, I tiptoe out of the building—with floorboards squeaking with every step.

Outside, I am a walking contradiction. Matching my deep disappointment and frustration over my failed session is non-stop laughter. I am undone. Unlike Saint Barsanuphius of Gaza, my spiritual quest can only be satisfied with pancakes, eggs and bacon—extra crisp.

Chapter 4 – Winter, Death, Dormancy, Renewal

Dying is easy, it's living that scares me to death.[1]
                                        Annie Lennox

In January the ground is frozen solid in these parts. Winter's icy arm reaches downward, requiring that concrete footings be at least 42" deep. The meteorologists on TV-8 warn of "Arctic blasts" and "Canadian Clippers." A mile or two in from the Lake Michigan shoreline folks brace for "lake effect snowfall." The big lake sheds its outer skin into the air and then snow clouds give it back with interest. A half-foot or more of snow is not uncommon in a single night.

In Pine County, where I live, we've tried various ways of coping with slippery roads through the years. Tire chains came first and then stud tires, but these were outlawed because of the damage they inflict on the roads. Now, salt or a salt and sand mix is judiciously spread, but the material sits idle as a tombstone if it's bitter cold.

After a Year's Hiatus, Retreats Resume
It's in this season of wind and chills, snow and rust that we gather for our second retreat. On Wednesday night I pack my bags. After work on Thursday I head for Kalamazoo, and maybe a whole different world.

The building of Seasons, the retreat center of the Fetzer Institute, was completed in the fall and our group is using it for the first time. There was green thinking in its construction. A crane like the ones used for skyscrapers lowered all the building materials to the site, saving every possible tree from the axe.

Disregarded

With the completion of the retreat center and our commitment to attend a two-year cycle of quarterly gatherings, our schedule begins to harmonize with the seasons. The letter I received indicates that the focus of our retreat with Parker Palmer is winter and its themes. Specifically, he's titled the retreat "Winter's Darkness and Death—Dormancy and Renewal."

Search for Self

Palmer opens our first full group session with a warm greeting. We listen to each other's accounts of what's happened since the first retreat. Palmer allows silence to settle over our circle and I see that his smile has changed into a look of concern. He's amazed at how hammered and unsupported we K-12 teachers are in our work. Part of this pounding comes from just doing business. We beat up each other because that's just the way it's done. "How can we care for each other and ourselves?" he has us ask ourselves. "What can all of us take from the retreat that will help us in our work and our lives?"

He suggests that the true self is the only place from where we can really teach. I realize that Palmer remains faithful to two themes, regardless of the season. We must find our unique identity and we must take care of each other and ourselves.

Palmer continues. "Like the dormancy of winter, we have gifts, intuitions and feelings preparing themselves to be awakened. If we can get into this season instead of resisting it, we can participate in the rhythm of life and bring forth its gifts, even out of the cold and darkness."

Winter is also about death. St. Benedict advised, "Keep death before you daily." This is not morbid advice, for his intention was to help us look at life in ways that make each day richer.

An early activity of the retreat weekend has us reflect on a childhood story that represents the true self. At what time was I most like myself? After time to think by ourselves, we form small groups. Listeners identify the gifts of each storyteller.

I tell a story of being a camp counselor at YMCA Camp Waukanee. "Once the campers were sleeping, counselors could meet in the lodge for socializing. Often we would end up eating a bowl of cereal or scrambled eggs on toast. Periodically, we would tiptoe up to the cabins to make sure our campers were okay. On this particular night, I sensed that an especially playful mood was in the air. One of the counselors produced enough cigars for everyone. The plan was to take a walk and have a smoke. Unfortunately, we were supposed to be in the lodge or our cabins—nowhere else—so the director or our campers could find us. I told my peers I couldn't go, but that I'd see them when they got back. As luck would have it, our camp director walked into the lodge and found me alone. He asked where the other counselors were, but figured it out while I searched for words."

As I end the story, listeners in my small group point out that I had demonstrated courage against peer pressure and a strong sense of values. I'd been a non-conformist in the best sense of the word.

I know that I tend to work at the edge of group life. I really enjoy working with others, but also attend to my need to do what I think needs doing. It isn't easy living at the edge, but for me the alternative is just as hard. I am also somewhat aware of my values system. Calling from Tennessee, Randy Misamore, a wise college friend of thirty years, said that I held myself to the highest values of anyone he knew. He also wondered if I was making my life unduly difficult. Food for thought.

In our small group, I change my role to that of listener and hear one woman tell a story about her early childhood. She returns from fishing and then places the remaining worms in the refrigerator to keep them alive. The next day she opens the white foam container and finds only dead worms buried in the dried peas of black dirt. She is overcome with guilt and sorrow from her involvement with the killing of living things. She was troubled by the incident for a long time.

To this strong, tough teacher the other listeners and I are able to describe her gifts of deep caring, a wonderful sensitivity, a willingness to be responsible and a very mature awareness of connections.

The sharing has a profound effect on me. We're intensely present to one another—unlike any other experience I've had. Whether I'm the speaker or a listener, I feel like it's a privilege, a gift, to participate. A new level of connection is being defined.

Each time we're directed to form small groups, we're reminded about our role as listeners. Each encounter must be approached anew—proceeded by the same focus and sincerity as the first.

We don't seek benefits from our roles as listeners, but they appear nonetheless. When the speaker shows a willingness to be vulnerable, I feel that I'm trusted—someone dared to share in my presence. With betrayal rampant in these times, that silent message is a healing balm. My colleagues are so open that two other gifts appear. One is seeing the sheer beauty of a unique being, the combination of talents, hopes, dreams and trials like no other. The second gift is a glimpse of the soul of another, that shy being that only appears under the safest conditions. The speaker slowly pulls back the underbrush and the listeners see the sunlight flooding an orchid in waiting. All this comes from biting my tongue hard, stifling the urge to add my two cents that would bankrupt the dialog. All this comes from something inside that's willing to put another soul first. From that comes grace. I guess there's even a fourth benefit from being a listener. I end up surprised at myself—I can slow down. I can listen. I can care deeply. In the end, what I thought would be a "nice chat," turns out to be a profound experience, a priceless lesson in the power of an honest and open encounter.

Poetry's Gift

Back in the large group Palmer describes that poetry is an effective aid to discussing matters of substance. Maybe poetry's edge on other written forms is its ability to illuminate mysteries that are beyond words. Poems come from the poet's unconscious and, at times, poets don't know what will surface next. They may not even understand all that they write.

Our task while discussing poetry, he explains, is *not* to focus on one interpretation. We should be open to many viewpoints, listening to others as well. When a poem seems difficult to understand, we can use this power of uncertainty to draw our curious selves into the mystery it attempts to describe.

With that introduction, we move into the theme of Winter and Death by discussing "Winter in the Country" by Mary Oliver.

Palmer reads the poem and then Marianne Houston does. I feel myself slip out of high gear as each reads with great sensitivity. No need to hurry now. My eyes keep returning to the lines that suggest the subjects of the poem are tragic figures, for they are unaware of their mortality. It is more difficult to live fully while denying the reality of death.

Regardless of how sinister something might be, I know that I'm better able to cope if I can acknowledge its existence. I realize that what I refuse to see always grows bigger and bigger. As my unclaimed fear grows, I wear myself out living in denial. Drained, I will start running on empty. Running, I will forever be chased.

Palmer points out that we can use the word death and not always mean the physical reality. We can use it as a broad metaphor. Death can represent the many endings we have in our lives—death of a job, income, meaning, a role, a belief, a love or a way of life. We fear these endings. We must move through and beyond them so we can fully participate in life. If we fear endings too much, we withdraw in an attempt to avoid pain and then life becomes a spectator sport. At this retreat, we'll benefit from reflecting on our metaphoric winters and deaths. We can "keep to our cell" and let it teach us what we need to learn. If we face our fears, they will shrivel from the encounter.

A Dark Probe

Palmer asks, "What is terror for you?" We find places to be alone and, in the silence, form a response. Terror for me is waking up and knowing I'm on the wrong road or in the wrong place or living the wrong mission. Terror for me is being unaware or being lost.

From my response I can tell that I have a need to be in control. I can't seem to embrace life as the mystery it is or enjoy it as an adventure. I see that much of my terror is self-inflicted. I am anxious over being lost and confused when I could frame such times as welcomed challenges. Life is a surprise party. It's my attitude that gives life's unpredictability its negative spin. How I view and respond to people and events beyond my control really defines them as life giving or death dealing.

Disregarded

In a triad, I tell about an incident when I was not in control, one full of challenge. Because of layoffs, I was at the helm of the high school band for the first time. "It was a Friday night in fall and the marching band had assembled on the practice field to do a run through of the half-time show before the performance. I grew more and more anxious as I watched band members march and play as poorly as I had ever seen them. There were musical breakdowns, then marching breakdowns. We stopped to reset formations that kept falling apart and had been solid weeks before. Game time loomed closer and closer. I was completely baffled. I finally motioned for a huddle and the students gathered around me in a circle. In my anxiety and growing anger, I let fly, "Folks, what's going on? I've never seen anything like this!"

"Faces grimaced, twisted, turned red and eyes glanced downward. The tears began to flow. They were dedicating their performance to a band member who had committed suicide the year before. 'We could have been there for him more. We could have supported him more. We want to do this to honor him.'"

I was out of the loop and the last to know. On the podium, leading the whole show, I didn't have a clue as to what was going on. This was terror for me.

The dilemma was large and the performance time pressed against us. The words came and I prayed they'd be adequate. "Can we agree to postpone this dedication? What I'm seeing and hearing right now will not honor anyone. This is a serious issue. How do we honor a person and respect the pain and the conflicted feelings of his family at the same time? Are we honoring suicide? Are we saying yes to creating a world of pain for our parents? We can't discuss this well at this moment; we have an obligation to fulfill. Can we agree that it would be better to discuss this issue on Monday?"

Here were students who had encountered death in a very personal way. For months they had been silently processing their grief and guilt and were now courageously coming to grips with it. There was no doubt about death being a teacher about life. Life had become more fragile and valuable and they saw the power of relationships. Out of the darkness something of great worth was being born in each one of them.

Chapter 4

Winter's Gifts

Back in our full group circle, Parker suggests we offer images of winter to the center of our circle and suggests that dormancy is also associated with winter. "What are physical signs of gifts that winter's dormancy encourages?" he asks. We provide a wide variety of images—good books, comfort foods, an extra blanket, wood fires, sleeping in, needlework, candles, and the special silence of a snowfall. We know winter is a time to hunker down in the worst conditions, to be as dormant as trees, seeds and grasses. Palmer offers that the dormancy of winter has a particularly powerful purpose and gift. It is a time that encourages attentiveness, reflection and awareness. As he distributes a poem, he continues. "While we sit in the season of quiet, we may discover how spent we are. To our dismay, we may realize we are exhausted. But a gift can even be hidden in exhaustion—release can follow."

Our letting go at a time of being worn out can lead to an epiphany, the unveiling of a hidden truth. I know this to be true from a personal story friends shared with me. The Rettenmaiers tell about going on a couple's retreat. The strategy used by the retreat master was to schedule meetings well into the night. Ted says that, in the grip of exhaustion, "Bang! Came the big breakthrough for us."

Linda Powell reads the poem in our hands, May Sarton's "On a Winter Night," and then our retreat group pans for gold. Sarton is alone. I suppose we could say "sitting in her cell." She stares into the fire, very much spent. Sarton realizes her exhaustion, but then an image appears in the flames: "A salamander...Gives tongue, gives tongue!"[2]

Wisdom comes.

The darkness of winter invites us home. There, we become still and our exhaustion gently dissolves the thick curtain between an epiphany and us. We allow the wisdom that is seeking us to penetrate by growing still and dropping our defenses.

Palmer helps us look at winter, death and dormancy from a variety of perspectives. He warns us about and then steers clear of what he calls "the irreversible gloominess" that can envelop a group that discusses winter and death. My dread of winter, metaphoric and real, softens from an appreciation for its gifts. Hidden in every dark image is a gift of light. Every question is an answer. Every image that captures me liberates.

Inner Strength and Wisdom

Friday evening is reserved for Clearness Committees. This Quaker practice helps an individual, the focus person, develop clarity about a perplexing personal issue. The whole process honors the ability of the focus person to handle his or her own dilemma—all of us have the capability to solve the problems that confront us.

Palmer remarks that it is rare for groups to intentionally create sacred spaces, but that is what we are about to do. In a clearness committee, committee members and the focus person are gifts to each other. His tone is unmistakably reverent. I can feel us settling into an even more respectful place than we've been previously.

It's is a privilege to be involved in a clearness committee. Though not the center of attention, committee members actually receive a gift of their own from their selfless participation. Members cannot offer advice; they can only ask questions. They are to be utterly attentive and stay at the edge of the space. The center is reserved for the focus person. Laughing too long or exclamations are taboo as they bring attention to a member rather than keeping the attention on the focus person.

One doesn't comfort a crying focus person. In our compassion to support them we can imply "Poor thing." The focus person is anything but that.

We are reminded to have faith in the process and that fruits of the experience will emerge in their own time, whether in the meeting itself or later. Palmer fields a question on how to ask honest questions. "Trust your intuition on what to ask," he says.

Two volunteer to be focus persons besides me. My clearness committee members are Dave Sluyter, Mark Bond, Mike Perry, Megan Scribner, Toni Rostami and Margaret Ells. Dave suggests that we use a small lounge in the main building. During our walk from Seasons to the main building, I realize that the members of my committee have the opportunity to mutter an aside, but they don't. The walk is silent preparation for what is to come.

Chapter 4

We arrange the chairs in the lounge and settle in. I take a deep breath and describe my dilemma. I'm working under a new principal who is extremely aggressive to those who express an opinion different than his own. I do share my opinions and they're not always in concert with my principal. The principal has divided our staff. He shares information and lavish praise with what my small group of colleagues has come to call "The Insiders." Information and support is withheld from us "Outsiders" and our input is discounted. The climate is dangerous. The Insiders are aggressive, enraged by misinformation supplied by the principal. As an association representative, I'm defending a number of teachers and myself against formal verbal warnings and written reprimands.

I've been head of the teacher's negotiating team for a number of contracts. Done well for my fellow employees, the role rarely wins approval from the administration. That role and my strong defense of colleagues only further cements my membership in The Outsiders. I'm also on the school improvement team and the most active members have become targets of the principal.

I think that the tangible control expressed by leaders of the district is driving people underground and that real growth of our school system is being stifled. In our current culture, few people find the courage to speak up. Without real dialog, we're stuck as an organization whether we admit it or not. I'm even concerned that few of us see ourselves as being stuck. Being the target of aggression, rumors and reprimands, I'm in pain. The faculty split hurts as much as being a target. I'm really concerned.

My dilemma is deciding whether to speak up with suggestions, regardless of the consequences, or not. If I speak up the pain will increase. Retaliation is almost guaranteed. If I remain quiet, I will feel as though I will not have fulfilled my responsibility to the organization. What am I to do?

I wait for the first question as members consider all that I've said. Then, the questions come:

How compelled are you to speak up?
(Smiling) I think it's genetic!

Disregarded

What might hold you back from speaking?
(Troubled) I think my family hurts when I'm in pain and I expect sanctions.

What alternatives are there?
(Guarded) I can work at being more tactful, make peace in some way. Attempt to lower the anxiety of my leaders by saying I don't want to run the show or criticize, but that I do want to help. They act as if I'm challenging them.

Do you view alternatives to speaking out as losing?
(Painfully) I think silence is already hurting the organization.

What do you say to yourself in a crisis?
What do you think you've learned so far in this situation?
Are you thinking of a career change?
Could a compromise be struck?
What do you see yourself doing in five years?
How do you view your leaders?
How do you view your fellow teachers?
How does timing your actions fit into this?
Do others think like you do?
Who might support you if you spoke?
Why do you feel the responsibility to speak up?
How would you describe your job satisfaction?

An hour and a half passes rapidly. Members display an astounding gentleness. The experience is like no other. I don't feel bombarded with questions. Members pace themselves and leave plenty of space for me to think and respond. I see that many are recording my responses, which they'll give to me at the conclusion. These people are honest and wise—selfless.

We move to the mirroring phase. Members echo what they have heard or seen. The best mirroring is a quote of the focus person, feedback that might loose a new discovery for me. Every attempt is made to mirror my own words, gestures, facial expressions and tone of voice:

Chapter 4

Your voice was strongest when talking about a career change.
You project strong internal direction in your responses.
You seemed to go deeply when you said you'd probably continue to speak up.
You seemed especially spontaneous when you said speaking up was genetic.
You acknowledged feeling alone when speaking up.
Your statements seemed to move from considering alternatives to no option but to speak up.
You seemed saddest when describing seeing students less with the new schedule that you're dealing with.

We then enter the final part of our meeting. It is reserved for affirmations:

You talked about your peers with affection.
You are a team player.
It's clear you try to leave the negativity at work to spare your family.
You understand your compulsion to speak.
You are honest and courageous.
You were fair and kind in describing leaders.
You have a good level of self-knowledge.
You aim for the higher good.

Clearness at Work?

I thank the members of my committee and share how grateful I feel. The process is gentle, but intense, and I find that it hasn't ended with the meeting's close. As I walk back to my room, images toss about. I keep returning to the stark contrast between the workplace and the retreat. Speaking up at work results in sanctions. Speaking up here results in affirmations. Sure, the workplace and the retreat are two very different animals, but the void is too wide. How far can we move the workplace toward creating spaces where people can be heard, honored and encouraged to use their talents? Does anyone dream of the possibility? Does anyone know that alternatives exist?

I wonder about further applications at work. What if the useless employee evaluation system were eliminated and in its place the opportunity for some form of clearness committees? With many educators being so unsupported and isolated, wouldn't this practice be an antidote? Wouldn't us "lone cowboys" develop connections through this practice? Wouldn't we come to know each other better as people and, in so doing, establish a community of support?

I cannot push back the longing created by the provocative void between the community of my peers here and the shards of my shattering community back home. I believe I've experienced solutions here. I'm feeling driven to share with my colleagues back home, yet, I'm coming to realize that my boss won't rest until I'm silenced.

Living Retreat Themes

In the morning our attention turns toward "wintering." Winter, the season, encourages us to "winter through it." How do we winter through the dark times? What tools do we reach for? What kind of attitudes do we call forth? How do we set our hearts in order to get through our winters? Many of us in the circle remark in various ways that persistence sees us through. Palmer helps us explore further, asking, "When were times where persistence sustained your work? What were the fruits of that persistence? To what do we want to make a life-long commitment? No matter how high the snow and strong the wind, what are we willing to walk toward?"

At the beginning of the retreat Palmer had asked, "What can we take back that will help us in our work and in our lives?" Now, we're brought full circle by an invitation to make connections between what we've learned here and our work. "How can we use our personal experience to intervene in our work situation? How can we best make a contribution? What excuses and permissions do we need to give ourselves so we can do the things we feel called to do, the things we haven't done yet?" As always, we are encouraged to find our own answers to these questions.

I jot down what I'm taking with me from the experience. The power of personal stories and poetry is a revelation. I now appreciate like never before the impact of wholly speaking and listening to each other. The Clearness Committee is a sacred tool I can use or help others use. Being present to others has new meaning.

Chapter 4

The gift of winter, death and dormancy has been revealed. All of these treasures could help a troubled world.

What can I take back that will help me in my work and in my life? Listing the solutions is easy—time, rules, worldview, and leadership. My excitement and resolve to contribute are real, but I begin to realize how difficult any intervention will be. It took willing colleagues, hours of silence and dialog to bear fruit. How can I describe what I've experienced here while hovering over the copy machine or downing a sandwich at lunch? My retreat colleagues and I haven't found words that capture what goes on here. And the more I survey the landscape back home, the more daunting the task looks.

I sense that I'm about to leave something at the retreat, some kind of burden best left here. This feeling is no more suggestive than the feeling I had at the closing circle of our first retreat. But what followed soon after was cathartic. I must be breaking open again. I urge more details to show themselves, but nothing comes. I tell myself that the recognition of just that much will have to do for now. Whatever the extra baggage is, I'm better off without it.

The talk of death and the searing cold can crack us open and set us free. The burdens we drag behind us can vaporize into the freezing air. At our closing circle, an up-to-now guarded Helen laughs heartily and through her chuckling says, "The work with my therapist went nowhere because I didn't tell him anything!"

Chapter 5 – Ambushed

We don't need protection; we need partners. If we had a few partners, we wouldn't need protection at all.[1]
　　　　　Donna Schaper, *A Book of Common Power*

　　I'm walking next door to congratulate Cliff Anderson. I've just heard that he's retiring mid-year. The floor creaks as I enter his room and I freeze, having caught him with his head down on his desk. I'm too far into the room to sneak out, so I walk in further. Startled, Cliff looks up.
　　"I've heard the good news," I say, and I offer my hand in congratulations. As we shake hands, I'm caught by a new sensation. I don't remember his hand being quite so delicate. I turn and head for a student desk. Suddenly there are deep sobs behind me. I whirl to see Cliff slumped over his folded arms, the desk holding him from collapse. I can't imagine what's wrong.
　　I sit like a statue. I'm surprised that I'm not embarrassed at this moment and I hope my presence isn't making my colleague uncomfortable. I feel something inside me take over.
　　Cliff is a math teacher. Although a man of few words, I've gotten to know him better than most since my computer lab has been close to his room. Both of my children had him as a teacher, saying he's tough but one of the best. Without our knowledge and any prompting from my wife or I, my daughter even nominated Cliff for *Who's Who in Education*. Both Cliff and my kids have said that it takes about three weeks to establish the necessary conditions in his classroom at the beginning of the year before any math is discussed. Everybody knows how to operate in the space and what's expected before the subject is addressed.

Chapter 5

My workweek often starts with a strong handshake with this tall and wiry figure. His position on the seniority list obscures the reality that he's up-to-date and full of passion for teaching. Offhandedly, he has told me that he rereads auxiliary material to keep interesting stories and details alive in his mind so he can share with students. He's curious about how this place works. In years when I've chaired the negotiating team, we have stood shoulder to shoulder in the hall and he has probed for anything I could give him.

I don't know how long we've been together in the deepening silence. In this encounter, time has been redefined. Finally, Cliff straightens and says that his situation "has been compromised." Something he said has been twisted around and the new principal won't let go of it. "It's best to retire," he concedes.

"Were you planning to retire this year?" I ask.

"No," he replies. "I had planned on teaching five more. I wanted to leave with forty years of service." His voice rings with pride as he says this. I hear that four decades of service carries deep meaning for him.

Cliff submitted his resignation, but the principal remains relentless. During today's classroom observation the principal dramatically looked at his watch, stretched his arms and yawned. More than salt in the wound, nothing short of annihilation will satisfy him.

I walk back to the room numb and then the anger swells. Slowly I'm learning that there is only one way to teach here—the principal's way. I'm angry at the injustice, but also with myself. I've been asleep to how dangerous this place has become, even though I've had adequate warning. I've had more run-ins with this man in a half a year than in twenty years of teaching. My boss is playing hardball and he's playing for keeps.

Winds of Change

At the beginning of the year I could sense Robert Danzle was like no other principal before him. New leaders usually arrive quietly. Their names change, but their behaviors don't. The sameness has caused me to wonder. The only explanation that I have for the pronounced conformity is that it comes from working in a highly structured system. Its influence is so strong as to make the majority of leaders act like clones of each other.

Usually, after a new principal arrives, little changes. One reason this happens is that principals are always given an obligatory year of grace to "get their feet on the ground." Should anyone say that we've had so many leadership changes that little has changed over the last few years, I wouldn't argue. But Robert Danzle is different than his predecessors. The clothes are upscale. The shoes are shinier, more expensive. A colored handkerchief bursts from his sport coat. His gait is haughty and his gestures are exaggerated. I feel my face flush with embarrassment at the staff meeting when he bows down on one knee and declares our school secretary "Queen Mother." All these new signals press me into thinking change is in the wind.

Early on, I'm disgustingly jealous of Danzle's confidence and his ability to charm the socks off of nearly everyone. I think these traits would be handy to have. My awe dwindles as the questions mount. One centers on his educational terms. I've had my nose buried in journals and books for a long time and his jargon is totally new. I've surveyed so much literature that I should at least recognize the terms he uses, but I don't. He's charismatic, but is his educational framework a glitzy bluff?

Ends Over Means

I guess that Danzle's charge is to create a master schedule that supports the formation of teaching teams. With this realization I feel my bitterness swell. Well over a decade ago, a few teachers here had undertaken an initiative to introduce team scheduling and two years ago Pat, Marilyn and I had done so as well. Could it be that our leaders are finally up to speed? Well, I quip to myself, one definition of a leader is the person who figures out what the people want and then gets in front of the parade.

Talk at the second staff meeting of the school year turns toward scheduling, so I send a memo to Danzle with my computer curriculum recommendations. I would prefer to see students for one full semester a year rather than a half semester. I point out that the benefits would be many and I am confident of these from a variety of experiences I've had and from my reading. The longer I'm with students, the better our relationships have been and the greater their growth.

I don't realize until later that, by sending the memo, I've become "a problem" to the principal. Developing a schedule with my suggestions would complicate his life.

Martha on Trial

This year we're experiencing the fallout from new state legislation that says teachers are not to touch students. Gone are the extremely rare cases of too much force, but gone too are thousands of hugs and pats on the back.

A number of parents have called regarding a classroom incident. Listening to Martha's version, I hear that the special education students involved were so violent to others that she was forced to physically separate students. One student, who lost his chokehold on another when Martha intervened, charged, "She touched me!" That's all it takes these days to put a teacher's job in jeopardy.

I'm an association representative, union advocate, and it's my job to work with the administration on Martha's behalf. Martha and I enter Danzle's office with a great deal of concern. This is a high-stakes meeting. If Danzle and Assistant Principal David Jenks side with the student, the safety of Martha's other students, as well as her authority to teach, will be at risk. The principal's opening remarks do not allay my fears. His words are friendly and professional, but the subtle undertone is "guilty." I'm looking at the detective, prosecutor, judge and jury rolled into one. My mind races through a meager list of options and out of nowhere comes the image of a clearness committee.

"I wonder if we could try an experiment?" I say.

"And what's that?" Danzle challenges.

I explain. "I'm familiar with a process that helps people find real insight in dilemmas. The only requirement is that you ask questions for which you do not know the answer. Your questions will help you and Martha look at the situation from a number of perspectives." As Danzle considers a response, a thought flashes through my mind. I've blasphemed—I've severely distorted the sacred process of the clearness committee. Many of the integral steps are missing such as the extensive preparation, the mirroring and the celebration of gifts. However, I take heart that the questioning may defuse a frontal attack of accusations.

Danzle and Jenks look at each other and nod in agreement. They then proceed with their questions. To their credit, they soften and work at understanding and I take heart in their willingness to try something new. Little by little Martha's philosophy emerges until I realize that I'm in receipt of a gift. In full display are her training, experience and heart. The bedrock is luminous, transforming the dismal space into a place of inspiration. Even as colleague and advocate, I'm taken well beyond my currently held perceptions of this woman. The meeting adjourns after we reconfirm procedures to be used if and when violence erupts in Martha's classroom.

Fixing Teachers

As part of our school improvement process, we've distributed surveys to parents. Basically we're asking, What are we doing well? What needs improvement? A few weeks pass and I've heard that most of the surveys are back. With all the work we've put into the school, I'm anxious for our school improvement committee to see the results, perhaps foolishly assuming that parent satisfaction will be better than ever.

Sue Hardy seeks me out at lunch. "I just found out that the survey results will be shared with parents at 2:00 p.m. today," she says excitedly. "Five or six teachers are named specifically. Our school improvement team hasn't even seen them yet. Plus, the report is tainted." Sue hands me a 35-page document and explains. The hand-written comments of parents have been re-typed. Some of the typed comments aren't carbon copies of the originals. Those that aren't slam teachers hard.

I throw my lunch into the wastebasket and head for Tony White's room to help validate Sue's perceptions. Tony is an association representative too; he's levelheaded and well respected. After Tony and I scan the document, Tony speaks. "Yes, there are

Chapter 5

problems *and* I do think teachers can be identified whether or not they've been named directly." I think so too.

Like Martha, Sue has been under a great deal of pressure from the new principal. She explains that even though she is school improvement chairperson, she had to ask to see the surveys. Hearing that the comments were to be shared with parents, she scanned the surveys and found the discrepancies. She has been named specifically in the report and, to her, it looks like part of a plan that is slowly playing out to "clean house."

Danzle's head hunting.

I believe that he's playing a dangerous game because there's a millage vote ahead. We sink or swim from the public's financial support. To purposefully tear down teachers, puts its passage at greater risk. We have to stop the dissemination of the results until we can get at the truth of the surveys and reach an agreement on how to present the report to parents. Sue and Tony ask that I immediately see Danzle and request that the summary not be shared at 2:00 p.m.

I find Danzle and Jenks together and explain our concerns, asking that the report not be shared today. Danzle bristles and says, "No, we're going ahead with our plans." From his manner, I can tell there is no room for discussion, but I persist. "I'm not opposed to facts, but opinion is not fact. Release of this information in this form at this time is no better than spreading rumors. There's a big difference between publishing a comment that identifies a teacher versus publishing that opinion with the teacher's name removed."

They refuse to budge. Danzle issues an adamant "No!" and ends the discussion by walking out of his office. I can't take no for an answer and walk with Jenks to his office, all the while pleading our case.

With only one option left, I finally state, "Since I haven't convinced you, you know I've got to call Mike Howard, our CEA President."

"I know you've got to do what you've got to do," Jenks replies in a measured tone.

I rush down to the lunchroom and ask Ruth Butler to take my upcoming computer class and she agrees. I phone the high school and tell the secretary, "This is an emergency. I've got to speak to Mike Howard immediately." Mike answers with a concerned voice and I go over the situation.

Mike asks in disbelief, "Don't they grasp the implications? Have you made it clear it isn't in the best interests of the school or the district?" I reassure him that I gave my best effort. "I'll be right there," he responds.

Shortly, Mike bursts through the door, emitting energy from every pore. Danzle, Jenks, Mike and I rehash both positions. No progress. Mike says that he's got to call our school superintendent and our MEA Regional Director. Both administrators leave so Mike can use the phone and they head to Jenks' office. They hunch over the phone and make calls as well. Before long, a colleague catches my eye and beckons me with his hand to step into the hallway. "The superintendent's office is on the phone with their lawyers," he whispers, and then leaves.

While Mike uses the phone, I close my eyes and search for common ground, but there is none to be found. Because of the time constraints and the danger, we're left with no room to move. Our position is ironclad, non-negotiable. They, on the other hand, could recognize that publication is possible at a future time and that, under reasonable conditions, our support is possible. We've expected to publish the results all along, but not without seeing it and not with discrepancies. The only hope that I see for the situation is from a softening of their position.

Danzle and Jenks return with the news. The survey won't be shared today. I let out a sigh of relief.

I thank Mike for his support on my way back to class. Just before the doorway to the computer lab, the energy drains from my body and forming a sentence for my sub seems impossible. I mumble, "Thanks, Ruth. CEA emergency…" I stand frozen in place, praying the students will give me a few minutes of peace to pull myself back together—and help me to refocus on why I'm really here.

Okay. Why am I here? I was drawn to teaching because I wanted to give back what I had received, but I find myself adrift. The critical need to defend my peers is severely eroding my time and energy to keep teaching and learning foremost.

Chapter 5

Repercussions

I leave school and wonder what tomorrow will bring. In my teaching, I try to begin each day anew. More than once a student who had exchanged heated words with me has been surprised at a smile and a greeting the next day. The approach helps derail the cycle of escalation. My hope is that we adults can start with a clean slate tomorrow.

When I come in the following morning, I find a short note in my mailbox from Danzle. "Please see me at 3:00 p.m. today. Bring an association representative." Since I *am* an association representative, I must be in trouble. At the appointed time I read through the formal reprimand charging that yesterday I left my classroom without permission. It's payback time.

Another Ambush

It isn't long before I'm presented with another reprimand. This time, I'm supposedly late for work. On the day in question, I arrive 25 minutes early but return to my car for materials when students are arriving. Danzle sees me reenter the building. He turns this event into high drama. I've committed the most heinous of crimes. I explain the situation, but Danzle doesn't accept my explanation, so the formal proceedings go the distance. I think how easy it would have been to be done with this issue, but apparently that isn't Danzle's objective. Put a teacher on the rack and keep them there. Tighten the chains at any opportunity, legitimate or not.

If I could become detached and see these incidents from afar, they would be tiny bumps in the road. But I'm too conscientious to do that. Students grow into teachers and remain in a system that is based on rewards and punishments. We have always lived by a creed to be "good boys" and "good girls," even into our adulthood and teaching careers. We've never left the crazy system that values blind conformity above all else. These small incidents are as large to us as truly serious crimes. We take even false accusations to our core and the accusation of irresponsibility seems like the end of the world to me. I'm crazy, we're crazy, and gifted manipulators use our craziness to full advantage.

Disregarded

What's the Secret?

Danzle's attendance at school improvement meetings drops off. Small incidents reveal that he's sharing *his* vision and asking for input from a small set of young teachers. They love the strokes and effervesce with enthusiasm. In general conversation they mention future plans and initiatives of which most of us are unaware. Their confidence and energy grows while some of us head toward a deep funk.

I'm overloaded with meetings defending staff members under siege. Every meeting with Danzle comes with two other meetings with the accused. I meet with the accused before the meeting with Danzle so I can become familiar with the situation and then after the official one to go over next steps. Danzle's method is straightforward and the tone is always the same—you're guilty, feel guilty. The initiating event for a fact-finding meeting, warning or reprimand is usually a phone call from a displeased parent. Danzle doesn't tell the parent to speak directly with the teacher as has been past practice, rather, he accepts the call and hears the parent's side of the story. When the accused colleague and I enter the room, the agenda is "shape up the teacher."

Much like the young teachers, students and parents love the strokes and the feelings of empowerment. Slowly I'm coming to realize that the students and parents are joining Danzle's parade. I'm gripped by a chilling vision of happy parents and students— but real teaching has taken a holiday. My best teachers have been those that challenged me, not those who pleased me. Danzle is pitting specific parents and students against his targets.

The parent/student/teacher bond is beginning to crumble, but only a few of us can see it.

Our school improvement team continues to meet, but we sense that we are purposefully being placed outside the loop. We believe in what we're doing and commit to remaining faithful. Besides, it's the law. Danzle comes right out and says he's above the law in what has become a chatty, weekly staff bulletin. I'm aghast at his hubris when he states that if he found a law he didn't agree with, he would disobey it. I guess that he's referring to Public Act

Chapter 5

25 and our established school improvement team. I had always thought, as a bottom dweller, it was *my* exclusive right to rebel.

Split Apart

Since Danzle's arrival, the staff has fractured into three groups. I believe Danzle has discovered that we're starving for praise and he creates the favored group by offering frequent and generous compliments to them.

I call those in the largest group "The Fence Sitters." These people face the challenge of remaining invisible, hoping to avoid membership in the other groups.

Of course, us Outsiders can't do anything right. A few are having minor problems with specific students, but don't deserve all the attention they're getting. Others are at the top of the salary scale, skilled, on the school improvement team, independent thinkers or a combination of these.

When he's not in attack mode, Danzle is irresistibly charming. He's funny, effervescent and confident. I've got to give the man his due. He has a large toolbox of strong traits. He suggests that the staff call him "Dazzle." It's another bigger than life gesture. "Dazzle" is over the top for me, but most gladly comply.

I develop a dislike for the Insiders, but I know I possess the same traits as they've shown. The reason I see these young ones so clearly is because I've had an experience here that opened my eyes. *I've* been played like a violin. Unknowingly, I was used to discourage school board members from serving another term.

Charmed to Attack

I'm head negotiator for the teachers. We're bogged down in contract talks so I go to the central office and meet with a negotiator from the administration. "Where's the solution?" I ask. In passing, he tells some terrible tales about the anti-teacher attitudes of a school board member. I'm shocked. At the next meeting with my negotiating team, I not only discuss how we can make some progress, I also share the tales told to me. At the next joint meeting of both sides, we let fly with both barrels at the board member. Justice has finally had its day!

Disregarded

The cycle repeats itself. At a one-on-one meeting, the anti-teacher and anti-education attitudes of another school board member are reluctantly shared with me. My negotiating team is only too happy to oblige again. At the next joint meeting, we spare no energy in setting the board member straight. "Can you believe that attitude?" we ask each other indignantly.

I'm back to see the administrative negotiator for a third time and another unsupportive school board member is discussed. Suddenly, my heart sinks as the light goes on. I'm hearing about Reverend Hoffman and I've had more contact with him than with the others. This time the stories aren't believable. I've been made a pawn and I've made my team a pawn to "clean house" for the administration.

At our next team meeting, looking at teachers Sam Scott, Ted Kessler, Denny McDunnah and Val Meitz, I say, "We've been had." They stare back in wonder while I begin to explain the discovery I've made. In unison, they grimace and slump as the realization sinks in.

It's because of this indelible experience that I find myself "adequate" to see the current situation. I can only see what's around me from having that same potential within me. I'm as gullible and self-righteous as the next. However, there's one element between the stories then and now that begs for my close attention. Are the Insiders being fed trash about us Outsiders, just like I was?

From Retreat to Work

I had wholeheartedly welcomed the respite of Fetzer's winter retreat. Even though its theme centered on winter and death, I returned from the retreat renewed. However, one of Rilke's sonnets has begun to haunt me. He advises, "Be ahead of all parting..."[2] but I have yet to understand his counsel. And he speaks of a winter that is "...so endlessly winter..."[3] That too remains opaque. These phrases frequently resurface and demand to be known, mantras in a foreign tongue.

Within a week my sense of renewal is gone. Danzle and I are alone in his office and we're discussing his schedule proposal. It doesn't address points that I made in October and I say so. His face reddens and he blurts out angrily, "Why don't you retire and become a consultant?" A chill runs through me and I feel tingling in my left arm. I'm under retirement age and need eight more years to retire. He wants me out and I can't go, even if I wanted to. The litany of meetings with Danzle washes over me, especially memories of Cliff Anderson. I suddenly realize more deeply that my position and the security of my family are at risk.

I might as well probe. "Be honest, Bob. Why the reprimands?" I ask. "You attack me—I attack you!" he spits. I have no idea what he's talking about. Is a difference of opinion an "attack?" He adds, "I hear you and Sue have had the run of the place." With that statement his intentions become even clearer. He calms down and describes the lucrative fees consultants pull in. He's masterful and I think to myself, "I'm the Eskimo and here come the freezers." The humor dies when the image of being forced out rifles through me again.

I really don't know how to improve the situation and I'm not above asking for help. Pat Knopp and I arrange a meeting with a number of wise high school teachers and tell our story. "What advice do you have?" we ask. Pat and I come away from the meeting with a sense of futility. We feel the compassion of our peers, but our colleagues point out the complexity of the situation, saying that most of it is beyond our control.

More Moves

Next, Danzle orchestrates the conditions toward a predetermined end. Apparently, the way to deal with the computer scheduling and me is to get the entire staff involved in the issue. He announces that a vote will be taken. The main question to resolve is whether computers will be part of the core curriculum or what he calls "the co-curriculum" (those subjects outside the 3 R's). Yet another division? At our staff meeting, Danzle gives each teacher a ballot while he explains the two choices. If the staff chooses to make computers a core subject, they agree to teach the computer classes. As Danzle says menacingly, "You had better know what you're doing every day you're in the lab. If you want to be responsible for computer instruction, write 'Yes' on the ballot and sign your name." Signed ballots. Hmm.

Most of these teachers aren't prepared to teach computers. The thought of adding more to their already full plates, coupled with the threat of intense scrutiny, adds up to a waste of paper. Voting in this context is like asking, "Do you want a Coke or hemlock?" The staff overwhelmingly says 'No' to the integration of computers into the core subjects. They become a party to splintering and isolation.

Two days later Danzle offers me a math position. With trust having evaporated long ago, I have to not only think about the offer at face value but also imagine how Danzle could have his way with me. It's hard to believe that the offer has been presented in good faith, even if it might be. Two days later I turn him down. I really like math and I would enjoy teaching it, but the master contract stipulates that a major or minor is required and I don't have either in math. I can only guess about what would have happened had I accepted the offer. Either I would have received poor evaluations, only to hear Danzle sadly moan, "We gave Jack an opportunity and he couldn't handle it." or my lack of qualifications would have been uncovered and I'd either be laid off or become a yo-yo, bouncing from job to job in the district. No thanks.

Since computer training was voted out of the core curriculum, I realize I will be part of what Danzle has been calling the "co-curricular group." I would realize much later that naming this group of teachers anything other than "core" created another type of fissure. Over time, the co-curricular teachers and their subjects became devalued because they weren't "core." I would learn that the students picked up on this distinction. They came to see their day divided into two parts—team time and non-team time. Non-team time simply didn't count. Any remaining importance of this small group was that we existed to provide planning time for the core teachers.

Trashing Revealed

I'm muddling through this year, still not connecting all the dots, mostly because I am part of a group intentionally left out of the loop. I walk away from meetings wondering what they really were about. Case in point:

It's early second semester and we've been released to meet

off-site as a co-curricular group to plan our part of next year's schedule. We represent art, music, physical education, computers and home economics. We've come to realize that we're, as Danzle has said, "the last piece of the puzzle." The core schedule has already been designed so the constraints are well established. I sarcastically think that the real question we are to ponder is "What can we make with bread crumbs?" In one sense we are a rag-tag group, laden with diverse interests because we are sole advocates for our subjects—one art teacher, one home economics teacher, etc. On the other hand, we've maintained our care and respect for each other. Maybe it's the Golden Rule that holds us together. All of us share the experience of being lone advocates and, because we understand our own vulnerability, protect each other.

A new teacher from core is present at our meeting, which is very odd. I know that a retiring teacher from our co-curricular group has been told not to attend because "subs aren't available." But somehow a sub is found for this young teacher? When it's my turn to share my vision, I urge those present to consider semester-length classes. My words set off the new teacher. I'm selfish. I'm doing this for myself and not for the kids. She's furious and she's going to throw a tantrum if we hold up teaming.

One dot connects to another.

The youthful enforcer must have heard some stories. We're the old fogies. We're selfish. We're against teaming. She hasn't been around to know that some of us worked years to get us into a middle school structure. We not only share her desire, our desire has preceded hers by many years. She's been fed trash. She's so aggressive that our mouths drop and we sit there stunned, left to wonder about her presence and how hard someone is cranking the rumor mill.

Phone Home

A week goes by. I enter the office to check my mailbox and I see that my boss is standing in his doorway. There's so much information flying about that I approach Danzle and clarify my position. "I'm in favor of teaming, but I'm not in favor of the current schedule under consideration. I think we can design something better," I say. My hope is that we'll use the next few months to consider alternatives. I know how creative we can be.

Sue Hardy walks up to both of us and says, "Jack, Bob has asked me to meet with him tomorrow and bring an Association Rep. Can you make it?" "Sure," I reply, and dejectedly think to myself that the chaos will never end.

Somehow, I leave work on an even keel and head home. The value of home increases with each conflicted incident. It's my safe haven. At home we care about each other. It's a place driven by love, honesty and trust. Home is the place where you renew your spirit for the next day.

The evening rapidly folds into bedtime and my head hits the pillow, with sleep following quickly. It's pitch black and Cindy is elbowing me, repeatedly saying, "Phone. Phone." As I try to wake up, I glance at the alarm clock and the bold, red letters show it's 2:00 a.m. exactly. I reach for the receiver and mutter a drowsy, "Hello," as I start to worry about our parents. On the other end I hear someone wildly inhale and then sputter a vicious, "You Fuck!" The void of silence is followed by a click.

"Who was that?" Cindy asks. I fake drowsiness, now gone, so as to cover up what's just happened. "Go to sleep, Cin. Wrong number." She emits, "Geez..." and rolls over. And for the rest of the night I listen to her breathe.

Crazy, Not Crazy, Crazy, Not Crazy

Some of us are curious about how things worked at Danzle's previous workplace. Did a staff split occur there as well? Were there scapegoats? A few days later, a colleague shares that he's made inquiries. Danzle's previous staff has the same widely held views as our staff. Some absolutely love the man; others refer to him as a back stabber. In some ways, the news is comforting. You can start to go crazy thinking you're as awful as the bad press about you. Knowing that our situation is a part of a pattern helps a little. Unfortunately, our new understanding does not point to any form of relief.

Once Fear's Inside

Danzle backs off for a while and I sense the irony. Even though he aims elsewhere, I can't let down my guard. I know the lull is due in large part to our association president Mike Howard, because he's been a strong advocate. Danzle cannot pass off his stories about me. Mike always counters with various forms of "I know Jack. Jack wouldn't do that. That's nonsense." Unable to sway Mike and up against both his personal and legal power, Danzle appears unwilling to waste time on me. Unfortunately, he's already had an effect. Fear and prudence slow me. "Maybe one minute from now I'll be attacked," I think to myself. I know it's hell to live like this, but under the circumstances, it's also foolish to lower one's guard. He invites me to go out for a beer with him. There's no way to know if his gesture is a sincere attempt at reconciliation or the precursor to doing me in with the jagged edge of a long neck. I reluctantly decline, demonstrating to me how distorted the relationship is, at least from my perspective.

Danzle's made examples out of a number of us, and I imagine that all of the "Fence Sitters" must be on notice, as well. I keep thinking that he's getting the opposite of what he wants. He wants "top performers," but what he's getting is shrinking performance as people sidestep the important stuff, refusing to tackle challenging issues of substance, as they try to remain invisible. Any job done well requires risk taking and initiative.

Yearnings and Learnings

I wait for other schedules to be presented, but none are forthcoming. It's hauntingly quiet around this subject and I'm puzzled. I expect a number of other choices to surface, since I know how Pat, Marilyn and I bounced many versions around, but the topic is off the agenda.

I long for the split to close and heal, but it hasn't. I want the Fence Sitters to take a stand and say, "No more! Enough is enough. Let's work together." I easily grasp that our split is painful to me—I value teamwork—but I fail to see the situation from a different perspective. I don't really understand that the pain comes from a deeper place. Like everyone else, I'm made for community.

Deep sighs break my concentration from time to time, telling me I'm stressed to the max. Occasionally, my left arm feels heavy and I pass it off as my imagination, saying to myself that I'm too young for *that*. Mid-afternoon my eyes feel strange and I name "it" fatigue. I'm becoming concerned about my health and I feel the double bind of being stressed over being stressed.

The Courage to Teach retreats provoke more thinking and reading. The gap between the culture there and the tension at work continue to fuel my curiosity. What causes groups to fracture? What do I name the seed that starts all of this trouble amongst us? What has a hold on my boss? How am I part of the problem?

I'm learning that I have power by staying with my convictions, but the downside is that I must be relentless to a fault. The realization that I'm too pig-headed, that I too want to win, is coming to light now. I'm likely "a problem" because of my passion and strong advocacy. In a better environment I might not act this way. I rarely feel heard or understood here and that impression keeps my advocacy fueled.

I begin to see that Danzle and I have something in common that keeps us going round and round. We use one tool over and over while many are needed. When Danzle encounters differing opinions, he resorts to using power to end the dialog. Such power is rarely just, and so he loses the support he needs through his own deeds. I'm self-defeating too. My persistence invites his attacks. I'm bowled over by my discovery that the terms I use to describe myself—"strong advocacy" and "persistence" are slick euphemisms. I've really chosen the same tool as his—power.

A Parting Blow

Maple tree buds burst into leaves and the end of school is in sight. An expectant, exuberant mood begins to spread through the student body. The rooms become stuffy by day's end and students leave with increasing zeal. This time of year a meandering bee can disrupt a serious lesson in an instant. The cloth window shades scratch against the oak sills as the building breathes in the late spring air, then breathes out.

The staff is converging on the all-purpose room to vote on next year's schedule. I enter and greet those I pass—getting angry glares in return. I'm startled. What's going on now? Danzle reminds us to sign our names to the ballots and explains that a new class has been added to our co-curricular area. It's called C.H.E.S.S. and it was approved during our co-curricular off-site meeting in January. I remember no such approval. We pass in our ballots and some staff look at me as if they've had the satisfaction of trouncing me, the bastard, real good.

I don't get it.

It takes a couple of days to figure out what happened. Danzle was busy. The day of the vote, he shared with some that I had just put in a last-minute request for a new schedule, complete with lavish computer time and full of selfish requests. I would be coming to the meeting to kill teaming and shoot down the work of the entire year. He lets loose a one two punch. I'm the source of the energy to insure a resounding vote and his story damages my relationship with some colleagues.

Ambushed again.

Naming "IT" Temporarily

I feel as if I've been eaten alive, my flesh picked clean. I don't remember ever feeling as fragile as I do now. At the edge of despair, I find a moment of solace – Julia Cameron's *The Artist's Way*. I stumble on her description of certain people that she calls "crazymakers."[4] Within a few pages she has captured Danzle and the rest of us in exquisite detail.

I've come to see the new "logic" that is wreaking havoc with our thoughts and emotions. The entire place has been drawn into his spurious drama: I am to be adored and revered. I deeply care about you. There is one reality and one agenda. I am pure of heart. Learn who I would have you be. I will explain your actions and motives to others. I will share with everyone the faults I see in you. I regret that others are enraged because of who you are. I'm sorry that my confidants are attacking you. The problems of this place are your fault. You are bad. You are alone. I will fix all of this chaos that you've created. I regret that you are forcing me to discipline you. Leave.

Cameron says that we're crazy and self-destructive if we allow crazymakers into our lives. I know deep down that if there is any hope for the soul of this school and my own, it is not in surrender so that we all become crazymakers. Hope for this place lies elsewhere.

I think back to the winter retreat and lines from Mary Oliver's poem, "On Winter's Margin."[5] It is the aloof and solitary ones that preserve and protect the possibilities of freedom and sanity, no matter the cost. We must somehow live outside this chaos in order to save ourselves and this place.

I feel like only my bones remain and I wonder over and over if from only a chalky skeleton can redemption come. Is *this* what Rilke means by the winter that is "so endlessly winter?"[6]

Chapter 6 – Spanning the Chasm

Out beyond ideas of wrongdoing and right doing, there is a field. I will meet you there.[1]

Rumi

Distracting thoughts race through my mind as I try to calm down. I'm behind the side curtain, stage right, in the role of Avram the bookseller during "Fiddler on the Roof." The group I'm in will run on stage as soon as a squabble breaks out.

As far as acting goes, I'm a square peg in a round hole—I belong in the pit orchestra or the audience, not on stage. It was easy enough getting here—no audition. My son landed the part of Tevye and our high school choir was short of male voices, so the director invited me to participate. There are four other men waiting here and I must say we look pretty authentic with caps, beards, worn vests, prayer shawls around the waist and high boots. The others grew out their beards too. I don't know about them, but I barely survived the wire brush stage, with dozens of variously colored spears curling back to impale me.

A group of male actors argue animatedly as they walk from the other wing toward center stage.

It's time.

We dash out excitedly and interrupt the foray. As I look from one combatant to the other and then at Tevye, I ask in a confused tone, "He's right and he's right? How can they both be right?"[2]

Ah yes, how can they, indeed?

Within two months of the show, the next encounter with my Fetzer retreat group would teach me that many contradictory pairs are really complex wholes.

Disregarded

Opening Circle

As I sit here scanning the schedule for this third teacher retreat, the irony of that line from "Fiddler" hits hard. We are here to explore the theme of paradox and I sit here musing. Okay, how *can* two "opposing" ideas be true? Palmer interrupts my reverie to welcome us here. He asks us to help create a few minutes of silence and so the retreat begins as all others have, with reflection. As I try to shift into the present, the baggage of the week begins to flake off, gradually at first and then gaining in momentum, until I feel the stark contrast between the peace of this place and the stressful workplace I left earlier this afternoon.

Palmer breaks the silence by reading a poem by Rilke. In "As once the winged energy of delight," Rilke challenges us to make connections where we haven't seen them before. Palmer continues, "I learned to stop holding my good self and dark self apart and, instead, brought them together. How can we hold paradoxes together better—mind/heart, subject/student, individual/community? How do you deal with the tension created by holding these paradoxes?"

His willingness to be honest and vulnerable invites me to do the same. Palmer offers that when he holds the tension of a paradox, his heart breaks open and he is stretched. "The only way for my heart to enlarge is to be broken over and over." I stiffen from the image of my heart breaking and think to myself, "Okay, Parker, you go first." I wouldn't understand for some time that, in order for new growth to be possible, a "breaking open" of sorts really is required.

As I see it, three paradoxes have been established in but a few minutes: 1) our *vulnerability* creates a *safe* place for us to engage with our theme, 2) it's *life giving* to be *broken* again and again, and 3) it is *safe* to *risk* an encounter with not just our light, but also our shadow.

As much as I want to embrace all that's offered here, the challenge is great. Breaking open? Confronting my shadow? Something inside is saying, "Not so fast."

Reflecting on Classroom Events

Our first activity has us dividing into groups of three to share

Chapter 6

a challenging yet positive situation from our teaching. Palmer had prepared us for this exercise at our last retreat, so we've come with notes in hand. We're invited to self-select our groups and find available places around the room to share our stories. I approach Carl, a well-dressed and upbeat guy known at the retreats for his enthusiasm for golf. Jane, a high-anxiety Erma Bombeck, joins us. Her short hair and modest earrings are offset by her dry humor. I hand my story to them:

> I teach computer science to 500 middle school students each year. All seventh graders take a 7-1/2-week course and all eighth graders take a nine-week course. Class periods are 43 minutes duration. The classroom is organized in a U shape with the student chairs facing outward. Placing the tables and equipment in a U shape is good for two reasons; I can see everyone's screen easily and it creates a large area for circle work. I have found one drawback to this arrangement—the students face away from me and the center of the room.
>
> At the beginning of class about four weeks into the term, I said good morning in a strong and positive voice. (There was no doubt in my mind that all students could physically hear me.) There was little if any response to my greeting. The students were already absorbed with the computer work.
>
> I got their attention and told them I had just suffered a put down and was concerned that I didn't exist. I was puzzled that no one had acknowledged my presence by responding to my greeting.
>
> I went on to say that I was very embarrassed about discussing this situation because I did not want to imply that I was attempting to demand their respect or friendship. Such an attempt would be presumptuous and useless. On the other hand, I told them how important a moment this was for me as a teacher and that I thought

it should not be ignored. I realized I could provide two things to think about: "being present" to each other and the purpose of good manners.

I explained to them that Americans doing business in South Africa have come to realize how cold and disconnected American society is. South African workers have approached American managers asking if they had done something wrong. The workers felt that they were getting the "cold shoulder" from their bosses. It turns out that American managers had not adequately acknowledged the presence of the workers as the bosses walked through the factories.

A widespread greeting in Africa is, "I see you." The response is, "I am here." or "You are seen." This interchange is a sign of connection and respect.

As I continued to talk, I could see that the students were relatively attentive, but many had their backs turned to me. I remarked that showing one's back to someone while they are talking is considered bad manners. Taking this position, I said, is another form of disconnection and disrespect.

I went on: Lest anyone be confused, good manners are as much for those exercising good manners as for those receiving them. Those who practice good manners improve their reputation and standing. Those who practice good manners become fit to live with. They are more apt to develop a circle of friends and colleagues.

I asked them to please let me know if they ever felt that I was distant or ignoring them. It was my intention to "be present" for them.

The next day, nearly in unison (but seemingly unrehearsed), I was greeted with, "We see you."

Palmer has asked us to discuss the paradoxes found in our stories. I tell Jane and Carl that I picked that moment because it deals with "being present to each other," a theme of increasing importance to me as the effects of our retreat community take hold in my life. Jane and Carl identify the room setup in my story as a paradox; it allows for whole class work but it also encourages disconnection. We also note the paradox inherent in encouraging a relationship that, at its best, would be spontaneous. Jane and Carl both say that they can relate, as teachers, to "taking risks" about discussing life issues when the expectation for us is to teach subject matter.

It strikes me that our discussion of "taking risks" is related to a term in the teaching field—"certainty." Work at your craft for decades and your certainty should be high. I agree in concept, but, throw in the unpredictability of people, and one experiences uncertainty. What is left to hang on to in such times is whatever bedrock you've uncovered within yourself.

Widespread Conflict

After we settle into the circle again, John's face grows troubled and he shares that his school staff is laboring under stress. As he describes the situation, I realize that his story is an eerie twin to my own. I see that the same three groups have materialized in his school—the Insiders, the Fence Sitters and the Outsiders. Because of off-hand remarks and subtle put-downs, an effective group of teachers have been magically transformed into the goat of the leader and the Insiders. The leader and the Insiders exist in euphoric symbiosis, exchanging kudos among each other. It appears that the majority of the staff is unaware of the amount of control and manipulation at play in the situation. John believes that some of the teachers have offered their support to the leader in order to stay in "good graces." While the Fence Sitters pose little threat and the Insiders keep the Outsiders pinned down, the leader has an open playing field. Identical script.

Is the fact that John's situation is such a carbon copy mere coincidence, or does it say something more fundamental about "the system?" Do these twin stories emanate from something in human nature, or is it a combination of the two? *What* is the spark for all of this pain? Another teacher in our circle describes a split and then another until I realize that conflict among school staff is much more widespread than I thought. I begin to believe that if I ever find a satisfactory explanation for all of this I will have found something of great value.

Intro to Paradox
Next, we brainstorm a list of paradoxes:

Spirit - Matter
Mind - Body
Contemplation - Action
Thought - Feeling
Light - Darkness
Masculine - Feminine
Heaven - Earth
God - Devil

We affirm that either/or thinking is fundamental to current Western culture. People mistakenly think of one pole of the paradox as good and the other as bad. That kind of labeling and judging destroys the wholeness of a paradox.

Palmer explains why we split paradoxes in two—we want to render reality lifeless. "The battery appears dead if the poles are disconnected," he says. "Life is easier when it doesn't reach for us." Splitting apart a paradox makes life simpler. Either/or thinking provides the illusion of control and both the ego and society decree that control is the ultimate solution to life's problems. When we pick a pole, it feels as if we're in charge – but that isn't the reality.

We need opposites. If we stay at the factual level, either/or works. The opposite of an ordinary fact is a lie. But, if we go to the level of truths, there are opposites that are true. In a paradox, the opposite of one profound truth is often another profound truth. We discuss that a classroom must have structure, but it must also promote freedom of thought and expression. I can encourage my students to use their inner resources, but I should also foster their openness to each other and to new ideas.

Chapter 6

What happens when a paradox falls apart? When we pick one pole and focus on it, our over use of that pole creates its pathological form. Solitude collapses into loneliness and community disintegrates into "The Crowd." If we choose between masculine and feminine we get either domination or submission. What can often predominate in society are the distorted forms of one side of a paradox.

Palmer continues. "Living and leading with our hearts exposed allows us to be fully alive and real. There is probably more suffering that one must acknowledge when living this way, but, at least for me, being fully alive and real is the only way I want to live." He ends by directing our attention back to ourselves. "Before we can get to matters at work, we need to work on matters of the self. We need to get in touch with the poles of life."

Thinking Paradoxically

We break out of the circle and, in solitude, generate a list of paradoxes found in our lives, attempting to notice how both poles are present. I begin to mechanically record a list of pairs such as control/openness, home/work but, as I continue, the exercise turns real. I notice a major shift in my thinking as the serious dilemmas at work emerge on paper. For most of these I've been conflicted over deciding to follow my heart or conform as in the case of designing our day. I could continue to advocate for a better schedule or fold. The operative word up to this moment has been "or." I know that each choice has a benefit, but I also realize that each has a down side. That's why the two choices form a dilemma. I reframe this dilemma as a paradox and now wonder how to be true to myself *and* still be a valuable team member. A second paradox of real concern appears on my list. I've been trying to decide if my school system is embarrassingly awful or at least average. Instead of exclusively looking at what's wrong, I need to find what to celebrate.

I see that when I use paradoxical thinking, I'm relieved of the burden of choosing one pole over the other, but a challenge surfaces when trying to "live in the middle." How does one "live" both poles when they are opposites? I have often chosen one pole over holding the paradox together because the choice felt simple and safe compared to the "middle way." Instead of having the comfort of quick and easy answers, the middle way comes with questions and a higher level of anxiety from being torn between the poles.

I am brought back to the present as we form a circle to discuss our thoughts about the lists we made. The fog begins to dissipate the longer we share and Palmer ends the session with: "Lunch! The reason we're here!"

Best Day

We reconvene by sitting in silence and imagining a best day and a worst day (certainly a paradox if there ever was one). For the best day I immediately think of a recent incident when I felt it necessary to talk with my students about being kind to each other. In that discussion, light eventually emerged from darkness. My students went from blame to ownership. As I scan my memory for a worst day, I first search for a catastrophe, but eventually I decide that a worst day is any day when my students and I just go through the motions. The fact that such days without peaks and valleys can feel so serene is deceptive; to me they are the worst of all days because no one is honest or engaged; no one is fully alive in the present moment.

Palmer reads an account of one of his best days and then asks us to identify whatever gifts we saw present in him in the situation. He listens intently as we comment on the gifts we notice. Now we are to do the same with each other in small groups.

Claire shares with Carl and me about "The Courage to Be Me Day" that she helped organize at her school. Claire is the youngest in our group, though no less wise, with sharp features and a love of nature. She describes the process before the event as one full of potholes. The event was cancelled twice because of conflicts. Facility availability and staff support were challenges requiring her patience. When the day finally arrived, the students had no idea how to handle the discussion topics in the self-directed groups. But by the end, a number of students reported that it was "the best day ever." One special education student bubbled over, saying, "I got to talk for five whole minutes!" Carl and I mirror back to Claire. We see idealism, individualism, perseverance, faith, forgiveness and trust, with the outcome being nothing short of liberation.

Carl, who teaches special education classes, tells about two students who would avoid writing and talking. Where other students would turn in multiple pages for their writing assignments, these two might manage twenty-five words. Carl then assigned a report on assassins. Hundreds of words poured from these two and they approached Carl to talk. "I just listened," Carl says in awe. He describes how the two talked about their own wounds and each walked away with a bounce and a smile. Claire and I tell Carl that we see patience and respect, a caring response, wisdom in establishing a generative process and a way of being a gentle and supportive guide.

It's my turn. I talk about going off-topic from computer subjects to discuss relationships. I had been noticing that as the students would enter my room, they would often exchange harsh remarks that left someone feeling hurt. On this day, I greeted my students and announced that we'd start class with a discussion. I helped them form a circle and passed around a discussion starter, a letter from a Lynn Minton column called "Fresh Voices" that I had found in Sunday's *Parade* Magazine. A teen from Texas had written:

> 'Why I can be mean'
>
> "You asked the question, 'Is it hard to be kind?' My answer is 'Yes, for a teenager, it is hard.' For one reason: peer pressure. My friends are most of my life. They influence me a lot. If you are kind to a 'nerd' or a person who is not thought highly of, you are laughed at. That can be humiliating. You want to be accepted by the 'popular' group so of course you are usually cruel to the 'nerds' from then on, to prove to your friends that you are not associated with them. Sad but true."[3]

I started the discussion by asking, "Can you relate to this letter, which was written by someone your age hundreds of miles away?" Yes, they say, they can. At first, accusations were traded, but then they were able to focus inward. Yes. They acknowledged that, once started, put-downs only continue in endless loops. Yes. They owned up to their part in the drama—all of this without prompting. They expressed a sincere commitment to create a better environment and the days that followed were conspicuously absent of conflict.

Claire and Carl cite in my approach a willingness to go off topic and welcome the opinions of students. They're generous with their observations of my manner, as they've experienced it on the retreat, believing that the softness, "sincere look" and calmness they see here were likely assets in my work with the class. I chuckle to myself, reflecting that only a few colleagues back home would recognize *me* in such a description. At work, when do we ever have the opportunity to know each other well enough to name each other's gifts? How many of us even think that identifying gifts is our responsibility to each other?

Modeling

We're invited back to the circle to talk about shadow. Palmer declares, "Every gift has a liability, a flip side. We must embrace the other side of our gift during times when it's misused or overused. The shadow side of a gift is often driven by us wanting to do the dance, to evoke and soak up the electricity."

He reads a description of his worst day, a day on which a class went poorly. He was teaching a required course for graduation and the students were distracted, dull. In the end, his patience is challenged. I see that his worst day was very similar to mine, with students going through the motions, present in body only. He asks that we comment on the situation in the hopes of promoting understanding but that we refrain from fixing or advising. "Don't advise or fix"—that's been a guiding principle at every retreat because, as he has explained, when we refrain from advising, our restraint unleashes that person's confidence in finding his or her own way. He shares that his gift is subjectivity and, in the situation we're discussing, he discovered the need for objectivity. The discussion of our classroom events takes us to the end of the afternoon. Palmer brings closure by saying that we don't really *lose* on the worst day because we can transform the situation into a learning experience. "Our best work results from being who we truly are, not from technique. The path of wisdom means living in the tension and holding our awareness of the paradox instead of choosing denial."

Days for Learning

The following morning starts with work on our own worst days. It's important to eliminate our projections. It will be most fruitful if we engage in this discussion without using others or circumstances as excuses. In addition, our worst day is to be shared in the context of "the opposite of a strength."

Our worst days end up looking not so bad after all. After hearing each story, I see that the initial seed of the worst day is always a good intention gone astray; I see the learning that follows the breakdown. The realization comes that on my best day I was subjective. On the worst day I was overly objective, to the point that my students reached for the off switch. On that day, I allowed the subjective/objective paradox to fall apart, emphasizing to extreme one pole over the other.

Behold a Truth

We next listen to a story entitled "The Angel and the World's Dominion." As Cheri reads, we discover its message. Moved by seeing human pain and struggle, an angel asks for the responsibility of the earth for one year. God grants the wish and it is not long before the earth and its people experience an unknown level of abundance. Gone are death and decay. The angel is overjoyed with the results until wailing is heard from the people. They have discovered that within this distorted abundance is a false blessing. Pained and confused, the angel begs for God to explain and God replies:

> Behold a truth...the earth must be nourished with decay and covered with shadows...and...that souls must be made fertile with flood and sorrow, that through them the Great Work may be born.[4]

Embedded in this story is an inspired guess at the master plan—that birth and death, light and darkness are dependent on each other. When a paradox breaks apart, all is lost. An endless string of sunny days results in drought. An endless string of rainy days results in flood. New life springs from light and darkness, from storm and respite. Paradox offers us the opportunity to embrace our worst days, and the shadow inside each one of us, as well as our gifts. Our health, our wholeness, rests in uniting opposing truths.

The story of the angel reminds me of another. When God is asked why God subjects Man to violence, pain, sickness and death, God answers, "It makes a better story." Viewed more deeply, beyond the intended humor, God's response carries with it the same truth. Richness and aliveness emanate from the better story, the more complete story, the one filled with paradox.

I try to apply our work here to my situation back home and I guess that my suffering can bear fruit. What good can come from my heart breaking open? At this moment, I don't know, but the question becomes a companion to others that will fuel my thinking and reading after this retreat.

Holding the Tension

We start the next session with a quote from Rilke's *Letters to a Young Poet*. "…be patient with all that is unresolved in your heart and try to love the *questions themselves*…"[5] Ah. Here is the permission I've been looking for—to be at peace with the confusion and anxiety that accompanies the tension of a paradox. Rilke says, "…the point is, to live everything. *Live* the questions now."[6] The answer to finding my way with a paradox is—there is no convenient, immediate answer—the journey is ongoing. My questions don't have to be answered; they have to be "held." In a world that convinces me that I must control everything, this permission is pure revelation.

Palmer asks, "What are the paradoxes you are willing to wrap your life around?" Workshops con us into thinking we'll receive a magic wand along with our name badge, that everything has a quick fix. Here, I'm invited to live a life of ongoing uncertainties. Come here and encounter something free that eludes capture.

Chapter 6

Parting Wisdom

During this retreat, we have not only learned new concepts, we have begun to think about their application. Palmer guides our final discussion toward the personal by saying, "Any significant inner work that I do for myself, I am ultimately doing on behalf of others. Organizations offer huge monetary rewards to violent manipulators who create further violence in their workplace out of a lack of inner work. There is a failure in not searching for a balance of activity and reflection."

We name the paradoxes in the classroom that we have come to see as important. Instantly the room comes alive as we call out many in rapid succession. It is obvious that we are far more adept at handling paradox now than earlier. We offer affective/cognitive, hospitality/rigor and a dozen more that are active in our classrooms and Palmer suggests others as well. Two of his are of particular interest to me. He calls attention to the emotion/intellect paradox, which affects all of us as teachers. He talks about the balance of stressing the academics in our work without beating emotion from the door. If we can't hold both at once, learning will take a holiday. Educators now realize that humans learn when they have emotions for and about something. No wonder my best teachers were the most passionate, I muse. Clearly, their passions were infectious.

Palmer also points out the big story/little story paradox. It's difficult to learn unless we can connect the big story and the little story, an important concept to a personal application. "Normally, the little story gets swept under the rug. I learned about the Holocaust as if it were on another planet, isolated in space and time, with no connection to me. Instead, I have to connect to the story close at hand. I have to see the bit of Hitler in *me*, how I am threatened by your difference and therefore must kill you off. Together, the two stories have immense power."

Laurie makes a remark that sounds like closure, "It's not a matter of *bringing* paradox into your life, it's waking up to the truth that it's already there."

Claiming My Learnings

As a final exercise, we write a letter to ourselves which will

Disregarded

be mailed back to us at some random date in the future, helping to keep the retreat alive long after today's closing. The most profound learning for me is that I must consistently regard people as paradoxical. By doing so, everyone becomes more approachable, especially those I've come to consider a foe. I now understand how inner peace is possible.

I will come away from this retreat with greater conviction in my work. What I thought were dilemmas I was unable to solve, zapping my confidence, turn out to be legitimate paradoxes. Even though the 7-1/2-week courses push me to cram in the content, today I give myself permission to do the affective work I've felt compelled to do. I'm shifting my emphasis on the pole called content to the middle of the process/content paradox.

I've been dancing around the positive pole of spirituality, only to recently learn of its inclusive nature—shadow must be embraced, as well. In me are gift/shadow paradoxes. I would do well to live close to the ground and embrace my shortcomings.

Back Home

I study the retreat's topics in the months that follow. My first book search reveals nothing on paradox, but, eventually, persistence pays off. The bibliography of a lone book leads me by a fragile thread to another and then each new find keeps the trail alive. I wonder if the world is waking up to the power of paradox or if that nothing has changed except my own awareness.

Palmer himself, it turns out, has written a book called *The Promise of Paradox*. I'm surprised by its bold, religious approach, which is different from the context he creates at our retreats. Palmer points out that the left and right and up and down reaches of the cross are a paradox. He writes that the cross means "the pain stops here."[7] With a growing sense of my own shadow, I see that the cross can symbolize the refusal to project darkness:

> …a way which transforms pain from destructive impulse into creative power…what we lose on the cross is the burden of falsehood and illusion… pain kills illusion so that truth can bring joy.[8]

Palmer's explains what a "dialectic" is. In the beginning, there is a thesis (a theory of how something works) and, over time, its opposite, an antithesis, develops. The tension between the two is the catalyst for "synthesis," the movement to a whole, higher state. Synthesis then becomes the reigning thesis and the infinite loop continues. I finally see what results from thinking paradoxically! It's *synthesis*, something "whole" and "higher," that results from holding the tension of a paradox.

Further into the text Palmer suggests that when we allow others to see our contradictions, our doubts, and our imperfections, we encourage and nurture community:

> When I think about the people with whom I have the deepest sense of community, I think of people who have been able to share with me their contradictions, their brokenness—thus allowing me to share mine. When we present ourselves to the world as smooth and seamless we allow each other no way in, no way into life together.[9]

Because of my retreat encounters, these are no longer words on paper; instead, they are a truth confirmed by my own recent experience.

While he addresses community in churches, I'm convinced his words still apply to workplaces:

> If true community is to flourish then the individual must flourish as well...In our corporate seeking, the individual must never be overpowered, never coerced into going along, never put in the position of an outvoted and embittered minority...As the church tests for corporate truth, it must always respect the word of God in the single heart, a word which may be too radical for the group to hear.[10]

How can I flourish in my work community? It seems to me that three fundamental beliefs must be turned on their heads. First, instead of believing my existence is justified by serving the system, the system could exist to serve me, so I can serve my students. Radical! In a perfect scenario for the world of medicine, for instance, the administration, nurses, lab technicians and consulting specialists support the doctor and patient. When I ask for support, I get the impression I'm a presumptuous inconvenience. Second, our decision-making could shift from the practice of majority rule voting to the much deeper and more meaningful process called consensus. Finally, we could sincerely respect one another instead of seeing each other as foes or pawns to be manipulated. If we believed that, for a given challenge, a single heart could hold the solution, every voice would be honored. From our experiences born out of heightened respect, we would discover that a word, which was "too radical for the group to hear," was the elixir the community needed.

Awareness Broadens

I chuckle while experiencing what I call "The Cayman Green Ford Phenomenon." When we bought our Ford Escort, we chose Cayman Green because we had yet to see a car in town with that color. It wasn't long before we were getting into cars that we didn't own! A sea of Cayman Green Fords washed over local parking lots. At stoplights we would be sandwiched between two others! Where had they all come from? We concluded that with our car purchase came an awareness upgrade for ourselves. Like those Cayman Green Fords, I'm beginning to notice paradox everywhere—not only in business and psychology books, but in literature and poetry as well:

> My object in living is to unite
> My avocation and my vocation
> As my two eyes make one in sight.[11]
> Robert Frost
> "Two Tramps in Mud Time"

Chapter 6

> It was the best of times, it was the worst of times, it was the age of wisdom, it was the age of foolishness...[12]
>
> Charles Dickens, *A Tale of Two Cities*

> If you want to lead the people,
> you must learn how to follow them.[13]
>
> *Tao Te Ching*

Voice from the Past

About six weeks after our retreat, my letter to self arrives in the mail and I open it expectantly. I see the words patience, Light, peacemaker, lamb. Risk being the lamb? It's my handwriting, but I wonder who the writer is. Seeing my advocacy for and defense of my colleagues through my role as union rep., who could guess that I not only want peace, I want to *be* peace?

The Retreat Comes Alive Again

The letter sparks a memory of the most profound activity of the past retreat. Palmer says, "Paradoxes are beyond words, so we are going to do bodywork. A body has a knowing that reaches back 50,000 years and further." We will physically experience paradox.

I stand as two others crouch on each side me, carefully grasping my forearms. I say "Go!" and the two give it all they've got, pulling down with all their might. I pull up with all my force, fighting back with one arm, then the other. Sweat runs off my forehead as we tug back and forth. Finally, I say, "Stop!"

I've experienced one pole. Call it struggle, resist—whatever. The three of us share impressions of the experience.

The scene is the same, but the instructions are different. I say "Go!" and the two by my side begin pulling as before. At the first tug, I fall to the carpet in submission and collapse.

I've experienced the other pole. The two activities have created a struggle/surrender paradox.

We reposition ourselves in the same way for the final part of the bodywork. I'm told to develop "soft eyes," to see all about me. I am to imagine my fingers stretching into the ground. My legs and feet are to be deeply rooted as well, for I must live between these contradictions.

On my command we begin again and I do my best to "live in the middle." I neither fight nor surrender. My two colleagues muster as much muscle and body weight as they can, but this experience is unlike the others. As my friends exhaust their energy and I have yet to feel fatigue, a single word forms in my head—"forever." So *this* is how we are to live in the center!

"Forever" echoes inside again and again until it folds into, "Do not seek the answers...*Live* the questions now. Perhaps you will then gradually, without noticing it, live along some distant day into the answer."[14]

Chapter 7 – Know Thyself

...I was a hidden treasure, and I desired to be known.[1]
                                                    Rumi

At a conference last month, I'm drawn to a Dominican Sister and introduce myself. Her name is Sister Sue Tracy and she is a hospital chaplain. As she smiles back in an uncommonly joyful way, I guess that she is medicine for many. I've been looking for a priest or nun to interview and she appears to be a prime candidate. From time to time reference has been made to our teacher retreats as a "formation program" and I've learned that the religious enter their orders and participate in formation programs. I'm anxious to answer a number of questions—What are the principles of formation? Do other communities help members identify their gifts? How is The Courage to Teach program similar to formation experienced by the religious? What impact does formation have on the individual?

In two short weeks, I find myself back at the Dominican Center in Grand Rapids sitting in a dining room empty except for my hospitable host, who smiles at me from across the table. Sister Sue goes through the schedule of her early years: chapel, silent meditation, Mass, breakfast, classes, lunch, classes, prayer, stations of the cross, rosary, recreation, supper, prayer, vespers, silence. "There was a structure to help us encounter God," she says. "The paradox was to be in the world, but not be worldly. Our schedule affected our values. It wasn't a cookie cutter approach. The individual was honored." She relates that, centuries before, her order was called Order of Preachers. Their emphasis was the search for truth. "We still have that same focus, but we've added hospitality and joy," she says, eyes glistening. I think to myself how well Sister Sue personifies that calling.

She describes the four Dominican "pillars" as private and common prayer, life-long study, ministry in any form and the common life (community). To Sister Sue, formation seemed to be "the encouragement needed for the quest for God, God the Be All and End All." Generally lasting from five to ten years, up to the "profession for life," the process is intentionally slow to insure that the Dominican way of life is right for the person.

So far, I can make loose connections between the programs—those of time, silence, and respect for the person.

Sister Sue shares that her novice director would keep asking, "What gifts has God given you?" Sister Sue would expect her encounters with her director to be opportunities to "point out my foibles, but, instead, she would only encourage gratitude." Sister Sue states in a matter of fact tone, "She said that I was made to have people drawn to me. My challenge was to draw those people to God." I think to myself about that living truth. Here I am, sitting in this unfamiliar place, miles from home, having been drawn to Sister Sue.

She adds that a spiritual director is a "spiritual mirror." That person doesn't push or point, but does try to call forth from the individual the experience that was shared for study. Her spiritual director would probe, "What do you do with this? Where is God in the muck?"

Sister Sue shares an incident that demonstrates to me the importance of journeying together, something that confirms my own experiences while on retreat. Sister Sue is in the interview before her "profession" and her novice director drops the bomb. "What are you doing out of your field?" she queries in an incredulous tone. In the eyes of her guide, her change in majors from English to biology was a worse fit. Sister Sue looks across the table at me and lights up, "Thank Heaven she saw me in the correct light!"

I ask Sister Sue about personal discoveries. "Befriend the brokenness," she offers enthusiastically. "Accept it. Self-awareness is vital so we don't project our brokenness onto others." I realize I've just heard another reason for self-study. One reason is to serve, a second is to become more effective in that service, and now another significant reason emerges—to uncover and honor our weaknesses, which helps us refrain from projecting them onto others.

She shares one more discovery. In her late thirties, Sister Sue realized she was not yet ready for a chaplaincy, something she had desired for a long time. While she waited and matured, cancer struck. "Cancer was a gift," she says. "It called me to a deeper level of life, call, mission and gratitude." Sister Sue relates that while in her forties and following cancer, she knew she was ready. I imagine how healing her presence is, for her chaplaincy is in the in-patient cancer unit plus the outpatient chemotherapy and radiation therapy clinic. At least from my viewpoint, Sister Sue has journeyed to the right place.

"During the early years was there much study of your past?" I ask. "No," she says, "we were focused toward what the order was all about and if we were a match." I ask about personality profiles. Sister Sue mentions Myers-Briggs first, and then says, "Later, I was introduced to the Enneagram. I'm a Seven, and you?" "I'm a One," I say. She bursts forth with, "Ah! A perfectionist! I know two poor sisters who struggle so to be perfect!"

I can't help but laugh, even if the joke's on me.

As I drive home, I reflect on the similar formation practices. Both programs honor the individual. The individual is not seen as one who needs to be fixed and reshaped. There's an intentional search for gifts; the community mirrors back gifts found in the individual. And, most recently, our retreat group has been encouraged to embrace our shadow, our brokenness, with the intention of reducing our projections toward others. Sister Sue demonstrates the fruits of a formation process—potent clarity of purpose and exquisite fit.

We Teach What We Need to Learn

Not long ago I took stock of what I'd learned from self-study and realized that I had accumulated enough materials for a class on identifying one's own gifts. It's the last session of a course I'm teaching at St. Andrews on "Finding Your Gifts." The local participants are mostly women, middle age upward. I have hosted retreats of my own before this class and I now realize that this project, like the others, has been a test run to see if I am capable of and comfortable with facilitation work.

As I look around the circle on this last night, some earlier moments come to mind. I had asked participants to pick five values out of a very large list and to tell how those values influence their lives. A mother of five sons said that the appearance of the Beatles on the Ed Sullivan Show had changed her life forever. It was the night long hair became "in." When a school administrator flicked her son's hair with a pencil and poked fun at it, the son left high school and never graduated. This earthy woman quipped, "I thought what was between the ears was more important than what was on them." She went on to say how difficult it was to teach her sons to think for themselves and then deal with the response from the system. The tale demonstrates the aim of education at its worst. The god of education can be conformity and its task to enculturate young minds.

I learn from the participants that many of us come vulnerable to the study of self. We come with the belief that we don't matter, that our hair has to be above the ear so as to please someone else. I begin to see how courageous my fellow travelers have been in coming here when they reveal what they've learned in surprise:

> "I've learned that I'm okay; that I do have gifts."
> "I learned that I do have real gifts and can admit this to myself in all honesty."
> "I even said a few nice things about myself—
> out loud even. That's a biggie for me."

These people are waging a revolution and I see that I'm a revolutionary too. Not only am I attempting to help them liberate their own gifts, but I'm fighting for my own liberation as well. As I look around the room, I feel real gratitude for what I've learned and I share with them one of my favorite teacher sayings, "I taught and they didn't get it, I taught it again and they didn't get it, I taught it again and *I* finally got it!"

Some have shared how Spirit plays a part in their work. Not

everyone feels that they are in the "right place," but all feel called. The school secretary in the group marvels at the number of opportunities there are each day to help staff and students. The emergency room nurse acknowledges how critical her work is. But these are clandestine affairs. While I can tell that their spirituality is not on their shirtsleeve, it is clear that it is an integral part of their work. It is a nurse on the children's ward who provides the most vivid image for me. As she makes the night rounds, stopping at each child and checking vital signs, she leans forward and says a little prayer over each one and does what she calls the "laying on of the stethoscope."

Our last activity is based on an experience of Joseph Campbell's I found in *A Joseph Campbell Companion*. Campbell and about forty-eight others spend a day considering what they value most and then participate in a ritual. They pick small objects that could represent those things and then are asked to give up their valuables, one by one.

Campbell's hosts have access to a cave, an environment that must surely heighten the experience. A cave we do not have, so I secure the only artifacts that will combat cement block walls, linoleum and the grumbling Coke machine—candles.

For the week's homework, students have asked themselves, "What are the seven things for which you feel your life is worth living?"[2] My intention is to help them identify and prioritize what they deeply care about. We are meeting in the church library. The students record their items on card stock that I've cut in the shape of stones. I leave the group and walk through the meeting hall and into the church basement, turning off lights as I return. When I arrive back at the library, we light each other's candles and begin our procession in the dark.

At the doorway to the library I say, "Surrender that which you value least." Each face glows from the candlelight as their brows wrinkle and they struggle over their decision. Eventually each surrenders one of their treasures into a wicker basket. The basket is left at the door. I will collect the baskets, reconstruct the order of the treasures and mail the results to each person.

We proceed to an archway, where, I again say, "Surrender that which you value least." Another courageous act of letting go.

Disregarded

We end our journey in the meeting hall and they reluctantly relinquish that which is treasured most. I'm struck by the thought that *I* must let go. I turn on a light and all blow out their candles. I watch the wisps of smoke rise toward the ceiling and deal with wanting to engage further while saying goodbye.

These people have shared how seldom they've been encouraged to look for their gifts. The class experience confirms a great need for this work. Small miracles have taken place here for which I cannot take credit. I've watched their gifts emerge as the class progressed, all because we intentionally looked for the goodness in each other.

Seeing into Being

For me, the gifts class drives home the idea that we can cast light or darkness on others from our own orientation. A community has the power to label any member a hero or heel. It depends on the maturity and perspective of the community. Shall community members act as mirrors or critics?

In my teaching, one of my favorite class activities is something I call "Schroedinger's Cat." Erwin Schroedinger was a physicist who, among other things, brought the power of "seeing" to our attention. I bring to school our African gray parrot's travel cage, stuffed with a towel. Before any students arrive, I place it on a table in the center of the open space. One step in the room and the curiosity of each student skyrockets. "What's that?" or "What's in there?" pops out spontaneously. "Wait and see," I mischievously respond.

When class begins I explain, "I've brought my cat. Sorry you can't see it, it's snuggled under the towel right now." Students move to the edge of their chairs and, invariably, someone rushes to the table to peer inside the cage. I explain that there is a button on the cage. Once pressed, food or poison will drop into the cage—*I don't know which one.* The room goes quiet.

I press the button and the silence hangs heavily. Then the questions erupt, cascading on top of each other—Did food drop down? Can we open the door? Did poison drop down? I answer none of these and counter with some of my own. "What are the facts as we know them?" "Is the cat alive or dead?" "What do you think?" "What is this problem really about?" "How can we apply what we've learned to our lives?"

Schroedinger points out that *only when we look do we determine* the status of the cat. Within the opaque container rests the potential of both states. In *our seeing* we bring nothing less than life or death to the subject of our attention. I cannot help but wonder how we would feel about ourselves and each other, and what we could accomplish, if we could see each other alive.

Panning for Gold

As part of my quest for self-knowledge, I read about personality. Three resources and a day off-site with the school improvement team greatly increase my understanding. From *Discovering Your Personality Profile, People Types and Tiger Stripes* and *Do What You Are* come descriptors of strengths, weaknesses and workplace conditions that would promote my success. In the Myers-Briggs world I'm an "INTJ" – "INNOVATOR of ideas."[3] In the Enneagram paradigm I'm a "One: The Reformer."[4] Mine is the "[m]ost individualistic and most independent personality of all the types."[5] Nothing like living on the edge, I quip to myself.

I learn of the likely traits of people with my personality type. People like me often persevere, possess enduring purpose, and are rational, direct, accurate, principled, and systematic. I regard problems as challenges, not as sources of discouragement. General descriptors include "relentless reorganizer," and "initiator or designer of changes." These seem pretty accurate to me and I note that membership on the school improvement team looks appropriate.

While reading *Do What You Are*,[6] I mull over a list of possible careers that are good matches for my type—writer, organizational consultant, administrator, university teacher, inventor and architect. All the careers look good to me. I've even dabbled in some of these areas already.

Those with my type can be too focused, faultfinders, perfectionists, unconcerned about social poise and self-righteous. Oops. I observe that these traits are the opposites of the positive descriptors. Distort a designer of changes and get a faultfinder. I realize that the potential dark news about myself deserves some careful reflection.

A thunderbolt strikes when I learn about an INTJ's optimal work environment and compare it to my own workplace:[7]
1. Allows me to develop and implement my ideas— (*a cold day in Hell...*)
2. Is full of new and relevant information— (*information is being withheld*)
3. Is relatively conflict free—(*currently a war zone*)
4. Encourages change initiatives and systems development— (*viewed as outside "my job"*)
5. Evaluated consistently and fairly—(*under slanderous attack*)

I've never given "fit" a thought! Am I in the wrong place? I'm drawn here. I want to be here. Yet, I can clearly see that, for my personality type, my workplace environment is well below "optimal." For the first time, I consider that there may be a fundamental clash between who I am and my workplace culture. I'm a relentless change agent in an entrenched organization.

Can lightning strike twice? There's more intriguing news about those with my type and the workplace environment. I read that I'm inclined to overlook resistance to what I want to accomplish, being especially inept at sizing up resistance and its causes. In addition, I would be more successful by recognizing that sanctions exist. The first statement rings true. I've conceded to myself more than once that I don't understand the politics of this place. I sputter over the second. Am I supposed to learn how to duck? Sanctions are warranted for theft, sexual harassment and not refilling the coffee pot. Are they legitimate for differences of opinion and change initiatives? I'm left to wonder about what contribution, if any, I would make if I acknowledged and stayed clear of sanctions.

The Past

I find the study on personality to be very helpful, but I realize that it's a waypoint, not a destination. We should study ourselves objectively *to go past* what we find. We are not our personalities, but we need to know them in order to move beyond them.

As I shift away from personality, I begin to notice magazine articles with titles such as: "Reinvent Your Life," "Take Control of Your Life" and "Design a Life That Works for You." While I believe that our lives are, in part, about self-transformation, I'm aware that our lives are trying to inform us. I would do well to discover the life already present. I should look to my past, maybe even to childhood. What has my life been trying to tell me?

While reading *The Truth About You*,[8] I try an exercise of looking backward at projects that I think were successful and most satisfying to help me identify my inborn strengths and motivations. What news about myself is buried in these projects?

1. Speaking and doing seminars
2. School improvement team activities
3. Independent learner
4. Wrote award-winning software that teaches money concepts
5. Authored a keyboarding/typing text for students
6. Authored school improvement pamphlets
7. Formed a family music group
8. Served as a volunteer group counseling leader in a prison setting
9. Wrote marching band drill and music arrangements
10. Planned and built a house addition
11. Served as chief negotiator for the teacher negotiating team
12. Established a Bandmaster's Conference for Army bands directors
13. Established a mobile DJ business

As I survey all of my project summaries, I see a pattern to build, serve, improve or meet a need. I'm someone who utilizes planning, learning, creativity and organization. I was often drawn to intangibles—ideas, principles, models or values. I tend to persevere despite obstacles. I tackled most of these projects on my own; for others I played a supporting role; but rarely was I the boss. I am left wondering if I choose the support role or if there have been few opportunities for me to lead.

Disregarded

I notice that most of the situations provided enough freedom for me to "succeed." The exception is my current workplace, the place where my initiatives are seemingly unwelcome.

Two serious statements from my reading stay with me, warning me that, like others, I'm capable of selfish acts subtly disguised as service. First, service to others can be self-serving. We serve to feel good about ourselves, to fulfill a need to serve. Taken too far, helping others could be a ruse for meeting my own needs. Second, just like everyone else on the planet, I will behave with my "preferred style" whether or not the situation calls for it. In the case of my personality type, everywhere there are windmills to be fought. Yet, I have already seen how our retreat group's commitment not to "fix" each other resulted in real growth. My learning here is that I should proceed cautiously before I decide to engage and improve every situation I encounter.

A Big Little Book

At one of the retreats, Palmer spoke about "a little book" he would someday write about vocation. I think that what I have in my hands must be it—*Let Your Life Speak*. Inside I read that no matter our role or job title, we will do what our true self urges us to do, that "…[our] vocation…will manifest itself in any role [we] play."[9] What is vocation at its deepest level? "This (vocation) is something I can't not do, for reasons I'm unable to explain to anyone else and don't fully understand myself but that are nonetheless compelling."[10] Vocation is what we end up doing time and time again. In my case, it seems as if I "can't not" stay away from improving organizations by encouraging them to support the actualization of each member.

Apparently, to discover my vocation, I must separate the wheat from the chaff. I must separate those things driven by my "oughts" from those things that I have consistently done from my center. Palmer encourages me to honor the mystery involved when he writes that vocation can be something that I "don't fully understand myself."

Palmer's journey helped him realize that it was better for him to work outside the organization than to be in it and full of frustration. My jaw drops as insight hits. I remember the thoughts

I had while noticing the striking difference between my working preferences and my current work culture. At work I'm battling to stay afloat in a churning caldron, but I *could* decide to climb out and walk away—I'm the one with legs. On the other hand, am I called to stay and make this a better place?

Those who have found their true selves and their vocation are said to be "authentic." What does an authentic person look like? Where are the examples we can look to for guidance? Palmer suggests that the people involved in movements are the ones who have found the pain of being unreal more severe than the pain administered by the system. These people choose authenticity and endure punishment at the hands of others rather than suffer the self-inflicted pain of living lives that are not their own. Pain is a part of a vibrant life and I see that a whole life is more difficult to live because it invites threats from without and challenges from within. A whole life, a life of your own, is more difficult to live than a half-life. But, the alternatives to wholeness are a life without vitality, one of slumber, fear or membership amongst the walking dead, the crowd.

Palmer explains that authentic people lead through their living. "When we live in a close-knit ecosystem called community, everyone follows and everyone leads...I lead by word and deed *simply because I am here doing what I do.*"[11] What is the charge of leaders? "Authentic leaders...aim at liberating the heart,"[12] that includes the hearts of others. He defines a leader as, "...someone with the power to project either shadow or light onto some part of the world and onto the lives of the people who dwell there."[13] Authentic people project light for the purpose of illuminating the treasures that are in each of us.

Palmer provides yet another reason to pursue self-knowledge. "If you can't get out of it, get into it!"[14] If I accept the truth that my inner life is a constant companion, then I can stop running from it and start seeking its treasures. I can find out what it's all about. Some sort of "turning" is required of me. Instead of abandoning my life, I can "get into it," living it with abandon.

What's a Hero?

Colleagues at the retreats had mentioned the hero's journey—

a trek into the unknown, the trials of the descent into darkness and eventual transformation. Pairing the word "hero" with my life is too much of a stretch, but I want to know more. Do personal growth and the hero's journey have common elements? I read Joseph Campbell's *The Hero with a Thousand Faces* and learn that a hero is:

> ...the champion not of things become but of things becoming...The dragon to be slain...is precisely the monster of the status quo.[15]

The hero's task is to release the creative energy that's being suppressed by the current culture. As I try to apply Campbell's work to my own life, three things come to mind. First, despite Danzle's efforts to reestablish unchallenged power at the top, our school improvement team is on a hero's journey. We are working to change the status quo, which, as I see it, is strangling staff and student alike. Our team is about new life. Second, I think of how I long to share with my colleagues the discoveries I've made at the retreats—about fear, paradox, gifts and community. Living those concepts would surely breathe life into a stagnant culture. But the experience is beyond words. I've heard other retreatants say the same thing. Even amongst ourselves we talk with great difficulty about what is happening to us. In addition, the work culture and schedule are barriers to deep discussion. Time to share is rare indeed. Finally, under Campbell's definition, we should *all* be heroes. The natural world is constantly "becoming" and so should we, for when a living being reaches equilibrium, the status quo—it dies.

Doubt

I begin to wonder if my zeal for improving organizations is my way of avoiding my own dragons. Am I resisting bad news about myself by finding bad news about this place? Am I casting my own darkness onto my workplace? Maybe I want nothing better than to spoil power's plans and unloose power's grip. But what if my intentions or especially those of the school improvement team are valid? What then? I think of the words of fellow educators.

Chapter 7

In *The Hero's Journey: How Educators Can Transform Schools and Improve Learning,* Brown and Moffett quote a teacher:

> I once had a superintendent who told me that people on staff were concerned about my level of enthusiasm and hard work. "It's not natural," he said. "You must understand that many people are intimidated by you—you are like a bright light. And bright lights show up a lot of dust.[16]

Am I feeling the resistance from some of my peers because I'm stirring up dust? Is that how you become an outsider? They continue:

> The isolation of the person with the vision was a theme that recurred in our interviews. One teacher stated: There are two characteristics that I have found to be common among heroic educators. One is an unquenchable passion. And the other is knife wounds in the back. If you have found a way to nurture yourself in creating your own unquenchable vision, then how do you find healing for the wounds? How do you deal with someone who says: "If I pull you down, I'll look better. Because if you're excited and passionate, what does that say about me?" It's a threat.
>
> If you are the one saying, "But the emperor has no clothes; there's a problem here," suddenly *you* can become the problem.[17]

I'm as independent as they come, but I know I need others to both poke holes in my foolish perceptions *and* help transform my school. But when there are too few fellow travelers, what then?

Trust in the Journey, Trust Yourself

I gain a great deal of clarity from this study, calm and confidence as well. Is there a lingering question? Yes. The one I must live into an answer concerns fit. Am I a good fit for the place I care about?

One thing is certain about my journey of self-study—I have resisted learning about "my heart." I'm haunted by the memory of crying at the bottom of my driveway after I arrived home from that first retreat. Why? Do I have a heart of stone? Am I so cold and unfeeling as to be able to bury sadness for years? I've tried to be self-accepting, but I can't embrace the image of a heart of steel. I think of the interview with Sister Sue and ask myself, where am I in all this muck?

A friend provides a blank Myers-Briggs Type Inventory and I fill it out a second time. I'm surprised at the results. Either the abbreviated inventory I took the first time has a large margin of error or I've changed. I'm not an INTJ. I'm an INFJ—F for feeling. It's not that I can't feel it's that I feel deeply. Epiphany. I've kept a steel exterior to guard a soft, vulnerable center. Now I see that it took our retreat community to break through that shell. I *feel* that this discovery has been worth all the digging.

I grab my journal and leaf through the pages, looking for a poem I wrote some time ago. As I turn the pages I realize that the absence of tears has been about the fear of being broken open, something that must be done again and again. I have resisted the enlargement of my heart. I find the poem I'm looking for and drift back to thoughts of the death of a friend.

Finding Tears

Annie,
I watched life leave you.

I knew you your whole life long.
You never criticized.
You were accepting.
You forgave.

Would that I treat all as you did.
Would that others treat me such.

Chapter 7

This has been a decade of funerals.
I have helped send too many
to their eternal rest.
They all depart, teaching.
The dead's lesson for me, the funeral rite—
a preparation for my own leaving.
The lesson is retold time and again,
and still I am dumb.

It is my decade of stone.
I've had no tears for these fallen.
Too distant in life.
Too distant in death.
And what is to be gained by feeling?

But, alas, Annie,
my grief for you—
hoarded from my teachers—
is honest.

I weep and moan.
I gulp and gasp.
Open…
Unashamed…

You are my redeemer,
for my heart has broken into life.

It was the years.
It was your faithfulness
and your eye for goodness,
that sparked my mourning,
so wild as to be—worthy.

You were my best teacher,
you, who have never been this still—
since I brought you home
from the kennel.

Chapter 8 – From Scarcity to Abundance

*The glass is neither half full nor half empty—
it is overflowing.*

Scarcity Everywhere

Danzle has told the 6th grade teachers that he will be placing Sue Hardy at their grade level. By encouraging students to come to him with their beefs, he's created such a stir around Hardy that the teachers are saying there's no place for her on their teams. Who wants all the trouble that comes with her? To me, it looks like another orchestrated move by Danzle to further alienate and discredit Sue. Understanding, patience, acceptance and compassion are scarce right now, especially for Danzle's targets.

Even while perceiving these deficits (and noticing my own judgmental nature) I know we're capable of so much more. I keep looking for something positive to celebrate, but from my vantage point the landscape is grim. Is there something wrong with my seeing or are things as bad as they appear?

It's April, budget time, and as I develop next year's budget I confront my annual pet peeves. The "spend it or lose it" directive always gets me going. I continue to recommend that unspent money be carried over to the next year. It's not that there's too much money, it's that I'd rather save it until I am able to purchase something substantial that I can use. Eventually I could save enough from yearly allotments to buy what I really need instead of depleting the money on sundries. What I need are disk drives. What I buy are disks. I'm told that carrying over dollars

Chapter 8

into the next year can't be done—all the while not understanding why. I've suggested to the co-curricular teachers that we pool our money and rotate the allocation of a higher sum amongst us. We would have more power than we do now while acting alone. No go. We view budget money as too scarce to risk trying anything different.

There's scarcity elsewhere. Many of us have been encouraged to read about and take workshops on "Choice Theory," a psychological framework championed by Dr. William Glasser. The expected benefit of understanding this model is increased student learning. If the model accurately represents how students really think and behave, teachers can tailor their actions to how students choose to value and commit to learning.

An important part of Glasser's message is "remove coercion." He contends that the enjoyment of learning and the commitment to it will be stronger in a non-coercive atmosphere.

I agree.

I think that coercion affects adults too. I believe that if teachers are heavily managed, they will heavily manage. It's a challenge to ignore the coercion aimed at us adults and to refuse to pass it on to students, but I'll try. Scarce here is the acknowledgment that leaders, teachers too, aren't walking the talk, that Glasser's model and heavy-handed approaches are incompatible.

An Attempt to Help

When it seemed like no one else was trying to mend fences, I wrote a memo to the superintendent. In the memo I laid out a plan to stop the war being waged on Hardy and then I sought the signatures of the other four association building reps. The memo started with, "We, the undersigned, believe that teaching and learning have become subservient to the struggle between Principal Robert Danzle and teacher Sue Hardy. This struggle must stop."

I was concerned about being partisan. We were already deeply divided. Defending Sue and condemning Danzle would only escalate the situation. I eventually came to write, "We prefer not to take sides on this issue. To do so is to violate our belief that what we are trying to build at our middle school is a partnership, a community, where all are accepted and celebrated." I emphasized that "Our sense of community is at risk."

I called Jason Richter, pastor at Community Bible Church, and asked for some advice on how to defuse this time bomb. While he was never my pastor, I respected him. From our discussion, I was able to write out a plan in the memo. "Our recommendation has four parts: containment, defusion, growth and reconciliation." I viewed the situation very differently than a hockey game where the referees let the combatants pound away until both are bloody and exhausted. That was what had happened so far. What I couldn't tell was how much knowledge the central administration had about this situation. I didn't want the hockey game approach, so I brought everyone into the fray by writing, "We redefine 'the situation with Danzle and Hardy' as a situation involving all of us—the school board, central administration, both principals, the association, staff, students, and parents" for, indeed, it really was.

Each phase had specific recommendations for both people. Sue's evaluations would be shifted to Mark Taylor, the new assistant principal. Danzle was to refer parent calls to him as well. Mark would look for and document Sue's strengths. Both Danzle and Hardy were to develop their own way of collecting information about their performance and establish growth plans. I made my best guess as to the root cause of it all. "Paramount to the understanding of this situation is the central theme of fear…Some of us acknowledge our own fears by recognizing our failure to intervene sooner in this situation." The final lines included, "We hope that at some point, reconciliation can come:

> You my brother or sister have wronged me in the past.
> I now understand that it was because you were suffering and did not see clearly. I no longer feel anger toward you.
> Thich Nhat Hanh"[1]

Falling Apart

The association reps and I had three meetings before the memo was sent. The night following our last meeting Mary Jo called me at home and asked that her name be removed from the memo. Talking with her husband, she had come to the conclusion that Danzle would most likely retaliate once he saw the memo.

Fred, another rep, went to the superintendent and told him he did not support the memo and then asked the superintendent to remove his name. I was stunned. He had indicated support for the rough drafts at all of our meetings. Seemingly out of nowhere, he backed down. It looked like we were falling apart. In particular, Fred blew to smithereens our credibility as a united group by going directly to the superintendent. Because of a fear virus, it looked like the letter was mine alone.

It took a few days for me to realize that I had played a part in the collapse. At our last meeting I had urged my fellow reps to have resolve in the face of possible retaliation by Danzle. I had painted a graphic picture of reassignments, fueled student unrest and bad evaluations—and they bailed out soon after.

After all of the work we'd done, I was left to wonder if the memo would do any good. A few weeks later, the superintendent thanked me for the memo and the effort to bring about peace. From that moment in time I had confidence that my superintendent knew about the riff. I still didn't know if the situation was being addressed.

A Lesson Learned

Thankfully, one experience during this time had its beginning in scarcity and its ending in abundance. I had volunteered to do jail ministry service and the day came for my group of volunteers to meet at St. Johns before heading to the jail. We confirmed our responsibilities—who would lead the singing, who would do the readings and who would reflect on them—then headed toward the county jail to conduct the service for the inmates. About halfway there we discovered that we had forgotten to pack everything except the doughnuts—no Bible, no candles, no matches, no guitar—just doughnuts. It was too late to go back, so we continued to the jail.

After we signed in, the officer at the counter yelled, "Door!" and his colleague in the control center nodded. A startlingly loud

Disregarded

buzz was followed by an even louder click that echoed down the hallway as the barred door opened. We entered the jail proper "naked," without our usual trappings. To our surprise, the service went well. In fact, it went very well. Vulnerable, and in the absence of props, we had dug deeply to find the resources patiently waiting to be tapped. The situation caused me to make a connection. In the 14th century, the German mystic Meister Eckhart wrote, "Blessed are the poor." He was talking about our souls, not our wallets. Resources had flowed when we were "poor." I learned at the jail that inner scarcity could make room for abundance. I began to wonder if all the scarcity I had been noticing was potentially a seed to a new beginning.

Maybe from donut holes come donuts.

School's Out

Late spring can even turn cynics hopeful, with hard buds and bulbs bursting into bloom. Everywhere there is evidence of promises fulfilled. May, with its jam-packed calendar, has lumbered into June. Finally, school's out and it is time for another retreat. I carefully read the advance letter. Palmer asks us to bring an object that somehow represents "summer." I whittle down my choices to a rock or a road map. The map would represent the family trips all members have come to enjoy together. I now plan them so half the time is spent in an urban environment and the other half in nature. A rock would represent the summers of my youth spent at the family gravel pit. The hardness of stone and steel was balanced by the love of my mom and dad. In the beginning, my parents were so strapped from purchasing the floundering gravel pit that the minister of our new church stopped at our house to ask if my brother and I needed shoes. All of that changed. Over time my parents' perseverance transformed a desolate place into a place of sustenance. Meister Eckhart, jail ministry and the gravel pit push me toward believing that something can be born from nothing.

Summer Retreat

As we gather at Season's, the Fetzer Institute's retreat center, I realize how wonderful it is to see everyone. Around the second or third retreat I had held a belief that everyone was maintaining a lovely façade, but now I've come to believe these really nice people are for real. We interact in a non-judgmental "container" with simple, but effective guidelines that help us honor each other. Here, I don't have the urge to keep looking over my shoulder for incoming rounds.

Of course, I think to myself, maybe these people have changed. My son has said as much about me. After a couple of retreats, he remarked that he thought *I* had been putting on an act, but came to realize that I had changed. I had softened. I had opened up to possibilities. Apparently, we will not leave the program like we entered it.

Part of what makes the Fetzer experience so rich for me is the wonderful food and the genuine support I feel from the Fetzer staff, be it hospitality or housekeeping. I find caring not only in our circle, but also anywhere I turn. Do I go overboard by saying Gazpacho soup, potato cauliflower curry and parsley fettuccini are healing?

The retreat themes are embodiment, community and abundance—interwoven concepts that are easily associated with summer. Choosing themes that fit the season, Palmer continues to help us develop an earthy rhythm in our lives unlike the mechanized ones so prevalent around us. He says, "Abundance will result if we truly feel connected. Community and abundance almost mean the same thing. What we need is *not* in scarce supply."

We share the objects we've brought that relate to summer. Eli starts off by saying that every year she hosts a swimming party at her pool so that her students get to see a different side of one another. Chuckles erupt when she adds, "My students get to see a different side of me too—in my swimming suit!" Linda explains that the grass around the tombstones is always overgrown in the spring and, for her, it's not summer until they cut the grass. Rich says he has two passions—teaching and fun—smiling widely as he raises his arm to display a golf ball. Summer camps represent summer for Mike, "I'm always impressed with how the kids and adults create community. Everyone takes care of everyone else." Mickey says that summer represents visiting grandparents, a time of freedom and going barefoot. I produce a roadmap and share how family vacations are glue for us, a time when we gratefully enjoy each other fully.

We concentrate on "community" first and a story is told about a medical school that decided to change its methodology from the traditional lectures and culture of competition to one of cooperative study groups. The medical students formed a community with the patients, doctors and each other. As they focused on and deepened their understanding of the patients, students' test scores went up. The story reminds me of the movie "The Doctor" in which a flashy surgeon (William Hurt) treats his patients as objects. When the doctor contracts cancer himself, he seeks out a colleague who he has disregarded, but who has demonstrated care for his patients. Through his experience with cancer, he discovers his errant attitude and, finally, his humanity and compassion.

Community is not a "soft" concept. Living in community involves struggles, frustration and just plain hard work. Palmer tells us that he's spent fifteen years in intentional community settings, eleven of these at Pendle Hill, a Quaker center for study and contemplation southwest of Philadelphia. He lists some of the values shared by the community members who live there: a deep regard for individual differences, a desire to be present to each other, support to speak one's truth and the willingness to wrestle for years until consensus is reached. In our retreat setting, we are not called upon to make many decisions; nonetheless, his phrase "wrestling for years until consensus is reached" creates a powerful image and offers to me an alternative model to what goes on back home. These Quakers, it seems, refuse to let time rule over them. Relationships are seen as more important than a hasty or forced decision. The idea of consensus also suggests that each person's contribution is valued, that the majority resists running over the quiet or radical voice, instead honoring and considering how such quiet or lone voices can be used to the advantage of the entire community.

Listening to him talk, I can sense the real love and appreciation that Palmer holds for the people of Pendle Hill and the experience he had there. I think to myself that I'd love to visit that

Chapter 8

place and compare the rules and quality of their "container" with the one we've established here.

We break into small groups to share our own experiences of community and then return to the circle to share the common threads and traits found in our stories. Many concepts emerge: commitment, trust, acceptance, challenging relationships, solitude, vulnerability and respect. Some comments address the shadow side of community: The "we versus them" mentality can fuel gangs and the militia. The root emotion that binds community members together can be hatred or fear. We note that many communities self-destruct.

We brainstorm obstacles to and benefits of community and discover that the obstacles outnumber the enticements three to one. Against our wisdom and need to form communities are our many human faults: fear of not getting our own way, jealousy, fear of dependency, competition and fear of self-revelation and self-disclosure. Palmer adds, "Community takes us into a complex force field—the reason we *don't* want to go there. A need is normally the trigger. We yearn for community and are scared to death about it."

We have developed a greater understanding of the benefits and the challenges and Palmer presses further. "Community is a gift. The question is, Are we going to open ourselves to it? We are all connected, so how do we understand what is out there and," he points to his heart, "what is in here? How shall we develop consciousness about the complex field around us and the one, no less so, inside? How can we hold this paradox?"

While much of our work in these retreats has centered on self-discovery, we are increasing our capacity for community as well. As we have used community to discover ourselves, we have discovered community.

The terrible sadness that surfaces in me at home comes from comparing my toxic work culture with the positive, yet challenging, culture we've established here at Fetzer. I believe in my colleagues back home and want to cry out that a gift is available.

Community *is* possible at work but we have to believe that it is possible, we have to be willing to create it, we have to want it so badly that we refuse to settle for less. Just as we too often teach students to excel but slight the building of community, so too do we push teachers to exhaustion and fail in helping them connect with each other. Among the many things I've learned here, I feel most deeply that community is the medicine for our wounds. Even with the severe division at work, I know the potential still exists. The big question is, "Where's the bridge?" How do we get from division to unity?

Abundance

We read the story of the loaves and fishes from Mark 6:30-44 and then offer our impressions of the overall meaning—"It's about being my brother's keeper...It's about modeling...Hunger and thirst...Trust...Seeing potential...Meeting needs."

Obviously, there's plenty of meat here.

Palmer then offers questions. "What condition are the apostles in? Why go to a lonely place? In that same condition, what would you want from a boss? What did the disciples receive?"

The apostles have returned exhausted and describe to Jesus all they've done. Jesus shows understanding and compassion by offering a boat and heads toward a quiet place so the apostles can rest. Jesus and the apostles leave together, but, anticipating where they are going, the crowd arrives at the destination before the boat reaches shore. We consider that the crowd may be hungry in two ways—body and soul—and want what the apostles have. We see that Jesus is a model of compassion and begins to teach to the throng, satisfying one of their needs. Compassion is central to the story. Compassion is necessary for understanding, garnering enough energy to look at the needs of another and respond. We must be sensitive and consider if there is a critical match—someone's need and me as a resource. We must ask, "When am I responding out of my own need versus my compassion?"

As the hour grows late, the apostles ask Jesus to send the crowd away. The implication is that the throngs can buy food in the distant villages, thus neatly taking care of the developing

Chapter 8

issue. Jesus turns things around—"*you* give them something to eat." We discuss that the apostles are willing to teach, but maybe not to feed. The apostles might think that the task is too large to handle, the resources scarce.

"How many loaves have you? Go round and see," sets the transformation in motion. "See" invites the apostles to discover assets over dwelling on deficits. "You" binds the apostles and the crowd together—from that moment there is only "we." Finally, "give," is the seed of community. Going from "they buy" to "we give," is the radical shift. So often Jesus displays a moral authority that shocks and challenges others. His knowledge of the potential of community is the source of his unshakable confidence, modeled so convincingly that a change in belief occurs. Framed in today's terms, the new belief is that the leader is not the only one with resources. While Jesus challenges, he also displays a confidence that the apostles can deliver. He shows us that leaders can be healers.

We discuss the dynamics of manufactured scarcity. The abundance of community can fall under lock and key. The boss holds the combination to the vault and you have to conform to standards before even thinking you can approach and ask for crumbs. John speaks from across the circle, "Conform and beg is a very long way from community and 'we give.'"

Of course, the result of the shift in thinking is that all are fed and the abundance of leftovers far exceeds the meager five loaves and two fish with which they began. We can believe that the feeding of the crowd is a miracle performed by Jesus or the crowd shared unselfishly all that they had. The most important truth seems to be that responsibility shifted from one leader to many. A new consciousness sparked new behaviors.

Palmer makes a powerful observation, "Five loaves and two fish is so feeble for a throng, that it could only be powerful with the right understanding and response."

We are asked to break into small groups to consider two questions—Where is it that I am living with the scarcity model, running scared that what I need isn't going to be there? And, Where can I celebrate that I've broken through to abundance?

Apparently, Mike needs a pit stop. He stands up and quips, "It's time for a break. Eventually we develop bladders the size of gerbils'."

Leading to Abundance
Next day, we begin by focusing on the relationship between leadership and abundance. Leaders can turn a shared view of scarcity into a shared view of abundance. Through leadership perceptions of reality can drastically change.

The concept of abundance stretches beyond material goods. Abundance is really about flow and state of mind. In the story of the loaves and fishes, the most important transformation was that of the people into community. There was a give and take without baggage. The exchange between community members must be genuine, unencumbered.

Jesus' form of leadership remains revolutionary to this day. He models flexibility, compassion, a different reality, empowerment, use of available resources and he demonstrates confidence and optimism that community can emerge. When the followers look to him for answers, he offers the power back, implying that the followers have the solution—that they are enough. So often we're led to believe that our leaders have all the power and intelligence. If we agree, our agreement is self-fulfilling. We also can create scarcity in other ways. If, out of fear, we hoard more than we need, scarcity becomes a reality.

Palmer says we'll wear out if we buy into and use a distorted belief system that says management is about overcoming resistance. The accompanying practices are characterized by actions that are rigid, predetermined, coercive, excessive and obsessed. "I get exhausted if I operate with energy and effort to get people to do something they don't want to do. On the other hand, if I offer opportunities that people really want to do, I can stay focused on a different form of leadership and not waste energy." An old saying comes to mind—you can catch more bees with honey than you can with vinegar. I think of Danzle and how Sue Hardy and I and a half dozen others could connect with him if he could work with us instead of pound on us. I have no doubt that, at the core, we want the same thing—a fantastic school.

Chapter 8

"They"

I listen as Toni reads "The Low Road" by Marge Piercy. It's clear that the poem addresses issues about being on the bottom, experiencing a "They" and, later in the poem, expanding "We." It begins rhetorically with "What can they do to you? Whatever they want."[2] After Toni finishes reading, we're asked to think of the next person that could become a "We." "Who would encourage us to take a risk to expand the community we call 'We?'" With that question Palmer points us toward inclusion instead of exclusion. And then he adds a remarkable observation—"The inner life is the withdrawal of projections on others and those of others toward me." His statement creates a powerful image for me. I see more clearly a place where people do their own inner work—deal with their own anger, demons, prejudices, fears and deficits and reject the trash hurled at them by others. Simultaneously done, rejecting projections and refusing to project, I see the potential for community igniting like a volcano and "They" vaporizing in the explosion.

Along the way we've learned the imperative of not going it alone. Alone, you're vulnerable, a sitting duck, something to be ignored or dismissed. When you join with others, even keeping your sanity is possible. So is organizing for action. Possibilities mushroom when we are moved to act.

I see that in my workplace there are too many "Theys"—and, sadly, I also consort in making these groups, not only by feeling their projections and their judgments, but by willingly naming them "They." The mysterious central office is a "They" whose members distance themselves by clouding over who makes decisions, always bent on hiding their vulnerability. And yet I help them become "They" through my judging and naming. Danzle and the Insiders are "They," as well. The group that probably bothers me the most is the largest in number by far. The Fence Sitters, by their sheer numbers, could define any reality they chose. They could say "Enough of this war. No more," and it would be done. Try as I might, I do not see their middle ground as leadership, the modeling of a better reality. There are no claims on our lives, no invitations, no courageous acts, no attempts at reconciliation from this group—only silence. I privately rant that they do nothing to help, but I'm the one who's experienced community. I know what it looks like. I've felt the power of "We" and now must look for partners. I'm the change agent. It's up to me to take the risks, yet I've been set up by Danzle. I'm like the Greek character Cassandra whose curse is that no one will listen…

Retreat's End

As the retreat draws to a close I reflect on what I've learned. There are many concepts that are fresh and important but I single out three in particular. First, I've discovered the perfectionist in me is a natural faultfinder and I now know that I'm apt to get hung up on scarcity. In the future I need to concentrate on what is present and not on what is absent. Second, I'm responsible for my own reality and increasingly responsible for sharing what I've learned. My new reality is that whatever is needed exists, be it time, patience, courage, intelligence or anything else. In meetings of which I'm a part, I should encourage us to look beyond our helplessness to the abundance possible with community. Finally, my confidence in the presence of abundance can quell my fear, breaking me out of a variety of behaviors that destroy community and obscure its resources. If I truly believe that what we need surrounds us, I can focus my energy toward summoning the patience to uncover it.

Leaving on a Jet Plane

This summer, our family trip is to the Great Southwest, but planning for it increases my sense of doom. All I know is that there is an immense amount of activity below my level of consciousness. When I sit, it feels like I'm moving. Something is having its way with me. There's a shift going on and I'm not in the driver's seat. We're three days away from departure and I want to blurt out, "I'm not going. You go." But I know there is no way for me to explain and for Cindy, Jenny and Joe to understand. Two days left and I nearly have to cover my mouth with both hands to stop from calling out. On the day before our departure, I feel like hiding until after my family leaves.

Chapter 8

I survive the flight and find some distraction in the sites and through my family. This is our first time in Las Vegas. As part of the planning I called Remy Travel to learn about the classic things to do here. "The show at Bally's is a 'must,'" the travel agent said. When the curtain opens and the showgirls appear in plumage and little else, I hear heartfelt tones from my fourteen year old when he joyfully yells over the music—"Thank you, Dad!" At least somebody's having a good time…

Next day, we walk the strip, pay homage to the slots and then head for the Grand Canyon. The drive takes much longer than I had hoped. As the day teeters on the edge of dusk and darkness, we wonder if we will reach the canyon in time to see it.

The parking lot is nearly empty when we arrive and we quickly walk to the rim. We're overcome from the sight, gasping in unison while scanning the landscape from end to end. I don't know what to do with the mixture of awe and appreciation except to let it carve something in me just like the Colorado River has done to this limestone and sandstone.

I relay to my family what I learned about the canyon during planning. We're looking at layers that were deposited hundreds of millions of years ago, well before the time of dinosaurs. The canyon itself has been made in a blink over the last six million years. Water has been the patient and confident sculptor, always finding a path to move forward—not a bad life metaphor.

The canyon disappears in front of our eyes as we're engulfed by darkness. The other remaining car in the lot pulls out. None of us are inclined to leave, to be in a hurry to shake off our first impressions. We sit on the warm sidewalk and softly share the experience. Soon, we're prone on the concrete, our backs soaking up the heat that's been deposited and then the unexpected happens. Stars appear, slowly expanding and brightening until some up and streak across the sky. We're treated to an extravagant fireworks display at the edge of our private canyon and we yell and laugh at each streaking meteor.

After breakfast the next morning we're at the rim again and we begin to enjoy the details dusk had obscured the night before. Wiry juniper, sharp yucca and low-lying scrub oak are scattered about as well as a few towering ponderosa pines. The colors of the canyon walls are more vivid by far than they were at dusk. Three of us stand at the edge and trade exclamations until Jenny asks, "Where's Mom?" We pivot to see her crouching and coaxing a chipmunk with clicking sounds and a handful of soda crackers. Cindy is being 100% Cindy.

I realize that camaraderie and the canyon sights are covering up the dread and confusion I've been experiencing. We leave Mather Point and find another viewing area to the west. I end up standing next to an older woman in a park service uniform and she looks through gold-rimmed glasses while she unabashedly strikes up a conversation. I get the strong impression that need and resource have somehow found each other. The canyon is a cathedral to her and she comes to mass and accepts the host in humility as often as she can. As we unwind in the motel at the end of the day, I record the encounter:

To the Edge

It is a time of shadow.
I am afraid to travel.
My soul is shifting so fast and so far,
that moving my body
makes me dizzy and anxious.

I have been to the shadows before
and I have seen pride and power.
Pride I wear, like clothes,
to cover me up.
I am afraid to cast off pride,
for then I will be naked—humble, insignificant.

I stare and feel small
and finally catch my breath.
I take a snapshot for my mind,
and many for my album,
for I am at the Canyon Grand.

Chapter 8

> An old women approaches and opens herself to me.
> She tells me of her walks to the rim each day
> to cast her eyes off the edge,
> to help her feel—humble, insignificant.
> Her words pierce my armor
> and I sense the reach of Mystery.
> Without question, she is a cosmic messenger,
> delivering these words to me.
>
> When she blends with the pine, I try to let go.
> And is this not the problem?
>
> How long before I can go to the edge
> to embrace what dances there
> and floats above the abyss?

I suspect that the mysterious shift inside me involves something dark and ominous, otherwise, it would have already happily popped to the surface like a fishing bobber. And I can only guess that "letting go" is the answer, something I'm not very good at:

> Now that I've let go,
> is this time
> like the other times
> I thought I had?

We reluctantly leave the area and head for Canyon de Chelly National Monument. Along the way we travel through Monument Valley with its spectacular mesas and buttes. So this is where so many of the auto commercials are filmed! I wryly think to myself, "Yeah, 'Built Tough' and I seem to be crumbling."

Part of the reason that we've come to the land of the Navajo is so that Cindy can take back to her students photographs of ancient dwellings, pictographs and petroglyphs. Following breakfast, we board an open-air flatbed truck with wide tires. Anticipation builds as the canyon both deepens and narrows and we sense we've left civilization. The riverbed is bone dry and the deep sand

Disregarded

overcomes many unsuspecting tourists, their cars sinking down to the axles.

It isn't long before cliff dwellings come into view. We marvel at the ingenuity, skill and determination of the fortress builders whose work embraces the canyon walls. We see ancient messages painted or etched in the stone. Our Navajo driver carefully describes a long history of victimization of the Navajo. He never says "Navajo" without following it with "People"—Navajo People—as if to remind us that the Navajo People are not objects to control. We take a long break to stretch our legs and I'm compelled to ask more:

Modern Pictograph

I see he is wise and has a sense of humor.
His first name is David, and
he guides us in a canyon of abandoned pueblos.
He is Navajo and tells of the horror
faced by his people with the Spanish,
other tribes, and the U.S. Cavalry.

The theme of each opponent is the same -
enslave or extinguish the Navajo People.
My government was not fussy about how the
deed had to be done -
starvation, saber, dehydration, disease,
exhaustion, broken hearts, rifle, rape.

We find ourselves alone.
I ask David how the modern Navajo People
deal with past injustice.
What do your people really want?

With a stick, he draws designs
in the sand of the canyon.
Is this to distract me? Himself?
Are these Navajo symbols?
Or are they meaningless?

Chapter 8

    He says that if the Navajo People need anything,
the leaders go to Washington and ask for it.
I nod as if I understand.
I regret the question
that turned us both into pretenders.

I'm stunned by this encounter. As David drew in the sand with a stick, I thought of Jesus doing likewise before answering. What an image! Did David politely dismiss me and deflect my question or is Washington the vault with all the goods? The themes of abundance and responsibility surface, even here in this arid canyon. Maybe a society can push a group so far to the edge that there aren't even a few meager loaves and fishes with which to start. Is this place so barren that abundance is impossible? Do successive generations of poverty confirm a reality or create a mistaken perception?

Does David really believe "you give" is the answer for the Navajo People or is David's answer an expedient response to the sappy tourist in front of him? Has David bought into the idea that only Washington has what the Navajo People need? Have his leaders tried to help his people live a different reality? I wouldn't be surprised to learn that David is wise and knew it fruitless to discuss such a complex issue.

David says that this is an age when the wise have become closed-mouthed. The wisdom that has been passed down for generations is being withheld from populations seemingly unfit for its hearing. I wonder, How must the masses turn around in order for the wise to speak? Who will lead this turning?

Next day we head south and west to Petrified Forest National Park and, as I look over the landscape, I wonder how vulnerable my protective shell has become. Am I reaching a point of breaking apart and opening up like these fallen sentinels have done? At Hoover Dam I ask myself, "What am I holding back? What is so darned awful that I've dammed it up and keep it submerged?"

Tomorrow we fly home. I realize that I've survived the travel while the painful internal shift continues. I've been rewarded for trying to move forward, like water against rock, because the family trip has been a gift. I'm sitting on the edge of the bed, listening

Disregarded

to the sounds of my sleeping family, when the unnamed force, loose inside, reminds me of its presence:

> No Choice
>
> I toss and turn.
> Nowhere can sleep be found.
>
> Slowly, I see
> I have been commanded to write.
> What muse is this that beckons?
> Am I to be a scribe?
>
> Jaws set,
> fists like stone, I resist.
>
> Yet, I cross the room
> and watch
> while my arm moves
> and words of a stranger form.
>
> Tell me, whoever you are,
> should I quit my day job?

Chapter 9 – Chili, Served Hot

A non-violent revolution is not a program of seizure of power. It is a program of transformation of relationships, ending in a peaceful transfer of power.[1]

Mahatma Gandhi

Earlier in the year I began to meet with a small group of teachers who would eventually help me confirm that my perceptions of the district were not unique. The meetings stretched into the summer of my shifting bedrock. I initiated the first meeting with my colleagues because a voice inside of me kept saying, Central administration deserves to hear "the truth" face-to-face.

What's for Dinner?
Tonight I'm cooking for eight. The menu is simple—chili, Caesar salad, cornbread and pie—February fare. I've invited six colleagues to my home to discuss their perceptions of how things are going in the district and to imagine how our association can become more proactive. I've picked these particular colleagues because they are not only teacher advocates, most having held union positions, they are education and district advocates. As I lower the heat on the chili, I realize that I'm feeling a new willingness to hear perceptions very different than my own, but I also want to have my own perceptions of the district confirmed. I'd like to feel sane.

My guests arrive in high spirits, even though this time together is being carved out of their own personal lives. I think back to the "recommended" social events that Cindy and I felt compelled to attend while I was in the Army. Food and conversation created organizational glue among officers and their spouses.

Disregarded

The mood remains upbeat while the chitchat stays exclusively on school matters. Mutual, recurring frustrations get their usual coating of dry humor. As we down dessert, I glance around the room and calculate that there are 154 years of experience gathered here. I wonder if we will struggle over the perceptions of our different worlds—elementary, middle school and high school. If we find common ground, I will suggest that that description needs to be shared with our leaders. I know that Palmer's handout on social movements has been subtly working on me, but maybe my isolation has been the real fuel. Maybe I've come to realize that being independent has its limitations, that going it alone will only take one so far.

Purging

With dishes in the sink, we settle into our circle and I explain our task. At recent association meetings I've noticed an increase in comments about becoming more proactive. We are here to give some initial direction to the soon-to-be-revitalized CEA Goals Committee. Maybe with our advance work, the goals committee can "hit the ground running."

Ted Kessler, who was on the negotiation team with me, jumps in first. "We can't move forward unless we agree on what our association is for." Just the kind of good logic I've come to expect from Ted. The discussion soon alternates between two themes: our desire to provide mutual support to colleagues and our general concern over what's happening in the district. Everyone seems to agree that we should be encouraging the identification and adoption of useful, system-wide programs that would help improve education—instructional models, brain research, scheduling and the like. Moving forward requires strong agreements and relationships, more powerful than current ones.

Mary Beth Norris, a language arts teacher, wants to know if "alignment" is a challenge for all three levels. Are teachers and administrators on the same page? Darcy Cole, an elementary Phys. Ed. teacher, quips about poor teacher buy-in for programs that are introduced by the administration. "It's like they toss bread out on the water, hoping that somebody will grab it." Trying to see the administration's side, I imagine how gun shy I would become

Chapter 9

after experiencing the resistance from teachers who fiercely value the freedom to teach in ways they choose.

We continue for over two hours. It's anything but neat and tidy, but I eventually sense an emotional thread—we're grieving. We've got to tell each other how it used to be. We've got to tell our stories. I think to myself, "The glue has dried up. We're breaking apart." Comments continue:

> "We're divided by department, grade and subject."
> "The old-timers used to 'handle us,' but we don't guide the new teachers as they did."
> "The social events have tapered off."
> "With an increasing number of teachers driving in from out of town, it's difficult to have social events."
> "When we used to have department heads, they supplied leadership."

Lea Ann Sullivan, a savvy high school math teacher, turns the discussion toward solutions—"But what should we *do* about all this?" We reach agreement on needing mentors for new teachers and bonding social events. The current structure stresses "task" so strongly that relationships have been slighted. We agree that we must help the administration move forward by at least telling them what we want and what we can support. While we need to bond with our bosses, we believe there is a step before that. We must get our own house in order by meeting solely with teachers—no administrator in the room. "With the teachers of one mind, the district could move forward," Mary Beth says. "There must be healing between members before we, as a united group, can work to heal the relationship with the administration."

Darcy adds, "We've got to quickly develop a support system for those who are ready to walk out of here, those who can't take the stress anymore." Michelle Mott, health teacher, addresses yet another group in need of support, "We've got to invite the teachers who have been alienated from the CEA and encourage them to tell their story." Artie Petroskey, elementary teacher, chimes in with his booming voice, "Yes! And how many of us have taken an administrator to lunch?" We all laugh.

Because it's late I take a stab at a summary. "It seems that we've been saying that the stronger the relationships among staff, the more likely we'll feel the support we need to teach and that increases the likelihood of our district improving." Artie interjects that my statement is close enough for now and heads nod. After everyone has left, I reflect on the evening. It seemed like a fine start. There was plenty of goodwill, sound thinking and energy. These senior staff members have not lost their passion, but I think back to Palmer's opening remarks at the first retreat that helped me wake to my own condition:

> Teachers aren't getting enough support. Our institutions are riddled with pain and we are disconnected from our colleagues...

I saw it in their faces and heard it in their voices. Most of these folks are hurting too.

Second Meeting

A month later, we meet again. The menu is the same, except we're having white chili this time. I've invited two extras to this meeting—Randy Leavitt, a teacher from neighboring Weaver-McKinley Schools, and Tom Thurman, an elementary principal in our own district. Leavitt used to be a band student of mine, so we go way back. Thurman is a friend and I know he cares deeply about our district. I think he's taking a risk by being here because he's at what some would consider a clandestine gathering. I explain to the group that Leavitt and Thurman are here to help us broaden our perspective. Leavitt can help us answer, "What's going on elsewhere?" and Thurman can help us with, "What's it like at a different level of our organization?"

Leavitt says his "journey" started seven years ago when he and another high school social studies teacher confronted their 40% student failure rate. They realized that something distinctly different had to be done.

As Leavitt continues I sense that in his district there is a good working relationship between leaders and followers so I ask, "How did the administration and teachers come to work together?" "A number of things come to mind," Leavitt responds. "Our education association president invited the superintendent to attend a Michigan Education Association conference on how to pass millage votes. A partnership was formed from that. We've had talks about how the EA can support the change process instead of getting in the way. We also started lead management classes for the administration. Each administrator goes through two classes. The administrators went from issuing orders to drawing out commitment and participation by teachers through invitation and inclusion. The transition from boss management to lead management gave people a voice and the feeling that what they said and did really mattered. We started with little things. In the beginning, we went after what we fondly called 'tissue issues.' If the toilet paper (tissue issue) was always missing from the lounge, we then brought it up, and the principal made sure the issue got taken care of. Trust was built when we were listened to. We took on bigger and bigger issues as time went on."

Leavitt is on a roll and it's obvious to me that he deeply identifies with their process. He continues with, "Another piece we tackled early and kept at was the 'change piece.' We had to change the culture. If you don't have the support of the administration, your entire process will die."

As I see it, the key ingredients for Weaver-McKinley were a willingness to tell the truth, a teacher initiative, a response in-kind by the administration, a redefinition of leadership and trust building. I'm encouraged from hearing these themes, because some of their themes are similar to ours. We're here to uncover our corporate truth and we're taking initiative.

Jon Perry, who teaches Special Ed., asks for more. "What other foundations did you establish?" Leavitt doesn't hesitate. "A vision was essential. We developed a vision that had three components—psychological, managerial and instructional. We knew where we were going. Another step was a twelve-day period we called 'Time for Change.' On those twelve days the students left an hour early and we stayed an extra hour to really speak and listen to each other. We got back to the essence of what we were about. School is a place where teachers teach and students learn and everything revolves around it." Heads nod in agreement.

Disregarded

Leavitt's story closely matches my own images of how change occurs in organizations. I see three major new pieces: mission, values and vision.

Artie asks Leavitt for "an example that demonstrates good relationships." "Well," Leavitt begins proudly, "our last contract negotiations took only twenty minutes for a three-year master agreement. A significant piece was that teachers had to commit to serious consideration of proposed changes."

I thank Leavitt for his comments and suggest we turn to our own district. Thurman takes the initiative, but declines to go first, "My stories are much more humble than that. Go ahead and dive right in. I'll add my two cents when the spirit moves." Realizing how vulnerable Thurman may be feeling, I nod.

A brisk interchange follows:

> We need to get along. How can we work with kids, if we can't always work with each other?
> We're separated, alienated.
> Most of us can't get a handle on where we're going. No program ever lasts for more than a year and a half around here.
> Parents have a much more powerful voice than us teachers do.
> I asked for a student to accompany me to a conference and was turned down. The student said, "Don't worry, I'll be able to go. I'll have my parents write a note." The students know we're at the bottom of the pile.

Here we are, at our second meeting and we are still grieving. It is obvious that these wounds run deep.

Finally, Thurman breaks in. "You've got to understand that I have no more power as an administrator than as a teacher. You carve out what you can and take what you're given and you have to work with that. Right now, my job is about putting out brush fires. Maybe someday it won't be. But, for now, if you want long-range planning to happen, it must come from teachers."

Chapter 9

Just a week earlier I happened to hear our superintendent remark that he felt powerless. Later that same day, a school board member said the same thing. Are we giving all our power away with that attitude or are we acknowledging our interdependency and the complexity of it all? I don't know. I'm also wondering if I'm a fool. I believe I have the power and responsibility to help create the future.

We thank Leavitt and Thurman for their help and they leave. I try to move us to the core of what we want to do—"If it were just up to you, what would you do?" The responses are aligned—build relationships—but the specific solutions are a little more varied. Will many small efforts and events cause a culture shift or should we go with "the big bang theory?" Eventually we realize we have to work on both fronts. Change will require a comprehensive, long-term effort. Both big bang events and the smallest of gestures are needed. Ted reminds us of something Leavitt said that we could say daily when talking with others—"Please help me understand."

Darcy adds, "We have a culture problem and, in our anxiety, we distance ourselves from each other to avoid conflict. Any further sign of conflict and we distance ourselves further. It's a vicious cycle." The silence that follows tells me that she has spoken true and that's my cue for closure.

Between Meals

In the days that follow, I mull over comments from the last meeting. Leavitt talked about "lead management"—a style that energizes followers and Thurman had said that long-range planning must come from teachers. Those images are quite different from what is currently happening.

I condense Palmer's handout on movements and send it to group members, suggesting that, "There are alternatives to top-down change." The act could look like the launch of a carefully crafted battle plan, but it isn't. What is foremost in my heart is the development of true teamwork, the likes of which appear to be developing at Weaver-McKinley. I could be satisfied with that.

Actually, I'd be ecstatic.

Disregarded

Eventually, it hit hard that we were beginning to live out some of the first steps of Palmer's movement model:

- Isolated individuals reach a point where the gap between inner & outer life is so painful that they resolve to live "divided no more."
- These people are driven not only by moral imperative but also by conceptual "reframing" of their situation.
- Isolated individuals slowly find each other in communities of support that operate by non-traditional ground rules.
- These communities function first to sustain people in a sense of their own sanity.
- ...these communities give leadership to a new range of "unexpected" people.[2]

We certainly feel isolated and I can sense a shared energy to do something about it. We are brainstorming solutions and that means we are reframing the situation as something we can influence. I not only feel the support of these people, I am regaining a sense of sanity—I'm not alone in my perceptions and feelings. Only the fifth element, involving the "unexpected" leaders, has me troubled. I believe any group member could walk into a room and, as sociologist Jennifer James remarked, "tell a story and transform the place."[3] But the culture has gone sour. Nobody can do that anymore. We've become too isolated and vulnerable to listen to each other.

Bottoms Up

In doing more homework on movements and activists, I notice that there seem to be three ways to deal with "opponents:" we can kill 'em, embarrass 'em or love 'em. I humorously think that there's a strong case for embarrassment. Irreverent community organizer Saul Alinsky, in *Rules for Radicals,* suggested that the attention of the white aristocracy in one city would be assured by buying a large number of symphony tickets, feeding an activist group from the black ghetto baked beans and then handing out tickets. To get us unstuck, we could have a stink-in!

Chapter 9

As adept as Alinsky was at organizing, groups would often fall apart after he left the scene. His successors learned that one of their main tasks was to help groups identify what they really cared about. Shared values help hold groups together.

When I think of the Fence Sitters, Alinsky comes to mind again. Stretching to make a point, he said, in his usual outrageous manner, that Gandhi was very lucky to have had the passive masses to work with. Alinsky puts words in Gandhi's mouth—"Look, you are all sitting there anyway—so instead of sitting there, why don't you sit over here and while you're sitting, say 'Independence Now!'"[4] We must work with what we have and start from where the people are.

I'm moved by Nelson Mandela's strategy, which is to love 'em. Mandela could have walked out of prison a terribly embittered man, yet at his inauguration he said, "The time for healing of the wounds has come. The moment to bridge the chasms that divide us has come...We must therefore act together as a united people."[5]

In my reading, I become aware of how strongly Gandhi's philosophy of non-violence influenced Martin Luther King, Jr. When white ministers from the north wanted to board buses and join their black brothers in civil rights marches, they were warned sternly that they would jeopardize the movement if they couldn't withstand fire hoses, dogs and nightsticks. Anything short of total non-violence would be violence, turning the oppressed into the likeness of their oppressors, hurting the cause.

After reading Thomas Merton's *Gandhi on Non-Violence*, I realize there is more inner work for me to do. While my goals are teamwork and community, I see that I'm also ready to overpower anybody to get there. I have been functioning from the assumption that as soon as I'm in the dominant position everything will be okay, while not acknowledging that nothing will have changed.

I'm convoluted in other ways too. Gandhi's philosophy is inclusive—there is no enemy; but I see the administration as a group separate from me, one to be overcome. While I pine for unity, it is most likely the unity that would come from others finally agreeing with me. Gandhi offers a superior framework.

Merton points out that unity of a people is the result of successful inner work by individuals. The transformation of self is the seed for group transformation.

Gandhi's inclusive philosophy was aimed at helping "the enemy" transform into something other than the enemy. "We" was the end result. Love demanded that there be one standard established for all. It was unjust to exchange roles, to overturn power only to end up with the larger share. To replace coercion or violence, there has to be dialog where there has been silence. I realize that the consistent response to my requests—"Your request is not in the best interests of the school system."—is a veiled form of silence. An organization or society practicing veiled forms of violence is deceptively "inarticulate."[6]

First Draft

With the next meeting approaching, I realize its time to put thoughts on paper. I slowly write the title – "A House Divided" and below it I write the consequences of our folly—"Every kingdom divided against itself is brought to desolation, and every city or house divided against itself will not stand."[7]

As I ponder what to write next, I remember making Palmer laugh when I said, "I was mute for months after considering the Quaker adage, 'Speak, only if you can improve on the silence.'" I also recall what Hemingway would think to himself in order to move forward – "All you have to do is write one true sentence. Write the truest sentence you know."[8] With my increased sensitivity to paradox, I have come to see that my complete sentences address only half of an issue. Thinking all of this has little effect on the hand that, again, has gone ahead without me.

When I finish, I'm at the end of a cathartic event. I type the report and, through blurry eyes, see that the report is encyclopedic. Move over Tolstoy. I've been faithful to what I've heard from our first two meetings, but I've also recorded my perceptions and the thoughts of organizational development gurus. The draft is too long, but this was my time to purge.

Our group hasn't discussed fear, but I've placed recognition of it in the draft so we can discuss it. As I stare at the word "fear," I wonder what committee members will say.

A surprising thought surfaces—I can't use school mail. The draft could fall into the wrong hands. What we are doing could be misinterpreted and, more importantly, Tom Thurman might suffer. Is my fear real or imaginary?

Big Reactions

Members arrive just as the pizzas come out of the oven. While we could talk about anything on this April evening, we stay with school topics. Following dessert, I pass out the report and its length is a surprise to all. Some colleagues read from the beginning while others flip pages, exclaiming "Whoa!" We both wordsmith and confirm our agreements, focusing intensely. Important words and phrases—fear, partnership, world-class organization and dialog—pepper the introduction. "Fear" bravely shows itself in the introduction and Lea Ann finds it first:

Lea Ann: Did we discuss fear? I don't think so, but it hit me that it's true. I believe it.

Jon: Do we all feel fear? Do we all feel isolated or alienated?

Artie: We probably won't get everyone to agree, but maybe people will support a variety of experiences.

Darcy: We haven't discussed issues with our principals and central administration because of fear. Are we courageous when we are in groups?

Ted: Some of us feel the need to gather data. I suggest that we don't. This is a *feeling* document. The justification of my position is how I *feel*.

After an hour's discussion, we decide on the following for the opening of the introduction: "Many of us have experienced increased feelings of isolation and alienation. This separation exists between teachers and between teachers and administrators. We also sense the distance that divides school employees from

Disregarded

parents and the public at large. We are a house divided. We can no longer tolerate this culture, the mechanisms that sustain it, and our own participation in it."

I've numbered eight main points and we move down to number one: "There is a need for personal authenticity." Committee members dive into the section, first reading about "The Abilene Paradox,"[9] a story of Jerry Harvey's that I've retold from his book of the same name:

> It's an extremely hot, sticky day. No one wants to stir. In the living room are a young couple and their parents. Afraid that the young couple is getting bored, father suggests a trip to Abilene. Secretly, the other three don't want to move, but eventually consent to go. The trip to and from Abilene in a car without air conditioning places an uncomfortable layer of dust on their skin. The food was awful. After their return, the son finally blurts that he hadn't wanted to go in the first place. The two women concur. The father then says *he* hadn't wanted to go; he was worried people were bored.

The story survives our scrutiny along with some of the text. "Many agree in private about the nature of our problems. Many agree in private about the solutions. We fail to communicate this. We don't tell people what we really want, therefore, our organization runs on assumptions."

We agree that remaining silent in a meeting and then creating a buzz in the hallway is like a trip to Abilene. Our silence co-creates a false, public reality. Then we act on that reality, inaccurate and fragile at best, while our private realities (possibly full of agreements) remain hidden.

The second section is titled: "There is a need for stronger relationships." It starts with a quote from E. F. Schumacher's *A Guide for the Perplexed:*

> ...we tend to see ourselves in light of our intentions, which are invisible to others, while we see others mainly in the light of their actions, which are visible to us, we have a situation in which misunderstanding and injustice are the order of the day.[10]

The literature I've read is full of examples of conflict in schools, churches, businesses and non-profits. We agree to insert, "We're not alone."

I've supported the claim that stronger relationships are needed with a list of "probable causes." Either/Or thinking immediately places us in competition with each other. Scarcity dominates our thinking so "One must fight for scraps." We have not learned to manage our diversity. We need models that help people find common ground.

Mary Beth urges that time management be added to the list. "Our concern is that we can't grasp a sense of direction. I look to Holt and Weaver-McKinley and a few other districts that are creating time to talk. We are hesitant to bring up important items at the end of the day when we're already spent. The time thing bothers me. We've got to build it in—find it and go with it." Darcy adds, "With time to uncover our needs, I think the question is, 'How can leaders help workers do their jobs better?'"

Time runs out, but Ted provides the specifics on how to re-write the next draft, ending with, "Jack, you've got to reduce 'War and Peace' down to 'A Brief History of Western Civilization.'" Everyone chuckles. I feel good inside from the generous spirit that's been present.

Second Draft

During early May, I rework the report using the committee's suggestions. We meet again mid-month. Over dinner, colleagues compliment me vigorously on my efforts—at making black bottom pie. That's all well and good, I muse, but how will they react to the report?

Disregarded

I've reduced the eight sections down to four. We begin by discussing the third: "There is a need for right followership." If we're going to point out how we think our bosses hinder us, we're going to have to own up to our own foibles, at least the ones of which we're aware.

I think that, as a staff, initiative and courage are not our strong points, but that could be said for countless employees who work in organizations. I have my own explanation for this phenomenon. I've had countless leadership books in my hands but only two on followership. We place so many expectations on our leaders that the importance of follower initiative is sorely overlooked. Everyone is content with this distorted arrangement of smoke and mirrors designed to deflect blame up or down. The leader's world is safer and simpler if workers are passive. Life is safer and simpler for workers if someone takes care of them and they have leaders to blame. It's a perfect arrangement.

I begin to think that our committee is scared of using the P-word in print. Avoiding the word "power" says a great deal. We are operating with a rule that demands we save face. If power is heavily skewed toward the top, we would not save face when saying so. It's not surprising, then, when Seymour Sarason's quote gets the axe:

> When political scientists have looked at schools, their descriptions and analyses have been centered on matters of policy and not on the uses and allocation of power…the failure to examine school systems in terms of the myriad of ways in which power suffuses them has rendered efforts at reform ineffective.[11]
>
> Seymour Sarason,
> *The Predictable Failure of Educational Reform*

A quote of Peter Block's doesn't survive either:

> Partners each have a right to say no. Saying no is the fundamental way of differentiating ourselves.

Chapter 9

> To take away my right to say no is to claim sovereignty over me. For me to believe I cannot say no is to yield sovereignty. If we cannot say no, yes has no meaning.[12]
>
> Peter Block, *Stewardship*

As members toss around some examples of how leadership and followership are intertwined, the words "dance" and "interdependence" come to mind. Change initiatives seem to go like this: Over time our bosses study a potential initiative of theirs and go through an intellectual and emotional process of acceptance. Our leaders then "spring it on us." During its unveiling, it feels like we're expected to be up to speed by the time the last transparency hits the overhead projector. The unprepared staff slams on the brakes. That dance has one partner with too little patience and the other with too much resistance. The reaction to leaders is to back off and offer something else. The result is a perpetual smorgasbord.

Artie's remarks relate. "I would really learn and change if I saw the administration commit themselves to something long term. I would do the same if I saw most of the teachers agree."

We discuss specific incidents in our district of another kind. In a nutshell, our leaders will propose a new plan and when our staff doesn't show their opposition to it, the leaders will simply implement it. When the time comes to give life to the new program, however, staff members are indifferent and little real change occurs.

Teachers rarely propose initiatives because experience has proven that their ideas aren't given much consideration. Over time, staff initiatives shut down to a trickle. Looks like we haven't come to grips with the "change piece" that Leavitt described.

I am pleased that a frank quote survives the knife.

> ...followers who give in to the pressure of authority even when it goes against their better judgment focus primarily on their "duty to obey." Exemplary followers...realize they have a corresponding

> "duty to disobey" when appropriate to protect the organization and even the person who may be knowingly ordering that a wrong be committed. In other cases, there is an additional duty—that is, to take action that leads to a positive contribution.[13]
>
> Robert Kelley, *The Power of Followership*

Which Way?

The fourth section is titled, "There is a need for leadership." We keep "the dance" theme alive throughout this section in print as we did in the last one. It's senseless to name a starting point in a circular pattern. Next, we acknowledge a certain irony involving fear and learning. When we feel anxious from being heavily managed, we tend to stop asking for any help. We think it too risky to admit to power that we don't know or can't do something, imagining that punishment will follow our disclosure; "not knowing" stays underground and that blocks our capacity to grow. Covering up our ignorance in a "learning organization" looks like the supreme irony.

Darcy speaks to the demoralizing pattern many of us have seen here, "Our leaders are violating us because they show no trust. We meet as committees, giving of our time and knowledge, and then our recommendations are ignored. Our leaders trivialize our lives."

Most of us agree that we don't have a sense of where our district is headed, but we own up to our part in the dilemma by acknowledging that we haven't pressed hard enough for the creation of a collaborative vision. Ted points out a bright spot, "I think the high school restructuring was a singular exception to common practice because the administration eased up on control. The restructuring worked because we had a true say in what was going to happen."

The report reflects this concern. We recommend collaborative actions, including: working on a vision, establishing a set of guiding values, using collaborative models and building trust. We declare that the manifestation of all these complex processes would be the result of personal transformation. Each of us changing would change the whole. "Authenticity, relationships, followership and leadership all stem from people doing their own inner work."

The Summary

The discussion remains upbeat. We add a statement to the report to reflect that "...we have every confidence that solutions are available...While each person can accomplish individual change, systemic change is needed as well...We want to build bridges and know that bridges cannot be built with blame." We end with:

> We are absolutely illiterate in subjects that require us to understand systems and interrelationships...For me, personally, one of the turning points was the day I had to say to myself: What do I want to do with the rest of my life? Do I want to spend it coping with politics and other organizational diseases—or do I want to spend it working on building a great organization?[14]
>
> William O'Brien,
> former CEO of Hanover Insurance Company
> *The Fifth Discipline Fieldbook*

We decide to meet the following month to tweak the report and lay out next steps.

Potluck

In mid-June, we reconnect. I marvel at the spunk of this group. School's out and yet all are present. Over grilled hamburgers and hot dogs the chatter centers on the "to do" projects all of us have put off until summer.

Since our last meeting, committee members had passed around *Gung Ho,*[15] a movie about relationships in an auto factory and tonight I've arranged for us to preview *The Abilene Paradox,*[16] which could be shown at an inservice training to get people thinking. After seeing the video, we wordsmith for two hours, finishing the report, and then develop a plan.

We decide to present the report to the association's board

of directors in September. We'll give board members a month to consider its contents and then ask them to approve it at their October meeting.

Because we believe that system-wide change must accompany individual change, I will give the report to Gordon Thompson, our superintendent, and then Ted and I will meet with him a couple of weeks later. We'll ask for part of the October inservice training day to show *Gung Ho*. After the screening of the video, we'll pass out the report. We'll then ask for part of the November inservice training day to show *The Abilene Paradox* and form small groups to discuss the report.

My colleagues have stepped up and are willing to lead.

Head Office

In late July I deliver the report to Thompson. Two weeks later he calls me at home and asks if I will be coming to see him alone. I tell him that Ted Kessler will accompany me. I wonder about the pause at the other end of the line, then dismiss it.

I pick up Ted on a muggy August day and we head for the main office. We enter the conference room and find Thompson, Brent Neal and Lynn Lightfoot waiting for us. None of these people are irritating, but I interpret the scene, and so many others like it, as "We need one more gun than you have." And that's irritating as hell. The word "trust" bubbles up. The irony surrounding trust is that you have to be vulnerable in order for the other party to show that they'll protect you. Trust can't be built while living in bunkers.

I ask Thompson how he would like to begin. He says, "Your report is a good match with our system-wide goal for better communication." I regain my optimism and think that we're off to a good start. Maybe six months of work will pay off. Thompson says, "From the limited number of administrators I've polled, there's a feeling that the report does not always give specific examples."

Well, I think to myself, if we provided examples, individuals would feel hurt and the bridges we are trying to build would all be consumed in flames.

Chapter 9

Thompson adds, "We'd like to use your report for our staff discussions." I wait for more, but Gordon looks for a response.

My heart sinks. We're offering to partner and they're after maintaining control. With an administrator, a power figure, leading discussion, we'll just be repeating what the report indicates is happening and must stop.

Thompson sees that I haven't jumped at his suggestion and offers that a teacher and administrator could lead the discussion. I decline. In our committee meetings I've heard members say that we first have to build relationships among teachers. If we put an administrator in the mix, it won't work. If I urge teachers to move out of their comfort zone while in front of an administrator, I'll look like I'm going after brownie points and colleagues will shut down in disgust. Either that or they'll be too afraid to speak candidly. I'm able to say, "You can't use the exact words of the document quite yet because our board of directors hasn't seen the report. You certainly can make any topic in the report the subject of discussion."

I'm anxious for details, so I ask, "What do you agree with most in the report?" I get the one thing I didn't expect at all—dead silence. Not one word. I rally hope for some small sign of a common bond and press further. "What could you generally agree with?" More silence. "Okay," I say, "What do you disagree with?" The silence grows dense as lead. It is clear that Thompson has brought the meeting to a close. I slowly stand and bitterly think, So much for your system-wide goal.

As I drive Ted home, he comes unglued. I've never seen him like this. He's twisted up in a knot, feet jammed against the floorboards and his body pushing against the door. Then I begin to understand. At his core, Ted's the initiator and sustainer of relationships. Ted's the one who most often calls me on the phone and says, "Can you go for coffee tomorrow night?" Like me, he's probably dreamt of something better ever since our first meeting in February—only to wake up to this nightmare. We're quite a pair. Ted's exploding at lift-off and I'm sinking into a dark, dark depression of ooze.

From my perspective, "Let's partner" is written all over our report. But we didn't even dance "The Minute Waltz." Who could turn down an invitation like that? Our committee created an opportunity whereby all of us could have looked backward and said, "That was the moment *we* came together."

I would not come to understand my part in this failure for some time. It must have appeared that I wanted too much control. I should have taken the crumb that was offered and agreed to jointly facilitate discussions. In their vulnerability, the administration could not handle more. If we had needed six months to work through our emotional and intellectual issues, surely they would need time, too. I had pushed too hard and too fast.

Of course all of this understanding does not quell the longrunning anger I feel inside. We had a chance to come together. In our imperfections, we could have been perfect. We could have bungled and muddled our way into a new relationship. What we offered was a partnership, what we got was a confirmation of our split. Like so much of our best work around here, this too looked like it would evaporate into the void.

Fragile Hope

One slim chance still remains for starting a dialog about authenticity and accountability. I'm part of the Professional Development Committee and we plan the inservice days for the staff. At our next meeting committee members choose the activities for October—without *Gung Ho*—but they agree to watch the video during a planning meeting for the November inservice day. I believe I've got a good shot at stating our case, so I do my best to ignore the voice inside that keeps repeating, "Last chance."

Gung Ho

In late October the Professional Development Committee reviews the film. The setting for *Gung Ho* is a small town with a defunct American auto plant that is being reopened by the Japanese. It's not long into the film before we see three distinct organizational levels operating in the factory. The top level is composed of exacting Japanese, at the middle level is a cocky American,

Chapter 9

Hunt Stevenson (Michael Keaton), and the American assembly line workers are at the bottom, wanting only to make cars the same way they did before the plant closure. After a roller coaster ride of false starts, a walkout, conflicting agendas and miscommunication, the characters do the only thing left to do—come together.

While watching the film, I think of the hero's journey. At the beginning of the story, unemployed Hunt Stevenson heads for Japan to convince the Japanese to reopen the auto plant. In an early scene we see Stevenson lost, standing in a rice paddy with business suit pant legs rolled up. Our hero has left the known world. In time he must return with an elixir that will save his homeland.

The Japanese reopen the factory, but the new partnership breaks down and Stevenson, the broker of the deal, is scorned from all sides. Alone, and severely depressed, he sticks his head in the barrel of an antique canon and opens his cigarette lighter as if to light the fuse. At this classic stage of confronting his shadow, he gains the capacity to be transformed.

In another scene, a Japanese worker desperately wants to leave work so he can be at the birth of his child. When asked if he wants to leave work, he says the opposite, "No. I want to stay and work."[17] We see he's on a trip to Abilene like many others in the factory.

It looks like the plant will close and the unwillingness of his Japanese colleagues to publicly own up to a reality they share, sends plant manager Takahara Kazihiro running into the river with his clothes on, "freaking out" in frustration. Stevenson happens by and pulls Kazihiro out of the water. Soaking wet, at the river's edge, the two grieve together. "We were this close to pulling this thing off. This close to doing it."[18]

Fortunately, transformation occurs. In a tense moment near the end of the movie, an impassioned Stevenson refers to a collapsed auto hurriedly assembled to make a do-or-die quota—"I'd rather have one of *these* cars *we* made *together* by hand. *Your* guys and *my* guys, together. Those cars stand for something. Those cars stand for something pretty great. I'm *proud* of those cars." [19]

After the screening, we talk. *Gung Ho* gets mixed reviews. I think that the hesitation comes from the rough factory language and some crotch grabbing. I guess that most wouldn't think twice about seeing the film at home, but in the prudish, legally wary environment of school, where only G movies are allowed, it's "out of the box" for a couple of people. But hope still hangs by a thread. We adjourn with the understanding that the decision to show *Gung Ho* will be made at our next meeting.

As I leave, I make a conscious choice to remain upbeat. With my deeper appreciation and belief in abundance, I know anything can happen. Transformation is possible and the potential for a galvanizing moment still exists. Time between our meetings could be a friend.

Blindsided

A couple of weeks go by and I can't understand why I haven't received notification of our next professional development committee meeting. I walk down to the administration office and speak with administrator Brent Neal. "When's our next meeting?" I ask. Neal smiles and says, "We've already met. You didn't show up, so we thought you'd dropped the idea. The activities are already set for November." I tell him, "I was never informed of the meeting!" as my voice streaks upward. A satisfied grin spreads across his face and I see that he's enjoying this moment.

Obviously, my exclusion was intentional. We were playing a game—I just didn't know it.

I can only conclude that it's over. Our very best intentions as a committee have been squelched. I bitterly recall Stevenson's and Kazihiro's lines that were spoken in a moment of hopelessness—"What a waste. This could have been something really big."[20]

In the months and years that followed, this would become ever clearer. Nothing about authenticity, relationships, followership and leadership would be brought up for discussion by either the association or the administration—at least not at any meeting to which I was invited.

Chapter 10 – Hanging by a Thread

No man is an island.[1] John Donne

The Courage to Teach Program has come to an end and with it the realization that the most formative educational experience of my life is over. As hard as I try, my appreciation for the gifts received does not overcome the feeling that a treasure has been wrenched from my hands. My colleagues had dreaded the program's end as well. At our seventh retreat, with the final one still looming ahead of us, Kathie Kennedy suggested we rename the last one "Our First Reunion" to soften the blow.

At the final retreat it was apparent that we had chosen celebration over grief, no matter how difficult. For my part, I brought everyone "bonkers." Worn on the head, the sparkling balls at the ends of the two metal springs bobbed joyfully, releasing the playfulness in all of us. I had stayed up well into the last night writing "The Top 53 Reasons to Join the Courage to Teach Program," including:

> You can go to the bathroom any time you want
> You get eight tries to go Aha!
> You already have your master's degree and were getting restless
> Fetzer advertised free birthright gifts
> You don't have to sit in rows.
> You can be part of an educational program that survives more than one year.

Disregarded

At School

Back in the classroom, renewed and reflective, I realize that I've set expectations for myself that are too high. No matter the conditions around me, I expect miracles. When the students walk in and I shut the door, I want a special place to materialize instantly, a place where learning is abundant and students are driven from within. Truth is, hard as I try, the results are often quite average.

Sometimes my shortcomings are related to conditions beyond my control. I don't teach in a vacuum. The students walk in with baggage in tow. I'm the innermost one of a set of Russian dolls—classroom, department, school, school system, state system and federal system—that looks all too much like its larger counterparts. I make the school, but the school also makes me. When I long to give my students leading edge experiences with technology, but have eleven year old computers in my room, that longing is not easily satisfied.

I'm stressed from countless computer problems and relationships gone amuck. What's this doing to my body? I know one recent retiree who had high blood pressure the last six years of his career. Medication did not help. Three months into his retirement, his blood pressure dropped into the normal range.

Just when I want to honor our connectedness as a staff, something pops up to make me wish I were disconnected. The most recent issue struck a solid blow to my effectiveness. The core subjects teaching teams have been continually stressing, to the point of distortion, the importance of "the basics." The majority of teachers have decided that the grades of co-curricular classes such as mine will not be used to calculate pass or fail grades. Only the four classes taught by the academic teams will be used. It isn't long before the students realize "this class doesn't count." It's a case of tyranny by the majority.

In addition, my days swing wildly. The school schedule has been designed around music classes—no problem in itself—but the unintended consequence is my classes are worlds apart in attitude and ability. Classes that meet during band time are void of music students and are surly to silent, reluctant to rebellious. If we're lucky enough, we somehow tacitly decide to endure each

Chapter 10

other. If we're not lucky, a war of frequent skirmishes ensues. And it is a war that I must win, for it is the ultimate failure of a teacher to lose control. When my computer classes are packed with music students I think I've gone to heaven. Student work is outstanding and we have the luxury of going off topic, one class learning the jitterbug as a swing CD spins on my drive.

The infiltration of problems created from without demand all the resolve I can muster from within. My reoccurring mantra: we make the organization and the organization makes us and when we fail to take care of the organization, it becomes a neglected child and rages in our face. Too many colleagues think that the organization is not a responsibility of theirs to influence.

Danzle Takes Aim

A new target of Danzle's, Jean Conway, asks me to come and listen to her story. Jean is in her first year here but she is an experienced educator and just walking into her math classroom gives me a sense of quality. Jean has had two meetings with Danzle and thought any issues could be resolved privately.

Jean says she is going to hold her ground. But she feels alone. I realize that she doesn't know Danzle's history and has been made to feel that she is the only problem in the building, the only naughty one. As she tells me her story, I can see that Conway has definite opinions on how to do her job. She has a high level of self-confidence similar to Sue Hardy's.

Near the end of our meeting, the tears come and she says that, with her cancer, she really doesn't need this stress. I marvel at the mix of heroism and hurt that live intertwined within. I say that, as AR, I would be happy to be present at all future meetings and that she should share her story with our CEA president. I tell Jean that she has joined a growing group—she's not alone.

As I walk back to my room I can't help but wonder if the rest of the staff knows about the two meetings with Danzle and if so what they're thinking. Do they see our newcomer as a poor match for us, weak in skills, or are they getting yet one more lesson in the consequences of being your own person, acting self-assured or standing your ground? How many on our staff have been intimidated into silence? How is their teaching being affected?

In the Rain

That evening, I do the black math in more detail. Danzle has now swung the ax six times, with one forced retirement, four casualties and one caught in a fight to the death. As I think back to a special moment when I asked Palmer for some important advice, I realize that the retreats continue to bolster me.

On one evening, Palmer and I happened to leave the main building together after the last session of the day. We were both headed toward the living quarters and as we walked I explained my dilemma about Danzle and my school. In the session just concluded he had been talking about the importance of not fixing others, not hurting people with our judgments and projections. Our job was to do our own inner work. It all made sense, but here I was, hurting from seeing so many people under duress at work. What could I do?

As we walked, the drizzle that had greeted us upon leaving the main building had intensified and found its way to my bones. My teeth began to chatter. Palmer stood patiently in the middle of the footbridge, oblivious to the drizzle, waiting while I searched for words.

"How can one live as you've described, not trying to fix someone and yet wanting to stop that someone from hurting others?" I asked.

Palmer replied gently, as the rain made a steady stream off the bill of his hat, "You bear witness. You say, 'This is what I'm seeing' and you offer your observation in love and friendship. Then you have to step back. You can't have an attachment to your observation. And you can't hold an expectation of change. You should reassure the person that they can 'take it or leave it.'" As anticipated, Palmer had had a wise answer. I began to consider bearing witness to Danzle.

Body Smarts

The retreats remain alive for me in other ways. The metaphor I discovered for myself at the first one is still intact and pops into consciousness occasionally. I'm a rubber stamp, issuing compliments and delivering good news to students about themselves. I don't like the image because I've learned that praise can distort others, but nothing's appeared to replace it. And still with me is the question, "What did Rilke mean when he advised, 'Be ahead of all parting…?'"[2]

The most haunting active memory comes from the "body work" sessions we did at the last fall retreat, now a little over a year ago. We were being guided to explore the size and shape of the container beyond our skin. After a self-conscious wave passed, I surrendered to discover how much "space" was around me. I shut my eyes and slowly moved my arms about as I probed for free space and walls. My container proved to be large. I could only feel a little resistance in front of me. I broke through the wall with my hands as I pushed outward and concluded that limits are of my own creation.

Next, we were asked to cup our hands and imagine placing our most valuable "gift" in them. "This is the gift that you give to the world," Palmer explained. He then asked, "How do you move to give it to the world?" When we were ready, we were to offer our gift. I cupped my hands and then extended my arms forward, offering my understanding of organizations and my initiatives aimed at helping my workplace. I was stunned from my body's response. When I offered my gifts with outstretched arms, I felt as if they had dropped and shattered at my feet.

As I stood with empty hands still cupped and a growing lump in my throat, questions hurled forth. Had I misidentified my gifts? Was I offering them in such a way as to invite rejection? Was my body simply reflecting past reality—that my initiatives had met with intense resistance—or was the bad news more central to me? As powerful of an experience as it was, I was unable to interpret its meaning. The gifts at my feet lay mute.

Driven by the desire to live authentically and contribute, I was unsure if I was doing either. Will I be able to account for my efforts? In the movie *Defending Your Life*, the character played by Albert Brooks dies and reaches Judgment City, a place where a person's life is reviewed to determine if that person will "move on" or be sent back to learn more. The review goes poorly for Brooks and in his hopelessness he weakly repeats over and over the seemingly empty promise that if he is allowed to move forward he'll "really, really try."[3] His entreaties are sad indeed.

Disregarded

I hold no hope for quick resolutions of these questions, but I return to the possibility of approaching Danzle. Maybe I can give witness. Maybe, in time, some of us can move beyond the protracted suffering.

Reduced Speed Ahead

At work I'm determined to address a number of issues, but first I need to know how staff members feel about them. For one, just a few teams have been assigned most of the at-risk students and no support has been offered for this intensified need. I've also heard that the academic teams feel overwhelmed with new responsibilities and they say they're "buried" with meetings. And with so much being asked of them, teachers believe an added planning period is necessary to deal with the increased demands.

The association representatives have identified other concerns. One relates to the targeting of individual teachers and the other the staff at large. Before Danzle arrived, parent calls were directed to teachers, but now complaints are directed to him. Danzle uses these calls to build a case against a teacher. At least with Danzle's main targets, parents are no longer referred to the teachers to jointly solve problems. He's even put this into print. The monthly newsletter that goes out to parents now suggests that parents call him, not a teacher, with suggestions or complaints. We have long insisted that problems should be ironed out at the lowest possible level; that practice has been changed without our concurrence.

I talk with the other building association reps. and suggest we host a meeting for teachers to discuss growing concerns. They offer that the dissatisfaction is mounting and we should become familiar with the staff's positions and uncover their recommendations. The ARs themselves are concerned about too much pressure from Danzle to excel and the ongoing three-way split of the staff. They're very weary from the tangible divisiveness between the Insiders, the Fence Sitters and the Outsiders. I suggest that we write summaries of what we believe are the issues and that we use them as discussion starters. The ARs agree.

Within three days the summaries are done and I reserve the all-purpose room and place meeting notices in each person's

Chapter 10

mailbox. Only a week to wait and maybe we'll have something concrete to work with.

Brazen Move

The day of our building meeting proceeds like any other. I realize that, with our three-way split, the meeting could go very badly. There's the chance that we won't honor each other's take on reality. And why should those who got the luck of the draw, of students or scheduling, agree to change their good fortune?

The final bell rings. After the students exit, I grab my CEA folder and head to the meeting. I check my mailbox on the way and find in it a memo from Danzle. He has cancelled our association meeting, saying that he already plans to discuss the topics at our upcoming staff meeting. Unbelievable. That's a new one—management canceling an official union meeting. Danzle honors no boundaries.

Back on Track

I call Drew Harrison, our association president, and tell him what's happened. He says to reschedule for the next week and that he'll see to it that it's not cancelled again.

I put out the announcement again and this time Danzle doesn't react. A little under half of the staff attends the meeting. A few core issues emerge. One is that the staff wants Danzle to stop pressing them so hard. "We do that to ourselves already," is the consensus. Everyone is feeling the pressure of higher demands without an increase in support. It's all supposed to happen out of thin air. If the support were there, staff wouldn't mind the increased emphasis on excellence. It's what everyone wants. Teachers share how the high concentration of at-risk students on just a few teams is making for "a very long year" and it's only November. A number of solutions are offered.

I agree to type up a summary of what's been said. We set another meeting date so we can determine if the summary matches the discussion. If it does, us ARs will meet with Danzle and not only discuss the issues, but also have something in writing for him to look at.

I get a call from Drew Harrison. Danzle has called him and

says I'm trying to stir up trouble. I tell Drew that as ARs we can't ignore the concerns of colleagues. We have to respond to them. I called the meeting in response to teacher complaints. The meetings help determine the level of concern. I agree to explain to Danzle what we're doing.

I inform Danzle that we would like to see him use a consensus process to address areas of concern. Part of our job as ARs is to honor the small voice and we want him to do likewise. We have to ensure that the "tyranny of the majority" doesn't violate any individual's working conditions. After the next meeting with staff, we would like to meet with him and share the summary of our discussions. "We'll provide you with a starting point," I say. I try to relieve Danzle's apprehension by pointing out that no grievance has been filed and that the topics haven't left the building. He shouldn't expect a call from our association president or his boss.

The next meeting with the staff goes well and, after it, the other ARs and I stay and discuss what we will share with Bob. We will insist on two immediate changes. Parent phone calls about teachers are to be directed to those teachers and the wording of the parent newsletter must do likewise.

For the first time, Danzle seems off stride as we assemble in the conference room. David Jenks, Assistant Principal, is present as are myself and three other ARs—Tony, Mary Jo and Nancy. I think that the most powerful people in the room are these three. Danzle and I are old news. But, if any of my colleagues speak to the issues, those issues will most likely be taken seriously. I think Danzle knows there's a risk in discounting our work, that we may really be representing way more employees than ourselves. And we are.

As we discuss the issues, Danzle relaxes because we offer some possible solutions and don't indict him as the cause. We've made lots of changes and now the kinks need to be straightened. What bothers him is our firm stance on referring phone calls to teachers. He throws out an anchor and appears unwilling to budge. We have past practice, logic and the resolve in our voices going for us. Finally, he agrees to the change.

Chapter 10

Seeing Gifts

Several days later, Sue Hardy catches me while hovering over the ancient copy machine in the workroom, the one that's putting an unwelcome dark line through every copy I make. She asks me to write a letter of recommendation that she can place in her personnel file. I recognize that this is a defensive move aimed at offsetting the "file building" that's been going on. I tell her that I'm glad to do it, adding, "I'll send you a copy with a nice big black line through it."

I understand Sue Hardy better than most. I've discovered many admirable traits in her as we've worked on the school improvement team. I've actually recognized a few of these traits in myself, although less developed. On a hunch I had asked her if she would be willing to fill out a personality profile, and she did it on the spot. Sure enough, her responses revealed that we shared the same personality type. We had the same sense of fairness and justice that demanded we not roll over for Danzle and a strongly independent nature that seems to make Danzle go mad.

With my new understanding of this small part of her I can better see that there's a clash between our independent personalities and the weaknesses of our community culture. But we have weaknesses too. We often baffle others. One of the suggestions for improvement for our personality type, I recall, is that we must explain ideas so other types can understand. When I am not clear, I am being myself, but I have a responsibility to make my best effort at communicating well.

There is a shared responsibility for understanding between the individual and the group, but groups often opt for blame. When that happens, "Please help us understand" gives way to believing everything would get fixed if someone would only "clean up their act." Once in a while we acknowledge that an at-risk student isn't "the problem," rather, a symptom of a dysfunctional family. However, we never seem to think about a fellow worker and our organization in that same way.

The Recommendation

I think about the stress that Sue Hardy and I are under and I think back to the movement model—"Isolated individuals slowly find each other in communities of support…These communities function first to sustain people in a sense of their own sanity."[4] A colleague has commented on the stress Hardy is under. "I don't know how she withstands the pressure. I would have been driven insane or would have been dead long ago from a heart attack." When the stress engulfs one of us, the long walk is made to the other's room and, without words, we ask to be pulled back from the edge. Something in the encounter says, "No, I'm not alone. Somebody sees the world like I do. At least one other person believes in me. There's at least one person who is willing to give witness to my life and what it stands for." It's barely enough, but it is enough.

I write the letter of recommendation. It's easy to do, but I wonder about the future. What if Danzle tries to fire her and the whole thing ends up in a tenure hearing? Will state officials be fair or is Danzle an extension of them? If Suits routinely support Suits, then the whole affair will not center on finding truth. I don't want to end up at a tenure hearing.

I write about how well organized Sue is and how she has the ability to formulate a plan and develop a realistic time frame for its implementation. I comment that she thinks broadly and deeply. She's worked hard to get everyone to speak at our team meetings—everyone counts. She's passionate about teaching and school improvement. Hardy uses research-based methods. She's professional, staying away from blame and negativity. She has even kept away from Danzle bashing. Amazing.

She adds extra touches to her classroom. Everything has to be just right. She looks for the expression of quality in process and product. She's done doctoral work, extremely rare for the middle school level, and completed an internship at the Michigan Department of Education. She has a strong sense of self. I close by admitting truthfully that she's taught me a great deal.

Higher Stakes

The next morning I'm looking over the shoulders of students as they work on a keyboarding exercise when Hardy opens the door and motions to me. As I approach I see she's revved up with emotion. "They're going for it!" she says. "Danzle's put me

Chapter 10

on an IDP." Sue intently searches my face for a reaction.

"What's that?" I ask. Hardy replies, "IDP stands for individual development plan. What it *means* is that I'm headed for a tenure hearing. I could be fired."

It's one thing to be canned in business. In business, getting canned might even be an opportunity. It's different in education. If Hardy's let go, no other school will hire her because they would have to honor her specialist degree and place her on the salary scale commensurate with her twenty-five years of experience. Not only would the rest of her career be jeopardized, so would her retirement. The "penalties" for not completing thirty years in the state retirement system are stiff. Cliff Anderson's forced retirement flashes in my mind again and I know that Danzle is capable of anything.

In the days that follow, Hardy explains the IDP. She says she will comply with all the requirements and deadlines so Danzle won't have anything objective to use against her. Even that's not easy to do because it buries her in paperwork, creating an even heavier burden and more stress. She asks me to go with her to Lansing and talk with a lawyer retained by the MEA. I agree.

As the days tick off until our appointment with the lawyer, I review the situation. Danzle contends that Hardy has problems with students. When she shares the names of students with a few of us, we realize that these students have presented challenges to us as well. Hardy explains that the students request to see Danzle, tell their story, and then come back gloating—behaving worse than ever. Students are encouraged to talk to him anytime. It looks like the file building is a simple task. The more voice students gain with the principal, the more wrongdoing by Hardy is implied. Students feed the parents and the parents feed other parents. Parents call Danzle. It is a well-oiled machine. Who sees this besides a paltry few of us?

Equal with the damage to Hardy is that to students. Does Danzle understand that he's a model? The message: "Ignore your own responsibility, judge others, go for the throat." These are lessons that should not be taught and never learned, most especially by young people.

Danzle states in the IDP that Hardy cannot get along with

staff. "Staff" includes Hardy's teammates. Two members have become frustrated while one remains supportive. I'm not aware of any quality team building that took place when teams were formed. Without capacity building, the classic life cycle of teams (form-storm-norm-perform)[5] has reached the storming stage. Do team members have this conceptual knowledge? If not, the "storming" could be misinterpreted as a personality problem. A scapegoat would have to be created. In addition, the chaos surrounding Hardy, yet created by Danzle, is bound to have a negative impact on team members. Hardy is seen as a problem. This "problem" is the same person I see as the most collaborative leader around. I believe that some of Hardy's teammates are not seeing the big picture.

As the number of students in a given grade changes from year to year, the sizes of teaching teams do likewise. A team can add or lose a teacher. Attached to the IDP is the year-old letter from teachers asking that Hardy not be placed on their teams. This letter is being used as a tool for dismissal. As I recall there were a number of things operating at the time the letter was written. Still in their first year of teaming, team members were just getting used to each other and *any* newcomer would have been unwelcome. Danzle was already well into his action plan, so Sue Hardy would bring trouble. Finally, Hardy would be most effective in our upper grades and the lower grade teachers wrote the letter in question.

I call the ARs together and we personally deliver a memo to each staff member who signed the letter, talking with them wherever we can catch them. "Did you expect the letter to be used in a case for dismissal?" A few step forward and say "no," which takes a lot of courage. We discover teachers who are willing to have Hardy on their team, especially those who have been on the school improvement team, but Danzle says in the IDP that there is no one willing to do that.

Hardy will not give her consent to be executed. She calls parents to explain her take on the student incidents. This doesn't work well. Danzle's fielded many of their calls and their minds were made up long ago. Besides, it's not easy for some parents to

Chapter 10

accept the wrongdoing of their children. Danzle orders Hardy to stop phoning parents. To obey is to lay down and die, so she disregards his directive. Danzle calls association president Drew Harrison and tells him to forbid Hardy to make any calls. With Sue gagged, Danzle can operate even more freely. Drew tells Sue to stop, that the calls are hurting her cause. I don't know of a tighter spot. Make a call and defend yourself and you risk angering parent, boss, and advocate. Don't make a call and the rumors fly about unfettered. I begin to wonder if Danzle's gag order is a violation of freedom of speech.

I read the IDP and see it's a conceptual disaster. It's really heavy on classroom evaluation and really light on advocacy for Sue. There is so little support offered before the evaluations that I can only conclude it's the test before the instruction. The word dismissal is used in the IDP. I wonder if that is a legal requirement at this stage or a personal touch. She's directed to gather texts and drown herself in the latest pedagogical material, but there is no one in the building better read than Hardy. The growth areas in the IDP are more outside the classroom than in, yet, failures noted during classroom observations will cause her demise. The evaluator? Danzle. It is Danzle who wants Hardy to relinquish her leadership of the school improvement team. He's the file builder, manipulator, ambush expert and one whose arrival coincided with the beginning of Hardy's nightmare. Power arranges the conditions to preserve or expand its power.

Maybe the most ominous part of the IDP relates to time. Hardy must transform in two months. Coincidentally, I hear a sound bite on the radio saying that tenured university professors would most likely be given ten years to show they had improved their deficiencies. One time span is as insane as the other one.

While on retreat, we had been asked to consider who we considered "they" to be. Who did we think was in our community and who did we feel was outside? That question comes to mind again. Who constitutes "they" for me now? Is the superintendent pushing Danzle, simply supporting him or unaware of the latest tactics? Does "'They're' going for it!" uttered by Hardy, include the school board? Again, I feel a surging need to yell, "Everybody in the room. Now come clean!" But it doesn't work that way. People at the bottom don't get to say who attends meetings. Even if they did, those present would say that those absent are the decision-makers. That's been a consistent pattern. No matter how high up one goes, bottoms only talk to messengers.

Legal Clout?

The long drive to Lansing is uneventful. Hardy and I find the law offices easily. The secretary offers coffee and we're ushered into a large conference room with an immense table. Hardy extracts pertinent documents from two thick folders she's brought. The lawyer enters and apologizes for the wait. Patrick Fenmore displays a big smile and his short frame exudes energy. He thanks Hardy for having sent materials in advance.

Hardy tells her story as I interject headshakes that confirm my agreement with her version. When Hardy finishes I add stories of my own, showing that others have been under attack. I try to help Fenmore see that Hardy is not an isolated case, that she's part of a large pattern.

Fenmore suggests that a description of the firm and his own experience might be helpful to us. I'm convinced from his narrative and his stellar personal record that he's our man. If we end up forced into a tenure hearing, we will be represented well.

Fenmore then turns to the tenure process. He bluntly says that the tenure board supports school boards and their administrations hands down. It's rare for a teacher to survive the axe. The system is distorted and unjust, but that's the way it is. I swallow hard, smothering a protest as he continues.

"Okay," I say, "but, what about Sue's case?" Fenmore says that it looks bad. It's his understanding that her file can be measured in feet rather than inches. Danzle has done his homework. "Doesn't truth count?" I ask in disbelief. He reminds me of the politics. "Power backs up power. That's how it is." Fenmore's best advice is to short-circuit the process before it ever reaches a tenure hearing in Lansing.

I'm numb as we walk out. I don't want to believe it's all so tainted. I try to reconcile Fenmore's winning record and his account of the tenure board batting 1000. It doesn't add up. I can only conclude that Fenmore's been his own spin-doctor. In the depressing ride home I rethink the situation. The support of colleagues—those who work shoulder to shoulder with you—is the most powerful source of support one has. What matters most is the level of courage of those who care. I remember president Mike Howard coming to my defense. His conviction in justice and his belief in me slowed Danzle. Our union dues don't garner power, our hearts and our relationships do. The power for justice resides at the very bottom of our organizations. It is found in the ground of our being.

Win-Win Request?

It's unhealthy working here and the joy has gone. I come to the conclusion that I can't stay. I love the idea of this place and, until now, leaving has been the most foreign of thoughts. Trouble is, I can't go. I don't qualify for retirement. I submit a retirement proposal to central office that I think is win-win. Over the long-term, my proposal will save the district money. For their part, the administration will get rid of one of their highest paid employees and one of their "problems." The request is turned down—too expensive and "we would have to do this for everyone." The response to my request implies that treating people equally is an important objective. If we're trying so hard to do that, why do we have Insiders and Outsiders?

Author James Autry points out in *Love and Profit: The Art of Caring Leadership* that equal treatment is, in a word, "hogwash."[6] I believe that a decision should be based on specific circumstances and how the organization can best serve its people instead of the reverse. Unequal treatment may be most fair. Autry urges leaders to be courageous and to "Trust the great majority of your employees to know that you are trying to do the right thing and that their time will come."[7]

What I Want

I wonder if there is any ray of hope that power will undo itself. Will the energetic pursuit of dubious ends backfire? Rumi, the thirteenth-century Sufi poet, knows he can be undone by going after the wrong prize. In the poem "Who Makes These Changes?" he writes:

Disregarded

> I dig pits to trap others
> and fall in.
>
> I should be suspicious
> of what I want.[8]

When I'm most honest with myself, I realize that I want the wrong thing, just like Danzle. I want Danzle to disappear just as he wants Hardy and I to disappear. I'm armed with more tools than ever before—an appreciation of paradox, a vision of community, belief in abundance, waves of gratitude—yet I can't find the key to reconciliation. Something's still missing. If it can be found, we'll all be released from our exhausting struggle. Something has to give way. Something has to break this deadlock. Danzle? Me? The Fence Sitters? What must be in our hearts in order to move the grace of Providence?

I know that I should seek a change in me, that option is under my control, but how does one get from anger, indignation and stress to peace? My God, what a stretch! Maybe the faithful use of these tools can help me find whatever's missing. I've got to keep walking in this minefield, still believing that in the middle of two opposites is the answer.

Diversion Needed

Gee, I've found a distraction! Shocking T-shirts worn by students are "in." They're appalling, but make me laugh in spite of myself:

I don't do Windows. But I'll clean your clock.
I do whatever the voices in my head tell me to do.
Runs with scissors.
Better buy some aspirin, this is gonna hurt.
I'm just better than you, that's all.
Take your sorry game off my court.
Dominate, Eliminate, Terminate
Yeah, right.
Losing is not an option.

Chapter 10

Take no hostages.
Smarter, Faster, Younger
It's not whether you win or lose, it's whether I win.
I'm an animal and I will eat you if I have to.
I'm with stupid.
Stop your whining.
Hold my medals while I kiss your girlfriend.
If you don't like my attitude, don't talk to me.
Nunya Business
You messin' with me? You're messin' with the whole family.
If it's too loud, you're too old.
Respect the game. Leave the court.
I'm not listening.
I don't wanna work.
How's my running? 1-800-EAT-DUST
Girls Kick Butt
No, really. You stink!
duh
See ya. Wouldn't wanna be ya.
What's it like, living without a spine?
Quit your snivlin and get a life
Get a straw. You suck!

Losing It

    I think again about the rainy night on the bridge when Palmer explained that one can bear witness to another. Without a doubt, an encounter such as that would be done in private and out of love. I wonder when I can see my way to create such a moment. But, right now, I'm beside another teacher who has come under scrutiny. Will these AR duties ever end?

    Like the other situations, it looks to me like another calamity has formed from nothing. George Tyner, a young colleague, doesn't understand the huge drama that is developing. I don't get it either. He has been told that his guidelines for helping students remove incomplete grades violates "policy," but neither he nor I have ever heard of the policy in question. Basically, he's giving students too much time to erase incomplete grades. George has been called to a meeting and, as AR, I am to accompany him.

Disregarded

We meet outside Danzle's office. When we enter, I see that a central office administrator is present, ratcheting this meeting to the max. The charges against Tyner, combined with Danzle's aggressiveness and the appearance of the central administrator are strange indeed. It's another crazy-making moment.

A letter of reprimand is being placed in Tyner' file. If he is at fault, I think to myself, it is a first offense to a non-existent policy and certainly not worthy of a letter in his file. The solution is simple—tell Tyner what's expected and confirm that he understands. I tell Danzle that the reprimand is unreasonable and I request that the letter be removed from his file. He refuses. Then it hits me. Tyner is Hardy's teammate and has been supportive of her. Tyner is being punished and pressured to choose. He can sink with Sue or abandon her. That is the only sense I can make of what's going on.

It's at the end of the day and the end of the meeting and my nerves are a guitar string. I look at Danzle, point my arm straight at him and blurt, "How are *YOU* part of the problem?" Danzle fires back, "*PUT* your arm down!" I hurl back, "It's *MY* arm and I'll do anything I darn well please with it!" In the charged silence I stand and leave Danzle's office, my arm swinging at my side.

I can't decide if I'm angry with Danzle or myself. *That* is not what Palmer had in mind. Me neither. And I just said about the dumbest, must juvenile thing ever. Danzle is a crazymaker and he's driving me mad.

Chapter 11 – The Last Straw

*Creating a powerful image of the future
will invoke a powerful urge to act.*

Chili committee members had said that our district's vision was unclear to them. I check in with other colleagues. "Do you think our school system has a clear vision? Do you know where we're heading?" To a person, even those I label "loyalists," say "No, not really." I probe each person further, "Would we benefit from a vision?" Without pause, each person replies, "Yes."

My belief in the need for a vision expands while reading Margaret Wheatley's *Leadership and the New Science*. Vision, says Wheatley, may not just be a future destination to move toward, it's very likely a powerful "field"[1] of influence, operating daily, encouraging desired behaviors from those who come in contact with it.

As I begin to search for resources that describe how to develop a shared vision, more than once I read sharp criticism of the top-down management style and hierarchical organizational structures. Both worked exceptionally well for the Roman armies, it seems, but today's organizations have vastly different missions. I learn that vision work can best be done by involving many. I find some excellent resources. *Future Search* by Marvin Weisbord and Sandra Janoff, among others, confirms the importance of vision. The tension between it and reality is a call to action.

Asking Permission

I write our district's System Planning Council, the steering committee of our school system, recommending that we conduct a future search conference. I'm given a spot on their meeting agenda and present the concept to the group along with written information:

> ...a very effective methodology of providing direction for an institution is the "future search conference." The conference will ask a very large group of stakeholders to recall the past, describe the present, and offer scenarios of the future for Crawford Area Schools. During the process, common ground is identified. The institution's trajectory emerges from the stakeholders' visions. Following the conference, many people lead confidently because they sense what to do from their involvement in the conference. What would it take to establish a future search conference that resulted in many people sensing the trajectory of Crawford Area Schools? Is a future search conference desirable and feasible?

I make as strong a case for developing an inspiring vision as I know how. The chairperson says that the council will consider my request and let me know of their decision.

The System Planning Council is made up of a group of my peers and administrators. Council members have done some good, shooting down ill conceived or poorly coordinated projects and projects pushed too fast, but they've also killed innovative projects. I usually know what they are against, but I wonder what they are for. What strategic planning process do they use? What's *their* vision?

Future Search Network

I decide to participate in future search facilitation training. Should council members agree to conduct a future search, I will be equipped to facilitate or help guide the planning phase.

I phone Future Search Network,[2] a non-profit organization that supports future searches globally, and Sandra Janoff answers. I tell her that I am interested in the training. I discover that the fee is too steep for me, but she graciously offers to lower it. The total cost is still too much. My brother asks his boss to fund my flight in recognition of a pro bono weekend retreat I had done for his employees. His boss agrees.

With that added boost I make the necessary reservations, all the while wondering how costs can be cut further. I'm reluctant to use family dollars to pay for the training and I decide to stay off site at the cheapest place I can find. Finances aside, I'm pushed forward by the need I see within the district.

Training in New York State

The flight to Albany is uneventful, and the drive on South I-87 takes me over rolling hills, the highway cutting into mountaintops and exposing steel gray rock. I find my motel outside of New Paltz, a long strip of rooms with doors exposed to the parking lot. It'll do. I place my bags in the room and head back out to make the evening reception. As I drive down New Paltz's main street on my way to Mohonk Mountain House resort, I feel a festive air coming from its tightly grouped shops that line the thoroughfare.

I encounter the first glitch of the trip at the bottom of the mountain. The guard at the gate is polite, but he says that I'm not on the guest list. No one passes this point without authorization. I offer particulars until he waves me on. I wind upward and it seems I'll never reach the top. Finally, the main building appears and its towering three stories loom above the lower parking lot.

I climb the stairs to the resort and proceed through the covered porch on its side. I catch my breath—a pristine lake stretches before me. I hadn't imagined a lake would garnish the top of a mountain. The oblong lake stretches to my right and is bordered by vertical rock cliffs on the near side and a wooded slope on the other shore.

I take the path past the boat livery and discover the conference building. I'm just in time. Weisbord and Janoff are walking about, warm and relaxed, helping people feel welcome. Participants mingle about, getting acquainted.

We settle into a large circle of chairs, introduce ourselves and share why we've come. We've been sent mostly from businesses and government—NCR, IBM, U.S. Treasury, Fannie Mae. We've come from California and Germany and places in between. Those close by remark that they're surprised I've come on my own. We go over the expectations for the conference and then we watch a video entitled "Discovering Community" that walks us through the steps of the future search conference while documenting a conference done in Santa Cruz, California.

I'm beginning to sense that what we are involved in goes beyond learning how to help others craft a vision. It's also about governance and justice. Weisbord confirms this when he says, "We are experiencing new forms of democracy. Not since the town meeting has there been such activity."

The meeting ends and I head down the mountain in the afterglow of sunset, feeling a mix of fatigue and elation. There's still the guilt of the expense, but I also have a strong intuition that the experience will be priceless.

Next Day

My two alarms go off within a minute of each other. In the bathroom, I turn on the hot water valve and run the water until steam rises. I moisten the instant oatmeal and top it off with a banana. Meals are the final cost-cutting measure. I shave and shower and make a peanut butter sandwich for lunch, also tossing an apple into my briefcase.

It's already humid when I leave the room. The morning sun reveals more details of the mountain than last evening. As I drive upward, I see that the foliage is thick and the silver dollar sized leaves of the undergrowth shimmer excitedly in the wind.

History Lesson

Weisbord begins the morning session with background information. He recounts how Kurt Lewin, who pioneered action research, also developed the concept of field theory (that people act in relation to a set of forces operating on them at a given moment) and an early understanding of change. As part of a research experiment Lewin secretly filmed children working with craft materials. For several sessions they were lead by a leader operating in an authoritarian way. The leader then switched to a democratic way of working. Lewin found that when the "authoritarian leader" left the room, the children stopped working. When the "democratic leader" left the room, the children continued to work on their own. The study also established that laissez-faire leadership (letting people do what they want) could have more negative effects than authoritarianism. So, already in 1939, the relationship of power to the ownership of work was established in a research environment.

Weisbord quotes Lewin who said, "Autocracy is imposed on the individual. Democracy he has to learn."[3] Weisbord adds that when he was managing a business in the 60's he had no behavior in his repertoire between telling people what to do and letting them do what they wanted. He too had to learn how to help people set goals, observe boundaries, and take ownership.

Social psychologist Solomon Asch uncovered two conditions necessary for effective dialog: each person must believe 1) that the discussion is about their world and 2) that the other person has the same psychological needs. Then and only then will each accept the other's views without sacrificing their own.

We hear about Fred Emery and Eric Trist, who studied whole systems and self-managed work teams and developed a future search conference model. Ronald Lippitt and Eva Schindler-Rainman, in their work together, emphasized "getting the whole system in the room." Combine these approaches and you get a democratic, inclusive process.

The pioneers tackled other questions, too, Weisbord points out. How do you help people move from looking for the "great mind" that will "save" the group to the point where people look at the resources within the group? "What can replace problem solving with its negative and discouraging aura?"

Weisbord is not only willing to honor the work of others, he is able to integrate their various contribution into a seamless whole. To these gifts of his he adds his passion and willingness to share.

He speaks informally, but his tone changes. "All these leaders have died. We're up to bat." After a long silence, a participant says, "So a future search conference gets the whole system in the room to study its past and present so as to create a future scenario that helps unleash what is waiting to happen?" Weisbord nods. Another offers in a playful tone, "So Marv, what you're saying is

Disregarded

that a future search conference goes against the two cardinal laws of training—get the wrong people in the room and deliver the training too late?" Everyone laughs and we take a break.

Act On What You Want

Sandra Janoff facilitates after the break. "The game is won or lost in the planning. Future search is a structured opportunity to do something people have never had a chance to do. How to frame the task is critical." She talks smoothly and slowly while displaying a constant smile. "Learning organizations encourage information to cross boundaries. We take on problems, but we don't problem solve. Instead, we look for an inspiring future."

I think Janoff's approach to problems is correct. I know that in our organizations it's been a crapshoot whether problem solving eradicated a problem or made it bigger. Author Robert Fritz writes that even when a problem gets solved, "…you do not have…the presence of a result you want to create."[4]

For the remainder of our time together, we are to simulate participating in a Future Search Conference. Janoff walks us through selecting a fictional organization for the simulated conference and establishing a theme for it. Around 11:00 A.M. we select "Building a healthy, sustainable Mohonkville" as our theme. We'll imagine being part of a community called Mohonkville and what we want it to look like twenty years from today. Next, Janoff helps us establish seven stakeholder groups within our community (government, education, health, citizens at large, etc.). We will run the simulation in real time, but periodically stop to discuss important concepts. Our model:

1. Study the past
2. Study present trends
3. Create future scenarios
4. Discover common ground embedded in the scenarios
5. Create action teams that work toward the vision

Future Search Conference Simulation

We begin after lunch. Janoff goes through the preliminaries.

Chapter 11

"We're here to get as clear a vision as possible and to uncover what we want to do. We'll create the future out of the past and present. The values that you uncover will take you forward."

Next, Janoff explains Swedish social psychologist Claes Janssen's 4-room apartment model[5] that represents emotional states experienced during change and explains that we will travel through all four rooms during this conference. When things are going well, we'll be in the room named "Contentment." As change confronts us and we find ourselves unwilling to confront certain challenges, we will move to "Denial." Eventually, we will find ourselves in "Confusion," a place of high anxiety, but there we begin to see possibilities and we engage in a sorting process. From Confusion we move to "Renewal," the room where we live our choices that address the challenge and eventually move us back to Contentment. "The 4 room apartment is what we experience when we are learning with others," Janoff concludes.

Next we're asked to follow the five ground rules displayed on an easel.

- All ideas are valid
- Listen to one another
- All information goes on flip charts
- Observe strict time frames
- Have Fun

I find the members of my mixed stakeholder group and we arrange our chairs in a circle. The registration packet had asked each of us to bring a relevant symbol of the future, and it's time to reach for these. Jane shares first. She's from a non-profit and she holds up a rubber bathtub plug and says she wants to plug the leaks of resources and talent that slip away when they are not used. Mike is from local government and he holds up a magnifying glass to help him see the needs of community residents. Larry is from business and holds up a pen that has one black ink end and one red ink end. These colors represent a vibrant business climate to him and his stake here is to help the local economy. Donna's symbol grabs me. She has a handful of foot-long pieces of yarn.

Disregarded

There's a knot in the middle signifying they're part of a whole, but she draws our attention to the ends—they're disconnected. She's a "citizen" and she longs to help people reconnect with each other. When it's my turn to share, I read Mary Oliver's poem, *The Summer Day*, which challenges us to thoughtfully choose a direction for our lives.[6]

I note that this activity isn't like the all-too-familiar icebreakers I'm used to from other conferences and workshops, the kind that has nothing to do with the content. This activity is integral to the process, helping us learn who is here, why we're here, and what values we treasure.

We Study the Past

Three long, blank timelines hang on the walls. Walking about with magic markers in hand, we individually record on butcher paper historic milestones of Mohonkville, the U.S. and the world. We then regroup and each group gives a three-minute summary report on the specific timeline assigned and analyzed—end of the cold war, the energy crisis, economic globalization, technology explosion. From the activity, I feel a strong sense of our historic roots.

We Identify Trends

A paper-covered wall is blank, save for a circle in the center with "Mohonkville" written inside it. Our task is to fill the wall with present trends. We are to construct a "mind map." As someone names a trend, Janoff draws a long line out from the circle and labels the exact name of the trend given by the participant—unprecedented economic boom, religious revival, quality movement, medical advances, decentralization, self-help. Related concepts get lines that branch from the main line. Unrelated trends get their own line from the circle's edge.

This time we form stakeholder groups to analyze the data we've created. I sit with all the educators. We analyze the mind map for what we believe to be important from our perspective as educators. The wall is our collective picture of reality and our foundation for the future vision. Although I was warned earlier,

I'm surprised to feel overwhelmed. I've been ambushed by information overload—chaos. Our group is working to make sense of the many rivers and tributaries drawn on the wall when Weisbord and Janoff call a break from real time.

Janoff says, "The key is to help people realize that they are talking about the same world. If we can do that, they will experience themselves as a community and they can see that they can live together, even with different viewpoints." Weisbord adds, "Everything is connected. There aren't boundaries—we manufacture them. To change a system, the system must interact with a greater world. We're bound to have people in the room who are under the thumb of power. Corporate future searches need in attendance customers, suppliers and others related to the corporation, but outside of it. These 'others' alter the dynamics and that promotes change. The organizational development litany has as its dialog—'The boss is a controller/The employees are like children.' But in a future search, there's no place to hide."

We Imagine the Future

We then re-form into our mixed groups and work on the future, attempting to create a vivid scenario. Business, government, health and education folk cross-pollinate. It isn't long before I can tell that we're aided by our diversity. My group sees Mohonkville as the richest of webs—seamless, collaborative, integrated, process-oriented, wisdom-based and value-based, anticipatory, immediately responsive, self-managed and self-renewing, with the caring for others at its foundation.

With these concepts in mind we design a skit to convey our vision to the other participants. When it is our turn to share, my group takes everyone on a guided motor tour with special emphasis on small, one-stop shops of support services that spread around the community and are staffed by volunteers. These places provide assistance well below their traditional costs and are able to respond in a fraction of the usual time. After presenting our skit to the entire group and seeing the other skits, I realize that our skit had many similar elements with the other ones, even without consultation.

Disregarded

Finding Common Ground

In the next portion of the conference we work to confirm our common ground. If we can't agree that a particular element in one of the skits should be in our preferred future, we will put it aside. The energy to move forward rests in our agreements. We reach consensus easily on a number of concepts: there are decentralized centers where people can receive support from highly trained volunteers, there are few government programs, volunteerism is the glue of the community, and citizen involvement is intense.

At Conference End

I realize that sometime during this process I've become a convert. The democratic environment and sense of community have been enough to win my heart, but there's more. I can really SEE Mohonkville 20 years down the road. I can work toward what I can see.

I get the proof I was looking for. This process can really help my school district.

Back Home

It takes almost two years for my futuring recommendation to bear fruit. I hear rumors that the school system will be involved in a futuring activity. A former school board president will do the facilitation. Prominent citizens and a mix of others are invited. I pick up on the news late in the preliminaries, but still ask to be included.

I'm turned down.

The rejection is a real jab in the gut. I brought this idea to the System Planning Council. I keep wondering to what degree these failures are by my own hand. What seems most likely is that political savvy and strategy are missing tools in my toolbox, but there's more to it than that. Is it reasonable to expect a response to my presentation long ago or anticipate the courtesy of being included?

I come to hear about the results of the futuring process via a brief report to staff given by a colleague who was invited. I get the strong impression that negative trends have been found.

Chapter 11

Our staff is warned of the dangers ahead. No action teams form. I feel ashamed of gloating over what will most likely come of this—nothing at all. It appears that even if we conquer drugs, rapid growth and inadequate funding, we will have, as Fritz pointed out, the absence of these problems, but not the inspiring organization we long for.

I fail at squelching the bitterness. Aren't you tired of spinning your wheels? How many times must your efforts be blocked before you wake up? The definition of insanity is to repeatedly do something that doesn't work. This organization is hell-bent on trouncing any ripple of real change. Its initiatives are deceptive disguises that maintain the status quo and control.

I realize that I better understand older colleagues. Many have had a slight detachment I didn't understand. Their words to me came in a variety of forms:

> The more things change, the more they stay the same.
> Don't bother.
> You can't push rope.
> I used to be as excited as you, but got tired of hitting my head against the wall.
> I feel I'm a fire, but then somebody throws water on me.

Everyone had been passionate and learned the lesson a bureaucracy teaches best. The warnings were there all along, but I needed to learn the same lesson for myself. I feel something deep inside shift irrevocably—I will not allow you to trick me again. You will never again get me to commit myself to you. You can no longer have my heart. You can no longer have all of the life energy I've been willing to give you.

Am I giving up? Have I become a traitor? No. I have been willing to eat instant oatmeal and peanut butter sandwiches for days and resorted to begging. I've been willing to try again after each rejection. But something has snapped inside. If I give myself to this organization once more and get hit with its resistance, I will have become a traitor to myself. There comes a defining moment when one must choose to guard ones' soul or surrender it to a contemptuous god. This god is unworthy of such a sacrifice.

Reconnecting

Three years elapse before I reestablish contact with Weisbord and Janoff. A major change process is underway in Southwest Lower Michigan and future search consortium members like myself are being invited to help. I'm selected to be a recorder for one of the future search conferences. It's clear that Weisbord and Janoff give me this opportunity to further my growth. I record the dialog among members of the Health and Wellness sector of Berrien County so the proceedings can be published and appropriately archived.

One of the purposes of this initiative is to determine how to address the troubling gap in racial makeup and wealth that has exists between the adjacent cities of Benton Harbor and St. Joseph. These cities sit side-by-side on the shoreline of Lake Michigan, but the St. Joseph River separates them. Some would say the river is as wide as an ocean. Can these communities heal wounds and unite for the common good of their citizens? The future search conference is one of eight being convened in Berrien County and funded by the Whirlpool Corporation. The conference, "will unite us around a common vision and avoid 'going it alone,'" Whirlpool CEO Dave Whitwam says. The first conference developed a framework for all the others: "To establish a set of interdependent world-class communities where diversity and inclusion are the foundation and where no one is left behind."

At the beginning of the conference, Health and Wellness participants share some symbols that have meaning for them. Pam Pappas, a dentist, holds up extractor forceps used to pull rotten teeth and says, "I use these every morning on people that can't afford care and have to wait so long to get care that extraction is the only solution." It's a telling image. People are, in fact, being left behind.

I watch Marie McCormick do her work as facilitator. She is an experienced future search facilitator, always mindful about holding the space for diverse and non-threatening dialog. She's high energy, and her comments project confidence and optimism. McCormick's good at explaining things simply—"A trend is an increase or decrease in something that is influencing citizens living here." During the preparation for the future scenarios she clarifies, "We're after the 'What.' *What* do you see people doing in 20 years? Projects are the 'How.' *How* did people make it happen?" Just like at Mohonk, each small group will convey as descriptive an image of the future as they can.

There are three conferences going on in the county this weekend. At night Marie probes the consultants from the other two sites over dinner, displaying a deep desire to improve her craft. My respect for these facilitators grows as I listen to what they care about. They want to create spaces where people can speak their truths and determine their own future. They want to help people reach their dreams.

Strong Impressions and Learnings

It is here in Berrien County that I see the power of a single voice. Most participants are caregivers, but one is from the recovering community. His name is Carl and his story captivates the others. He speaks with an authority and a passion that can only come from life experience.

> Even when a person decides to turn their life around—they can't. The system looks so confusing, a person doesn't know where to begin. When you've been on the street for a long time, the simplest decisions are too hard. People on the streets need simple help—guidance—the complexity is a barrier. People on the streets are left out in the dark. Once they have a history of need, often they're not given a chance with employers. The only way into an inpatient drug rehab program is through the courts system. You've got to break the law to get help! Then, you've got a police record!

I'm deeply convinced that Carl's presence is helping create a different vision than the one that would be created in his absence. Carl's remarks drive home the point that, to make a difference, you have to show up and speak from your heart.

The absence of two other community segments works in the

Disregarded

opposite way. Youth and alternative medicine practitioners were invited, but none are present. I wonder how the vision would differ had they come.

It's clear that participants fervently want to connect; the premise here is that if the right spaces are created, people will do so. As various small groups present their future scenarios to the rest, this long-frustrated desire is let loose. Without knowledge of each other's work, three of the groups' visions merge into one these now-disparate cities on the edge of Lake Michigan. As the third group concludes, "We are no longer two cities with a river that divides us, we are one city with a river running through it."

These are moments of magic.

As I listen to the scenarios, I *see* what Benton Harbor and St. Joseph can become. I have experienced the power of the process again. Others know this power as well. McCormick remarks to me in the lobby of the motel, her voice tapering off in wonder, "I can't put my finger on it, but of all the types of work that I do, there is *something* about a future search..."

A Local Future Search Conference

While I was unable to help sponsor or participate in a future search conference for my own workplace, the opportunity has arisen to facilitate one for residents of my own county. As I wait for participants to arrive, I trace the steps that have led up to this moment.

How humble was our beginning! Five of us citizens had named ourselves the Trust Committee. We'd been placing articles in the local newspaper that highlighted moments of cooperation between two or more groups. We had also placed the articles into a pamphlet entitled "Case Histories in Cooperation." All of us belonged to Pine County Futuring, a group of citizens working toward a preferred future for the county. When we met apart from the large group, we asked ourselves how we could contribute to the futuring mission. We ended up committing ourselves to sponsor a future search conference. We had no formal status, no officers, no charter, no office space, no mission statement, no budget—nothing except each other. We had operated in open

Chapter 11

space, a place short on rejections and resistance, a no man's land full of potential. Since we had hardly existed in concrete terms, power hadn't wanted us dead. We were like a slender stalk pushing its way up through a tiny crevice in the rock. Yet, from the most fragile of existences comes the conference.

We gained strength quickly after making the commitment. We invited seventeen people to be on the planning committee and, except for one who had health problems, all had accepted. It was a talented, high-energy group. To the person, each member made important contributions.

Local industry and small business supported the conference with their donations, demonstrating to me how the private sector is often the key to making things happen in the public sector. The Pine Community Foundation provided a large grant to fund an outside facilitator. The Woodlands Institute offered their site for three days at one-third their usual rate. Our county newspaper, The Observer, printed a series of informative articles in advance of the conference.

From afar, Sandra Janoff of Future Search Network provided advice and helped manage the process of finding facilitator candidates. Ferne Kuhn of the Kuhn Group from the Philadelphia area was finally selected. Ferne and I have talked extensively on the phone and e-mailed for four months and she has stayed overnight at my house for the two full day meetings we've had with the planning committee. The rides to and from the airport have been a delightful mix of everyday conversation and professional sharing. Her experience and passion have assured me that the conference will go well. With her mentoring and my experiences at Mohonk and Berrien County, I feel confident to take on my first facilitation role.

The Conference Opens

We have placed chairs in a circle that, to me, represent equality and unity. The conference begins with the combined words of Marge Piercy's poem "Councils"[7] and my own. Planning committee co-chairs Alyssa Allman and Kevin Main strongly recite alternating stanzas from opposite sides of the circle…

> We must sit down and reason together.
> No one should stand over another.
> The quiet ones are invited to speak.
> The restless are urged to listen…

End Result

The conference exceeds my dreams and, with it, comes a deep respect for county residents. I invite all participants to form a circle for the closing. Ferne suggests we go around the circle and those who choose may comment on their experience here. It isn't long before we've joined hands.

Ferne is on my left and we're hearing overwhelmingly positive comments. I squeeze her hand, a gesture that means, " Did you hear that?"

> "Most effective event I've ever been to."
> "It was an honor to be invited."
> "This is the only conference I've attended that will make a difference."
> "I didn't know so many people valued the same things that I do."
> "I'm grateful to have met such interesting people."
> "Because we've reached common ground, I know we can confidently work toward our dreams."

Businessman Paul Guerra is on my right and he shares his reflection on the conference. He's been to many meetings of this sort, but this conference is different—something positive will definitely result.

It's my turn and I describe how grateful and inspired I am to have watched enthusiastic citizens engage so deeply. It becomes difficult to share my appreciation for Ferne with the circle of fellow citizens—there's a large lump in my throat. Ferne took on the facilitation assignment knowing that mentoring a stranger came with the task. "We went from being strangers talking over a long, thin wire to becoming friends and colleagues. Her experience and wisdom taught me a great deal. All of us here must have noticed how Ferne honored our words by holding the space for all of them."

A laugh comes from the circle when Ralph King says, "I've enjoyed holding hands with Anthony White."

The conference ends with stanzas suggested by Marge Piercy's poem "The seven of pentacles."[8] Kevin's and Alyssa's voices urge us to widen the circle:

> Weave real connections.
> Weave ties that are real.
> Together, build what calls you,
> calls you from your dreams.

We release our grip on each other.
It's over.

Cleanup

While I begin to help with tables and chairs, a strong sense of accomplishment lingers. I can't help but note that my efforts are blocked at work yet supported outside of it. As I make a trip to the van with materials, questions push for an answer. Can we create organizations that honor the passions, talents and dreams of its members? Can we create organizations that welcome change initiatives from the bottom as much as from the top? Can we create organizations without a top or a bottom? Do enough of us really understand the value of shared vision to seek its formative power?

I remember the parting words my son Joe's favorite college professor had for him at graduation time. Professor Kate See from Michigan State University, a wonderfully wise woman with a deep understanding of social institutions, had just four words for him—"Never join a bureaucracy." Maybe that's perfect advice for me. A bureaucracy is a hermit crab—something active in a dead structure. To cast off its shell, leave its rigid, safe haven, would be to choose adventure, choose life.

Chapter 12 – Minuteman

The fateful question for the human species seems to me to be...[If] their cultural development will succeed in mastering the...instinct of aggression and self-destruction.[1]

Sigmund Freud

The fall rains taper and my vigil for the first snow begins. The sun's rays graze the front yard when only a few months ago they were burrowing into the soil. Eager leaves that have fallen, dry and curl. They tumble or slide on their edges across the driveway with the sizzle of frying eggs. The immense highs that spoke of connectedness and wholeness are gone. For me, fall is the season most difficult to endure. Fall. Its name says what is going on inside. Fall. Falling. I've toppled from forces within and without. Only an arid landscape remains. I wonder if I'm becoming ash or drying out to re-ignite.

Cindy is celebrating her fiftieth birthday today. Her venture out into the world is short-circuited, while still in the garage, when her car emits a weak click upon turning the ignition switch. Although I'm the one who must take care of the problem, the symbolism delights me: turn fifty and your battery goes dead. Fortunately for Cindy, the repair is simple; unfortunately, my battery isn't so easily fixed. As I trudge back in from the garage, I wonder where the seed of hope is hiding in this repressive fog.

Little did I know that this time would become one filled with valuable discoveries.

December Wind

I sink into the couch and close my eyes. The house is still, save for the alternating whirs of the refrigerator and furnace.

Chapter 12

Once in a while a windowpane snaps in the tug-of-war between the inside and outside air. Eventually, I open my eyes and begin to focus on the commotion in the tree outside the window. A bright red male cardinal shows itself and another joins him and, soon, another. It's the most blessed I've felt in days.

Thirteen days separate today and the winter solstice, but it reeks of anticipation. The air is like a razor, ready to slash anything still alive, and capable of producing a white blanket to hide the homicide. The cardinals take flight and I become absorbed with the animated ornamental pear tree beside the front walk. The wind is picking up and the leaves shimmer wildly. More leaves are wrenched from their branches and I have a strange sensation that the wind has somehow made its way to my core.

Part of what feels so unsettling is that I've been on a journey toward an unknown destination. I could proclaim an end to my search, celebrate all that I've learned and be justifiably content. I've rejected that urge for something I barely sense still lies ahead. How strange of me to offer so much effort toward such a vague hunch.

The warm sensation on my cheek travels slowly to my lips and its salty flavor sends me searching for news. All of my being works to solve the mystery that is whirling inside. Finally, truth emerges. *I'm going to die* courses through me with savage force. Insight and dread compete for supremacy. The clash resolves rapidly and with utmost certainty. The persistent dread is replaced with the awe of discovered treasure, bestowing the feeling of a hard won victory. I know what it is to be "ahead of all parting." I have moved into and through my death. Beyond the limitations of logic, at the deepest level ever, I've encountered my mortality. But the surprising result of this meeting is liberation. Released from this unthinkable burden, I feel incredibly alive. In my head, I've known all along about my fate, but a deeper realization had to manifest. My discovery is at the emotional level, a matter of the heart.

What seemed to come out of nowhere in an instant has really taken years to appear. Hadn't I been on two retreats about winter and death? Hadn't I helped bury friends? Hadn't I purposefully read on death and imagined my life snatched from me? None of that was an accident. But this moment is spontaneous, unorchestrated grace. That which lives deep inside and cares most about me has urged me forward to reach this waypoint.

Our journeys are to progress toward the light, more life. In squandering our energy by investing in a defensive stance, we will most surely lose our treasures, reducing light and life. Our distorted fear of death will not stop with our bodies; it will broadly spread into the metaphoric realm – death of career, income, love, status, faith, and meaning. To bolster our courage, we must remember that spring follows winter and new life follows death. The response we must make to our mortal condition is an unconditional acceptance that invites light and life. We must be ahead of all parting. We have to move forward into the heart of the matter in order to have abundant life. Our hearts have to be broken open in order to grow into understanding. I think of Palmer's advice—"if you can't get out of it, get into it."

I celebrate this moment with a journal entry:

December 1st.
It is coming out of the west,
invisible, but relentless.
The maples have long been naked,
but now the leaves of the pear tree
are being forced to choose.
Some cling. Others are pried loose.
Some willingly let go –
floating, flying, diving.
Between bursts, a third are perfectly still,
while the rest shiver and shake.
Rust colored are the sky sides;
their underbellies gold.
Will this laying bare take more
than a day? Three?
At full gust, all wag in unison
giving tongue to what
each has learned since May –
or have known forever.

Chapter 12

I am drawn into this sacrament completely
and, with each gust,
am washed, am washed.

Other Heart Matters

I make an appointment with Dr. Wahl, our family physician. My heart has become an unsteady friend, pausing ever so briefly, and then pounding like a bass drum. At other times it begins to race as if someone yelled "Fire!" I've begun to feel unnerving sensations in my left arm as well.

Dr. Wahl listens to my description of the tensions at work and then to my heart. Alas, in the safety of the exam room my heart beats a reassuring pattern. I sense that Dr. Wahl is a little skeptical of my complaint, but he remains faithful as ever and orders a test. He shows more immediate concern over my description of work. This is a small town and the rumors of power gone awry must have preceded my visit. He pauses before moving beyond the familiar boundaries of stethoscope and script pad into the dispensing of non-medical advice: "Jack, one always has to be vigilant. If you buck the system, it's apt to bite back real hard. From the rumors I've heard, I'd advise a low profile and a great deal of caution on your part." I consider this good advice, but I don't see how I can avoid Danzle and my responsibilities as an association representative.

Two days lapse and I report to be fitted with a monitor that I'll wear for twenty-four hours. Patches are applied to my chest that have wires connected to a recorder. When an erratic heart "episode" occurs, I'm to press a button on the monitor and that will mark the recording tape for a technician to interpret. I'm supposed to document on paper the beginning and ending times of all my activities. I leave the hospital with a large bulge underneath my coat.

My daughter Jenny has come home to attend the annual Christmas play with me at her former elementary school. The heart monitor is too big to ignore so I explain the situation to her with a tone that dismisses my concern. "Dr. Wahl is being overly cautious." It's a lie, but one meant to put her at ease. As we sit together watching the play, the first episode comes. A big thud follows a pause in my heartbeat. I discreetly reach inside my coat and press the button. Jenny throws a puzzled look, but I don't acknowledge it, pretending to be absorbed in the performance. During the second episode minutes later, she grabs my arm in concern. Her eyes dart about, searching my face for clues. I smile back and then look at the stage. The kindergartners are belting out a wild chorus of "I Want a Hippopotamus for Christmas" when I reach for the button again. Jenny's face turns white with fear. I whisper, "It's nothing, Hon. Don't worry, I'm fine." She's not convinced and I hate the fact that she's been drawn into the stress of my work.

Three days later Dr. Wahl shares the results. Sure enough, I wasn't imagining things. Wahl loses me quickly in medical jargon—tachycardia, bradycardia, PAC's, multifocal PVC's. His best guess is that my body is producing adrenaline. He says, "Your body is ready to fight or flee. You're under a lot of stress. What can you do to get out of your situation?" I tell him that I ask myself that same question often, but no answer has come to me as yet.

High Stakes

What can I do, indeed? I'm in a bad spot. My health is being affected, an ambush is likely, I'm short of the needed years to retire, and I've received a rejection to my retirement request. When I call the MEA regional office I explain that, at any moment, I could be forced out like Cliff Anderson. With my health in jeopardy, the security of my family has become paramount and the only thing left for me to do is to develop a strong defense. My phone calls and subsequent meeting with the regional rep don't help. He's caring enough, but he delivers news I don't want to accept, "Being forced out is mighty hard to prove. It'll be a case of 'he said, she said.' It will be your word against the word of your boss."

The stress pushes me to places I would never think of going. I meet with a local lawyer, Tom Dykehouse, a man I know to have a sharp mind and high moral standards. I've come to know

Chapter 12

him through a mutual friend. He's moving, so we wind our way around boxes to his desk. He listens as I describe the situation and offers the same message: "It may be exactly as you say, Jack, but the evidence is difficult to collect and the charges harder to prove." He suggests that I see our town's local labor relations expert, who happens to be a lawyer that he respects. I thank him for his time and open my checkbook, but the more I insist on paying, the more adamantly he objects.

Within two weeks I'm able to see lawyer Herb Matthews. His office décor is understated, with family pictures being the focal point. As I again tell my tale, Matthews takes notes. I ask him if he can put a legal label to what's going on. He says the proper terminology is "constructed termination." Finally, I have something concrete to grab onto. If what I say is true, he goes on, and the court's decision goes in my favor, Danzle will have been found to have constructed events that lead to my dismissal. Matthews' tone is discouraging. He doesn't think I'd have much chance of proving my claim. "Besides, you haven't been terminated," he points out. I briefly share the stories of Anderson and Hardy and about the physical symptoms I've experienced, adding that, "I'm trying to *avoid* termination and death."

Matthews leans far back in his chair and stares at the wall while tapping together the fingertips of both hands. He finally asks about the damages I would seek. I explain that if I were terminated early, it would likely take six figures to offset the financial losses. I can tell by his frown that Matthews is wondering if I'm an ambulance chaser. He's not sure if I'm here for justice and protection or big money. He remarks that the amount sounds very high. I go through the steps that I used to figure compensation and his face registers concern for the first time. I guess the numbers have helped him see the gravity of my situation. With a shift in his chair and a comforting nod toward me, he appears to have become an advocate. We part with the understanding that, if things get worse, I will be back.

I'm glad I went to see Matthews, but I sarcastically think to myself that the legal system of ours is most like a mop. The mess must be made before you reach for it. It would be "better" if

Disregarded

I had been terminated and were already in financial ruin. We'd have something concrete to deal with. It would be "best" if I died from the stress, then, I'd be taken seriously for sure. One has to be in a deep hole before anything can be done and even then, with the system seemingly supporting the powerful, getting out of a hole is very unlikely. My most depressing realization is that Danzle would probably have no trouble "proving" the myths he's constructed about me, while it would be almost impossible for me to prove the opposite.

Psychology Classes

So what *can* I do? If I can't affect the outcome, I guess I'll have to consider careers following my premature "retirement." I think about how much the retreats have affected me and wonder if I might be successful working in that area. To test this out, I conduct a few retreats to see if I have what it takes and the results are encouraging. But another possibility comes to mind. Perhaps I should become a mental health counselor. I take psychology classes to determine my fitness, gauge my interest and to help me better understand the psychological underpinnings of the formation retreats.

Why can a group be such a powerful resource for each of its members? I learn in a class on group counseling and from reading the work of Irvin Yalom that groups can offer their members a baker's dozen of therapeutic benefits. It's easier to understand why the retreats were so powerful.

In an introductory course I discover that there are around a dozen major psychological models. Most counselors seem to concentrate on one or two for their basic philosophic framework and then borrow tools from some of the others. Many of the models accept existential concerns as part of their understanding of the human condition—we share concerns about aloneness, freedom of choice, death and the meaning of life. I also learn that the majority of those seeking support suffer from either depression or anxiety.

As a course on self-defeating behaviors makes clear, anxiety is the root cause of these ineffective actions. An unexpected event or difficult situation evokes fear. Fear in itself is not the demon; it's a warning mechanism and a stimulant. What we do with our fear is what transforms it into a deforming force or an invitation to say "Yes" to adventure.

But, too often, we choose various self-defeating behaviors—procrastination, avoidance, blame, to name a few, as a way of disowning and covering up our poor choices. "I'm too busy." "It's the rule." "I did it because of the pressure." Phrases such as these reveal our attempts to get ourselves off the hook.

Eventually, the consequence of a poor choice arrives and, ironically, our worst fears materialize. We often end up getting what we feared and tried to avoid. If we fear rejection and choose to be aloof to avoid it, we are likely to become lonely. If we fear failure and choose not to try, we are likely to experience failure.

As I learn more about existentialism and self-defeating behavior, I become more convinced that fear is the tyrant in our lives. Our distorted needs for safety and control manifest into behaviors that squelch life.

Primitive Tribe

Ernest Becker's *Escape from Evil* proves to be a valuable read. The puzzle pieces that I've been holding for so long find their way home.

Since the time before fire, humans have organized themselves into tribes and waged contests in order to prove their strength. "Winners" temporarily convinced themselves of their invincibility. Modern man is no different. The passage of centuries has done nothing to change man's need and related behaviors. We're still driven to compare ourselves with another—and to come out on top. We must compete and win in order to give ourselves a feeling of superiority and, therefore, relief from the vulnerability we really feel. The feeling of invincibility we seek cannot be obtained in solitude. We need each other.

Groups divide in order to conduct this win-lose ritual. If the divisions are unbalanced, a unilateral move takes place. The weaker division becomes the scapegoat, the whipping boy of the stronger. "Taunting and humiliating" adversaries or "torturing and killing them…adds to one's own size and importance"[2] and keeps alive the feeling of significance and durability. This meanness results when man's aggressive side balloons out of proportion to his capacity to love and nurture.

Regardless of which subgroup we belong to, we begin to sense our shadow. We despise our feelings of inferiority and vigorously disown them. In the words of Carl Jung, we look "...for everything dark, inferior and culpable in others."[3] The scapegoat is the creation of the dominant, but fearful. Becker writes, "It is precisely the split-off sense of inferiority and animality which is projected onto the scapegoat and then destroyed symbolically with him."[4]

It's ironic that we don't dare use our sensibilities to overcome our instincts. Most of us don't dare to buck group conformity in order to be ourselves for fear of sticking out, because "...it is dangerous to have a head."[5] Having your own head would place you "at the cutting edge of evolution"[6] and be a threat to others. In our conformity, we perpetuate the primitive ritual.

Where do some leaders get their power? There's yet another need of ours that can be met through group conformity. Humans also need visible gods. We create a human god, a "manna figure," so we know where to look for the distribution of goods. But in order to receive goods from this god, "the boss," one must become compliant. The compliant give away their own sovereignty, further empowering and deifying the manna gods.

Only now does all of this come together at a deep level within me.

We have been afraid.

How thickheaded I've been. "Be Not Afraid" has been working on me since the Vermont conference and only now does it ring true with full force. The scenario described matches what's happening at work. The anxiety provoked by the changes at work pressed some to identify scapegoats—the Outsiders—in order to relieve their internal conflicts. We have recreated the ancient, but ongoing drama perfectly. We have not transcended our original nature. We are primitives acting primitively. The suits are a ruse. The seed of destruction is our existential concern—our sense of being ever so fragile—our fear of death. If fellow workers knew that they were performing a primitive ritual, would it be such an embarrassment as to cause the whole arrangement to collapse?

Elsewhere, I learn more. We are not mineral or vegetable; we are animal. Many creatures have eyes that are situated in their skulls to best scan all about for danger. These are the hunted. In *A Natural History of the Senses* Diane Ackerman writes that humans have "predator eyes."[7] Our eyes are set forward. We have the potential for deadly attacks. Each one of us can be dangerous. And from reading brain research, we should know that our emotional responses form faster than cognitive ones. We're as suited to growling, attacking and jumping to conclusions as we are for displaying reason and restraint.

From these discoveries I more fully recognize how fear influences us and I'm reminded of a powerful passage in Palmer's writing:

> Indeed, fear is the counterpoint of every great and good human virtue: fear, not doubt, is the counterpoint of faith; fear, not hate, is the counterpoint of love; fear, not greed, is the counterpoint of generosity; fear, not betrayal, is the counterpoint of trust. It is fear that deforms our lives; it is fear that snaps all the great virtues of their power to reform our lives.[8]

During the Nights

My recurring dreams have turned ugly. Each night I explore a huge, unfamiliar mansion, reluctantly moving from room to room, compelled to open each door, even though what I loath will be on the other side. I guess that dark news is coming because nothing of light could come from a mansion full of cold-blooded creatures. I keep these dreams to myself. One doesn't come downstairs in the morning and, over Cheerios, say that you've struggled all night with closets crammed with eels.

I scrounge for a picture I took last fall of the moonflowers along the fencerow. They're perfect examples of what I need to do to live in this awful darkness. I need to be vulnerable and open to move forward.

Disregarded

Wonder of wonders —
the moon flower.
While the maple trees catch fire,
the moon flower quietly takes its leave.

The stalk, so tan and bleached,
gives back its moisture to the air.
The leaves have no pretense about age.
They close, shrivel and droop,

asking to be passed through the flame.
But the seedpods linger.
All are a delicate green.
Each pod is a silent fortress.

The royal hued stems lead
to the sharp spines which protect the seeds.
Hundreds of seeds. Hundreds.
But each pod knows, from its center,

all must be risked.
The pod must break apart
for the seeds to be flung.
It must be vulnerable.

To stay safe behind its spines
is to refuse everything.
Birth and death are
in this solitary being.

I sense an eternal cycle.
I feel the mystery.
And, for just one moment,
I understand.

    The terror of the nights begins to spill into the days. I wonder if Palmer and the Fetzer Institute expected our journeys to reach this place or if this is more of my own doing. What I really

Chapter 12

think is that I took the retreat program and went overboard. In so doing, I've undone myself.

Morning Message

The sounds of breakfast preparation from the kitchen reach upstairs as I finish shaving. The comfort of the day is that it is like hundreds of others, a note in the persistent rhythm of a Bolero-like song. The compensation is that the days come and go with regularity regardless of my state. Each day *must* be getting me closer to whatever is drawing me downward. I take a step toward the stairs and then come to a dead stop.

"You don't know much."

I look around the room for an intruder. There is no one here except me. I stop breathing and wait for Cindy to call again, but I know the voice is not hers.

Slowly, I surmise that my learnings have taken me too high. I must have used my intellect and learning as weapons and rank, and maybe I've wanted what other primitives have wanted—to be king on the hill. I have wanted to be special, special enough to feel powerful, powerful enough to give meaning to my life. I decide that I have probably been a pest as well. I have pushed for change with a great deal of energy. What's worse, I've done so, not just for all the good it would do, but also from my own need to contribute. I conclude that gravity's pull is to be my friend.

The image of a ladder comes to mind, probably planted by Mirabai Starr's translation of *Dark Night of the Soul*. I have climbed high and, now, strong is the sense of rushing downward. Starr writes that one experiences "exultation" followed by "humility." "God is at the end of the ladder. The ladder rests in God."[9] I have come down. I'm as low to the ground as a squash.

I recall that the voice inside was absolutely neutral. Rather than flinging a stinging, razor-sharp arrow meant to hurt, "You don't know much" was offered in love—exquisite love.

Brokenness

Days pass. Yet another realization comes. I sense that I am being companioned by my shadow. I'm surrounded by it, but astonished at the outcome. I feel good. I'm reconciling myself to myself. The biggest revelation is that, as a perfectionist, I am finding my salvation in my faults. As I welcome and accept their presence, I feel at peace. I'm broken. I'm becoming whole. The dryness and the darkness have lead to wellbeing.

Being a squash isn't so bad.

I retrace my steps and identify critical moments in my journey. The return home began on a winding road that lead to the first retreat. Community, with its unconditional acceptance and help in discovering gifts, made it possible for me to accumulate enough good news about myself to face my shadow. The decision to work diligently to identify my gifts turned out to be a most crucial, beneficial one.

Power in Vulnerability?

"The most precious human gifts are rooted in weakness,"[10] writes Jean Vanier in *From Brokenness to Community*. I now realize the voice of love, the voice of communion, came to me when I was in need, not otherwise. The gift I received came when I was vulnerable. "…[H]ealing takes place at the bottom of the ladder."[11] Power is benign. It's when, as individual or tribe, we seek it for the wrong reasons that we cause terrible damage. Healing is found in humility and weakness.

I'm taken with Vanier's story of Armando, an orphan with severe mental disabilities who cannot walk or talk. Brought back from the edge of death, a condition Vanier attributes to having been rejected by his mother, the love of the community supporting Armando encourages his own eyes to say, "I love you."[12] His presence is therapeutic to those who hold him. Vanier concludes that if, in his brokenness, Armando can heal others, so too can we in our brokenness. We can come to believe that fully being ourselves, shadow included, can be a gift to others. The space created by community is the space to grow into the acceptance of who we really are. We have a right to this space and a true community gives this blessing of freedom. Us Outsiders deserve this freedom like everyone else. All of us are, Armandos. Out of our mutual brokenness and hard won realizations can come healing and a strengthening of community.

Chapter 12

My reflection on brokenness yields another useful discovery. Ownership of my faults urges me to admit that I have played a part in provoking my neighbor. In my advocacy, my pride, my knowledge and my need to win, I have incited a riot inside someone else. Before I begin to call the person who rages at me my enemy, I should stop short and realize that the enemy is really inside me. But I must love my enemies. It is through this commandment that *I* can become whole. I have to accept my shadow in order to love myself. Wholeness isn't possible without recognizing and loving one's own brokenness. Once this process takes hold in me, the brokenness of others is no longer an abomination to me, rather, a shared bond. When I sense someone's shadow, I immediately think of my own and judgment quickly yields to connectedness.

Metaphor

During this time I revisit my metaphor and I'm not greeted by the familiar image. No. I'm a Minuteman. Much like the patriots of the American Revolutionary War, I have taken up arms ever so reluctantly. I love my homeland, still willing to swear allegiance. But I have been provoked and assaulted repeatedly and have been forced to defend my neighbors as well. It is only after experiencing so much violent disregard for my own sovereignty that I am left with no choice but to say, "No more."

I focus on what speaks most true about me in this new image. I begin to believe that my gift is loyalty—faithfulness. I have been faithful to this institution while being besieged by it. Mingled with the shadow aspects of my efforts is a core behavior that could serve an organization well. While I haven't been compliant, I have been faithful.

Reflections

I survey the events of this season—I'm mortal, I don't know much, I'm a primitive tribesman, I must go low, I am broken, I can become whole—searching for the lessons in these powerful experiences.

"Be not afraid" had been eating at me for a long time and

encouraged me to learn that fear is the great challenge in our lives. We fear many things including change. We somehow fail to see that the world is constantly evolving. What is more dynamic than this world—newborns, volcanoes, migrations and thunderstorms? One of the few constants *is* change.

We fear our dark side as well, but our shadows hold immense promise. An acceptance of shadow can nourish the process of unity with one's self and with others.

It is now clear to me that our nature easily succumbs to dividing, scapegoating and warring. We are unable to see that winning and being on top means nothing more than being primitive and self-serving—afraid. If we are conscious of our warring nature, we can refuse its calling.

In psychology classes and at the retreats I learned that projection is one of our most frequent behaviors. Few acts are more hurtful. In our vulnerability, receiving a well-aimed barb feels terribly destructive. Criticism, no matter how seemingly minor, blasts away at our bedrock. We must learn that our "seeing" is terribly flawed. We don't realize that when we look at a scapegoat, we are seeing our own cast-off shadow. To see a fault in others is to have that fault.

I'm astonished by one revelation – I'm not a victim. The burden of thinking "poor me" has vanished. To "be ahead of all parting" is to miraculously move through one's fear and beyond one's own needs. Death is not the victor and, with the strength of wholeness, neither are the projections of others. Compassion for others is the result of deep understanding. I believe my colleagues are hurting. The real victims at work are the victims of their own fear. I come in contact with their issues, but I am not a victim. Compassion for them is possible. Hopefully, mine is not an elitist compassion that says "poor you" and really means "lucky me," but the kind of compassion that can only be offered to a colleague at eye level. Most surprising of all, I no longer see the most trying people at work as evil. They are hurting too and, with these new understandings, the separation I've felt between us is evaporating.

I've come to realize that we are all connected because of our differences as well as our similarities. We are, each of us, unique, and *that* is precisely our similarity. To be human is to be connected to all beings living and non-living. I knew all of this in my head, but it was my heart that had to break open into understanding. I felt total connectedness during peak experiences surrounding the retreat program, but relearned that truth more deeply while in the shadows. These learnings merge into a tangible gift, a tool of sorts. Finally, I've been given a path toward healing.

What If?

At one of the retreats Palmer had remarked, almost off-handedly, that part of what we were doing was "building capacity." We created a safe space, new to most of us. We learned relationship skills. We found new ways to look at the world. We developed ground on which to stand. With such a foundation, the winds of change can be weathered and our shadows need not be cast onto others.

Well before the initiative at my workplace, we should have been developing capacity. We should have been growing our community for its own sake and the ability to hang together. The lesson for me: weave strong threads of community before forces test the fabric.

Personal and organizational change are matters of the heart and personal change is instrumental in facilitating organizational change. While gurus and authors regularly urge us to work off of their change checklists, they often neglect to mention the personal journey required from each of us. Our organizations can change most readily if each member is working toward growth. A broad initiative to help each individual grow would indeed be a challenge, but absolutely essential if transformation is a serious goal. Instead of feeling defeated by this realization, I hold immense hope for the workplace. If my obstinate heart can break into greater understanding, so can anyone else's.

I'm convinced that our fears and destructive behaviors can be transformed by the power of love that our journeys uncover. Our organizations can even become true communities. Through love we can remove the barriers between us—we can become squashes:

When the head priest walked out into the field behind the temple, he found that his squashes had divided into two groups and had begun to fight. The priest yelled, "Stop!" at the top of his lungs. He scolded the squashes and told them to sit quietly. When peace returned to the field, the priest told them to feel on top of their heads. Each discovered a vine that led to all others. "We are all connected!" they exclaimed. "What a waste to fight." From then on the squashes lived in peace.[13]

Chapter 13 – Pendle Hill: Community

Community is a place of pain and conflict, for people reside there, but it is also a place of liberation and resurrection.

The sign reads "Welcome to Pendle Hill: A Quaker Center for Study and Contemplation." As I turn in, I feel a rush of gratitude. It's been a long day on the road. I shut off the ignition and take in the silence. A check of my watch reveals an eleven and a quarter hour trip from home to Philadelphia. I ease out of the driver's seat and carefully stretch from side to side. I slowly walk over to a large map of the center and get my bearings. I'm supposed to register at Main House.

I've come to Pendle Hill to learn how these people hang together. What are the secrets to staying connected at work?

First Impressions

As I walk to Main House, I pass a brick structure to my right labeled "The Barn" and see a sign posted in its doorway—"Morning Meeting 8:30–9:00." I know the sign refers to the daily religious service of this community, but what that entails is so far a mystery.

The exterior of Main House looks like most of the other buildings—stone exterior on the ground floor, white siding on the second floor and a style that says "colonial" to me.

Unfamiliar food smells greet me as I open the door. The warmth of Main House is comforting compared to the chill outside. The oak floor gives off casual creaks as I move straight down a hall and into a large room. I introduce myself to a woman dressed in a fleece vest, tennis shoes and running pants. With a

Disregarded

broad smile she introduces herself as Elizabeth and remarks that, "We didn't expect you until later, but this is good. You can join us for dinner."

Elizabeth and I walk out into the cold and head for a house-like structure named Waysmeet, which lies just beyond criss-crossed paths. It dawns on me that Elizabeth could have just pointed to Waysmeet from Main House, but she made the extra effort to be hospitable. I feel welcome here and appreciate how that feeling counteracts the one of vulnerability I have.

As we enter, I can see living rooms to both sides of the entryway and that stairs lead to guestrooms. Elizabeth says that I'll be in the only room without a key, but I won't need one. She's convincing, but I remember seeing security alarm signs posted in the front yards of homes no more than three blocks away. I think to myself, "Maybe I've found a safe place, an oasis." Elizabeth exhibits a charming economy in her speech and I like the way she sums up the condition of my room, "Nothing is new, everything is clean."

After Elizabeth leaves I walk out to the van and begin to chuckle. Formerly tan, it's white with salt, telling community members a stranger is in their midst. I unload the van, but save the unpacking for later. I enter Main House again and hear a large mix of voices until chimes sound and the room goes still. A voice announces the menu with flair, "Curry over rice, rolls and spinach with nuts in yogurt sauce." The buoyant voice asks for a moment of silent prayer.

I find a table with one empty chair. Shirley, Jesse, Jonathan and June Etta introduce themselves as dishes are passed family style. I'm asked if I'm "on sojourn." I pause because the phrase is foreign to me, but in the context of the question I believe it's honest to answer, "I am."

Shirley inquires, "Are you a Quaker?"

I answer that I'm not. I'm here to interview residents about living in community.

"How come?" Jonathan asks.

"The question that brings me here is 'What can the workplace learn from intentional communities?'" I've been to a number of

Chapter 13

retreats lead by Parker Palmer and he spoke affectionately of this place.

June Etta offers water from a pitcher. I ask if she works at Pendle Hill. June Etta "works outside Pendle Hill on Tuesdays and Thursdays, doing witness work." And Jesse? "I'm a chaplain at a Washington, D.C. hospital." I exclaim how happy I am to be here after a long journey and Jesse chuckles as he recounts his initial arrival at Pendle Hill. He was college age and it was the seventies. He had driven the long trip from Detroit in a lumbering ambulance. Elated to have finally arrived, he broke the serenity of the campus by driving through it—the red rotating beacon flashing wildly.

I've already absorbed strong impressions of this place and at least some of its people. It is clear that the people here reach out to strangers and are called to service. My sense is that this is a refuge for them, a place of companionship, food and rest to which they can return after long days of service. Renewed, they can step into the world again.

Review of the Day

I return to Waysmeet, make my bed and unpack. I enjoy the serenity of my room as I allow myself to feel how tired I am. The book I've brought helps me unwind until it's time to turn in. I climb into bed and review the day. At the start of my trip, I had almost turned back. The temperature was one below zero and the roads were heavy with snow. At thirty-five miles an hour I figured it would take me twenty-five hours to reach Philadelphia—not acceptable. I found the right lane of the interstate to be a skating rink. When the windshield turned to milk glass from the salt, I went for the washers and nothing happened. I felt as if I didn't have a chance of making it at the rate I was going.

The light penetrating the overcast seemed to be brightening so I decided to postpone turning back. Interstate 80/90 was no longer slippery, but its pure white color from heavy salt applications gave me the impression that I was driving over snow.

Finally, the overcast clouds broke apart and the washers began to work. Red barns with black or silver roofs gave way to white barns with green roofs. Tabletop fields stretched into rolling hills, then mountains. An occasional barn sign advised that I should indulge—"Treat yourself to the best, Chew Mailpouch." The road signs just west of Philadelphia, their unique names bespeaking a distinct heritage, began to signal I'd reached the end of my trek.

As I recall my first impressions of Pendle Hill, a final thought breaks through the drowsiness, "Have you come to study community or have you sought it for yourself?"

Day Two

Breakfast at Main House starts with chimes. Today's leader attempts to play a full-length symphony on the three bars of the chime set until all present are laughing heartily. "Pancakes!" is followed by a request for silent prayer. Only dinner is served family style so we split into two lines and slide trays along rails separated by stacks of pancakes, yogurt, raisins, bagels, cold cereals and an assortment of fruit.

Between bites I begin to take a more studied look at the dining area. The linoleum floor looks ancient, but it's polished clean, with heavy metal strips securing the seams. Dark wooden ceiling beams run the same way as the strips. Sturdy ladder-back chairs surround the rectangular pine tables and a large fireplace is at the east side of the room. Simple. Made to last. There is freedom and energy in this sparseness.

Meeting

I ask those at the table if I would be welcome at the morning meeting. The response is a strong "Yes" and I pick up another example of Quaker simplicity. What I had called "The Morning Meeting" is simply called "meeting." As I walk from Main House to The Barn for meeting I see many others converging there as well. Inside, I reach for a coat hanger and stand frozen as I read a large poster resting on the coat rack.

> Friends Worship
> We are met in a great task when we meet in worship, no less than to realize the Divine Presence

> and to create an atmosphere in which that Presence and Power can touch us into fuller life.
>
> Once we remember this, we cannot but approach the occasion with reverent humility and the desire that nothing on our part may hinder or disturb.
>
> It is something holy and wonderful we are trying to build together—the consciousness of the Presence with us here and the reality of communion with God.[1]

The walls of the worship area are white brick one third of the way up and white wainscot the rest of the way. There are four sets of wooden pews set parallel with each wall, leaving a large square open space in the center of the room. The cushioned pews are comfortable and the ceiling lights around the perimeter create a soft ambiance for the fifty or so of us gathered. The Quakers believe that God speaks directly to each one of them, making an intermediary such as a rabbi, priest or minister unnecessary for daily worship.

Everyone settles in, eyes closed. The room becomes still. I think of the Quaker adage that fits this setting: "Speak, only if you can improve on the silence." I wonder if there will be any outward sign that the spirit is present. Most of the half hour has elapsed when a troubled voice fills the room and the speaker shares his concern over world violence, the shrinking number of Quakers, the confusion of purpose, and lack of Quaker witness concerning world peace. He laments that an earlier time saw Quakers with clearer and firmer resolve than now. Shortly thereafter a female voice, full of sadness, expresses regret over the escalation in the Middle East. "There is no unified voice for peace." I'm touched by the sincerity of these people, their voices filled with real pain.

Following meeting, introductions and announcements are made and a young girl stands to speak. With surprising authority and optimism she announces youth conference activities that are yielding international collaborations of youths for peace. I can

Disregarded

see nods of agreement from the younger worshipers and think they might be showing another side to reality, not negating, rather, giving balance to the discouragement in the older voices.

I stand and introduce myself and mention that I've come to interview residents about community. I surprise myself by saying more. I'm moved by the despair of the speakers. I try to speak, but pause until the lump in my throat recedes. I finally say, "The strongest and most effective people I know are authentic people and the Quakers, I have come to realize, are the most authentic people I know. This place is like—can I say a breathing meditation?—a swinging door, a breathing in and a breathing out. Out for service and in for food, rest and community, then back out, over and over. This place is alive!" A number of people shake their heads in agreement. "Much of the rest of the world is asleep. Can you ask anything more of yourselves than to be awake and fully alive?"

A few more introductions are made and meeting is over. A woman approaches and introduces herself as Bobbi Kelly. She tells me she can do an interview now and has arranged for three others. I know from an earlier phone conversation that Bobbi is a long-time resident and I'm eager to speak with her.

Bobbi Kelly: A Practical, Long View of Community[2]

I open by expressing appreciation for Bobbi's willingness and warn her that I've got seventeen questions. Bobbi smiles and utters a short, "Well!" that expresses surprise, but I feel her commit with determination to my interrogation. I learn quickly that, like many others who have come to Pendle Hill, Bobbi came as a student to discern her future path. She returned in 1988 to become a staff member in housekeeping, then became a cook and is now in outreach/admissions. Bobbi suggests that her situation is a little different than most residents. She's from the Philadelphia area and "didn't have to leave an entire life behind." I ask, "Why do you stay?" She responds, "I like mixing it up with people, and having the support of others is nice as well. I like the work I do and it's a nice place to work. My commute is one hundred yards. I hate commuting."

Chapter 13

How might Pendle Hill be different than other communities? Bobbi walks to a door and opens it for a young child while she talks. "We're a retreat, conference and education center. There is a permanent staff, but also a large population that comes to live here and then leave. The permanent staff maintains traditions and the short-term residents join a flowing stream, a non-exclusive community that one doesn't expect to live in forever. One of the fundamental reasons we survive is that we are supported by a non-profit corporation. I wouldn't want to hold together this community without it."

I ask Bobbi for her personal definition of community. Bobbi's responses closely follow my questions. "Well, Parker Palmer said something that I liked. Community is the place where a person you can't stand arrives the same time you do. That person leaves and another just as irritating arrives."

Bobbi moves into an explanation of guidelines that help sustain Pendle Hill. "There are unspoken messages you get from the atmosphere. You have a daily job—don't forget to do it. We honor people's privacy and solitude. A closed door is understood. We know we need to deal with conflict when it surfaces. We work at, struggle, with conflict resolution. We do informal coaching on the side, believing in the essential goodness of people. We live and let live, honor diversity and accept personalities."

When asked what words she associates with community, she indicates, "I think I value openness the most. You can be private but not secretive. Safety is another word—safe but not totally comfortable. Something will always shake you. I value that."

An important question I have has to do with how they establish space. In the Fetzer retreats, Palmer was able to create a safe place for people to share and I wonder if safe places exist in all communities and whether or not members know how to create those safe environments in which to live and work. "Bobbi, what do you know about creating and sustaining space?" I ask. "Well, community creates space, it does, but I'm not always sure how it does it. It can be within buildings or spread over green spaces. It comes from very deep Quaker values. We answer to God; we work to respect others. Some people have it in their souls and

209

that carries others until the others learn how. Sometimes the inefficiency of group decisions is a blessing. The process is filled with struggle, but the respect demonstrated for each other turns out to be a gift in the end." Bobbi recounts a time when an architect was hired to redesign the kitchen. The cook disagreed with the design, saying that there could not be doors where the architect had drawn them. The conflict became an important community decision. Another was the barn door I saw dividing the two large rooms of the barn. Should it be removed during the renovation and become a work of art on the wall or remain a functional part of the structure?

Although I'm intently listening to Bobbi I allow a thought to capture my attention. Her down-to-earth view of community contrasts sharply with my dreamy view. What I'm receiving here is an exposé from someone who has lived a communal life for a long time. I'm hearing the day-to-day, life-as-it-is version of community.

"So what's the negative side to community?" I ask. Bobbie smiles. "I don't want to get rid of anything. I didn't know how irritated I could get until I came here. However, I learned that everyone is someone's best friend. You learn to let go of irritation. There's always a potential of rampant gossip because we know each other so well. It's rarely malicious, but we have to remain alert. Like a village, people fill roles and sometimes they aren't seen outside those roles. Elsewhere a person might have a number of personas as they move about—work, home, church, card night, etc. We have to look at the person, not the role."

When I ask if she knows any Quaker sayings related to community, Bobbi replies, "One I can think of is 'It's better to ask forgiveness than permission.'"

She doesn't even pause for reflection when I ask, "What do you bring to this community?" "I bring a sense of humor, a practical approach, flexibility and straightforwardness." Nor does she pause when asked what she receives from the Pendle Hill community. "I receive friendship and support. A broken ankle laid me up and I learned the strengths and weaknesses of community. Nobody gets unconditional love or everything they need. Community has taught me that not all expectations can be met. No community can do that. We all need love, but the media paints pictures of Utopia, giving us huge expectations and then we go off and try to find places that do that."

"So, Bobbi, do you have a metaphor or theme for Pendle Hill?" Instantly she replies, "The story of the blind men and the elephant. Each touches a different part and they can't agree to what it is."

And what advice do you have for the people of an organization who want much more than the culture they have? "Be forgiving! You don't have to go away to have community. Don't go looking for the perfect pot. The point is to make the pot. If you want community you have to build it, you can't go and get it. You can build it anywhere, but community is never guaranteed. The way we do things is holistic, egalitarian. We use a process we call 'meeting for learning.' We ask a question and we use collegiality to learn. We assume everyone can deepen the understanding of others. You can will it, but you have to do certain things. The right management style will foster it, but the people must want it, feel that they *have* to have it. Attitudes foster it. If you have this attitude, that you want to build it, people respond. They want it too."

Our time ends. I thank Bobbi and then walk back to Waysmeet for a breather. The interview was full of insights. Bobbi responded to each question without hesitation, giving me a strong impression that community is in her blood and bones. Community isn't some untouchable, ethereal conceptual model, it is a pair of comfortable, old walking shoes. What I discover from talking with Bobbi is that community can be a practical way of life.

Tom Jenik: Living Light on the Land

Bobbi had told me that my next interview would be with Tom Jenik in Main House. Tom and I meet in the hall near the entrance and head for a living room. As Tom enters he turns over a sign suspended by a string from a nail so it reads, "Meeting in Progress." Most of the doors to public spaces have similar signs so, in an instant, rooms can be transformed into spaces for private group work. I'm enjoying the discovery of simple, informal and effective ways to do business.

Tom's beginnings match Bobbi's. Tom came to Pendle Hill to figure out direction. In his youth Tom had really wanted to do woodworking, but was told that he was too smart to work with his hands. His visit to Pendle Hill nine years ago allowed him to reconnect with and act upon that longing. He came as a ten-week student and never left. Tom says a co-worker has a phrase for Pendle Hill: "pained by the potential of the place."

Having been a teacher, a businessman and now in hospitality at Pendle Hill, he has learned that no job is perfect. He pauses to think and speaks slowly. "But here, the whole package is nice. I feel useful in helping provide a space for others to come and study and reflect. I'm an extrovert and my hospitality role feels natural. I also like living light on the land and I can do that here."

I hear satisfaction in his voice when he says, "This is a place where people ask how you are and sincerely wait for an answer." There's one issue he thought he would resolve, but has found out that it will be ongoing, "How does one satisfactorily live and work in the same place?"

He quietly offers, "Community is a by-product of service," crediting Parker Palmer with the observation. Working on things that matter most encourages deeper relationships. He continues, "This is a place that tries to minimize learning the rules by violating them. We try to help make guidelines explicit little by little. We're after people who want to join in our projects and don't calculate all the while how much time they're giving. It's also wonderful when people take on any job that needs doing even if it isn't their assigned responsibility."

Tom is deliberate. His answers come slowly. The first word Tom associates with community is acceptance. "You accept a person you can't stand. You learn how day by day, but you never give up your own integrity to accommodate, otherwise there would be resentment. Another word is love. Yes. Love. But it's more practical. And the spaces we create here come out of a respect for each individual. People walk by and can tell if you want conversation or not. Students meet with a mentor once a week, but that

Chapter 13

mentor accepts what that person wants to do even if the plan changes once they're here. We do our work with a sense of ministry such as housekeeping for guests."

On the phone, Bobbi had mentioned that a process of re-evaluation of direction was underway at Pendle Hill and I ask Tom for his impressions. He leans forward. "In other settings I got my fill of magic markers and flip charts. I have to be careful of my cynicism. It's helpful to be a community of inquiry, but it's got to be practical. Change is hard to come by and I'm unsure of how much we'll change. I do know that you can't change without knowing who you are. An important question for me is, 'How long do you seek versus go with what you've found?'"

Tom believes that he brings honesty, trust and a straightforwardness to the community. His hope is that he is modeling "Do with what you have" through his repair work and "maybe living a simple life, not allowing the financial fears of retirement to overtake my life." He continues. "I try to be fully present to my work. We manifest God through loving acts. That's a belief that inspires me. Dan Wilson, a former director of Pendle Hill, once asked me how I was doing. I said, 'It's a little hard on my ego to be making beds and cleaning rooms. It was easier to say that I was teaching at a university.' Dan Wilson then said, 'Remember Brother Lawrence. It takes a strong ego to do what you're doing.'"

I sense that Tom is unfolding and he says as much. He notes that he's doing things he never thought he would and, as evidence of having found his calling, he is "seeing a positive response to my work. I've received unsolicited donations to the wood shop. Money. Machinery."

I ask the final question. What advice do you have for the people of an organization that want much more than the culture they have? I'm comfortable with the long silence that ensues. Finally, Tom says, "Our process and our model of governance are efficient, inclusive and egalitarian. Organizations can greatly benefit from using processes that minimize differences in status. Something else people in organizations would have to do is get over being comfortable with scapegoating and non-action. Living in community is difficult work. You must consider how your actions affect others. One person did the newspaper crossword in ink, early in the day. Later, a group wanted to do the crossword and, well... We're better at talking about what's working. But we've got to take seriously the challenge of working at community. How do we get along here? We keep reminding ourselves that if we can't do it here, in our work and family settings, we can't do it in the world."

The personal styles of Bobbi and Tom are very different. I think of Bobbi's use of "inefficient" and Tom's use of "efficient," but don't believe they're at odds. They speak to the paradoxes found in community. It seems to me that the comparison demonstrates the diversity that exists in any group, but maybe most comfortably here. With just these two encounters, I'm beginning to glean how complex community is. Bobbi's metaphor comes to mind. Community *is* an elephant that can be viewed from an unlimited number of angles.

An Adventure of a Different Kind

Back at Waysmeet, I change into business attire. At lunch, I feel out of place in a sport coat and tie. Jason, a college-age student taking classes here, remarks that I look "fancy." I explain that I've got business to conduct outside of Pendle Hill.

After lunch I'll observe corporate training done by the Avalone Corporation staff for its own employees. In fact, I planned my trip east around the training dates.

I think about the steps that led me to Avalone. Months of searching finally uncovers an important explanation for why relationships at work can go bad. *Seeing Systems* by Barry Oshry is "the mystery explained." We're living with systemic forces that we don't see and our ignorance keeps us captive, reactive and embroiled. Oshry explains that each level of an organization has its own unique experience—its own type of pressure and emotional baggage. People at the top feel immense pressure to perform. Middle managers feel pulled apart from those above and below them and workers at the bottom feel unappreciated. We respond to these emotional burdens in classic ways, most of which are self-defeating, including blaming others. Oshry offers life-giving suggestions. *Seeing Systems* became dog-eared faster than any other book I'd read, with underlining and exclamation points scattered

Chapter 13

throughout its pages. Working in a building with a divided staff is the deepest wound and the ultimate pain for me. His advice is that I shouldn't take personally much of what goes on at work—root causes are often systemic.

I called Oshry at Power and Systems, Inc. and asked, "How can I learn more?" Barry's business partner and wife, Karen, made arrangements with Avalone to have me observe training designed by Oshry. It's in the form of a simulation.

As I head toward the northwest part of the city, I feel as if I am leaving one world and entering a very different one.

I look for a parking space in the Ace Conference Center's massive parking lot. There appear to be none, even on the grass. Cars are parked bumper to bumper and I realize how much corporate America is investing in training.

The receptionist gives me a map of the center and points toward the two rooms used by Avalone. On the way to the rooms I see that all others are full, corporate names posted in the frames beside each doorway. The place hums with activity with brick and thick carpet working to soften the commotion of the hundreds of people who fill the place. I find the first room and it's empty. The frame beside the door says "Hope," a challenging reference to Oshry's simulation of life in a hierarchy.

On my way to the other room I notice open areas with stuffed chairs and inviting displays of food and drink. I find the Avalone group on a break, with employees standing and talking in small clusters. I smile and greet the first person I see. It happens to be trainer Jim Petraco with whom I've been in contact. He says he was on his way to find me in case I had gotten lost, and then introduces me to co-trainer Ray Keller. "There's been a change in plans," Jim explains. "You'll be participating instead of observing." Earlier, I had promised Karen and Jim that I would meet their expectation of not disrupting the training—I'd be invisible. I realize that a very different mindset is now required, but I'm already on an adventure of sorts and consider the last minute change to be good news.

We make our way to seats in the conference room. I grab glances at my surroundings. There are nineteen participants, three of whom are female. Each wall displays charts and posters. A white board covers one wall. The training resumes and all of us focus on a slide with the title, "This is what we call partnership:" The next slide presents the definition. "Partnership is when everyone is committed to the success of our current process."

Jim changes his tone of voice, signaling we are nearing the simulation's start. "In most traditional work situations, we can find four groups of people—Tops, Middles, Bottoms and Clients." Ray takes over seamlessly and says that there are unrealistic conditions we'll experience during the simulation. "In this simulation you will have limited time to complete tasks whereas, back at your workplace, there is always enough time to complete what you need to do." Someone shouts, "Yeah, right!" from the back of the room. I realize that Ray's playful sarcasm is his way of saying that this simulation has real elements in it.

He tells us his expectations. Engage deeply—really live the assigned role. In particular, we should be mindful of our interactions, especially our reactions to the encounters we have.

Jim weaves through us, asking us to draw a role assignment from a cloth bag. We draw tags marked "Top," "Middle," "Bottom" and "Customer." I'm to be a customer. Once Jim's done, we've become a hierarchy with a customer base. All I know at this time is that the company provides creative solutions to customer problems. I will approach this company and request their services.

Oshry has devised a number of techniques to encourage our buy-in, turning the simulation into something real in our minds. Bottoms are asked to remove their shoes. With just this simple gesture, they more closely resemble true Bottoms who lack resources and feel vulnerable. Bottoms are given socks to put on so they can traverse the hallways. We move to the "Hope" room I found earlier.

I scan the room. Three tables for Bottoms are crowded together and placed within a taped area. Bottoms have to stay inside the tape. The message: the ten bottoms had better know their place. There's a table for the three middle managers in the center and a table in the far corner for the three Tops. The three other customers and I are seated in chairs against the wall opposite the

Chapter 13

Tops. A horn sounds the beginning of the first workday.

The three Tops huddle together and talk in earnest with furrowed brows. Within seconds they already exhibit signs of pressure. The Middles begin to talk, but look much more at ease. Some Bottoms look bored and others begin to crack jokes.

The Tops approach and I'm greeted with handshakes from all three. They make a promise that one of them will talk to me tomorrow. I watch them turn and leave, knowing nothing will happen today. "Today" was actually thirteen minutes long, but it shares the characteristic of an eight-hour day—not enough time to get everything done.

The horn sounds and the day ends. I make a few notes in the reflection log that's been provided to help me capture what it feels like to be a customer, how I look at the others in the room and anything that happened of importance.

The horn sounds for the beginning of day two. I stand and walk over to the Tops' table. A young woman named Beth says she's been assigned to help me with my needs. She diplomatically asks if she could schedule an appointment with me in a few minutes. I agree. I realize the Tops are still getting organized and are trying to juggle their internal and external concerns.

Beth approaches and she suggests we use the Middles' table to discuss my needs. From written instructions I know what I need to do. I describe that my company wants to develop a network of national radio stations within the next five years. I believe that, "the profitability for radio has not been maximized. What creative programming can your company create that would begin to move toward that potential?" I also describe what I want our relationship to look like. Although not guided by any script, I tell her what I truly want. "I want our relationship to be seamless, collegial, reciprocal." Beth promises to meet with me on Day 3.

The horn sounds for the close of Day 2. I use the log again to record a pattern. I feel warmly towards the Tops because I've had contact with them. The Middles and Bottoms are unknowns and, probably because there is no relationship, I write down what I'm thinking, "Can these people deliver?"

We move back to the other conference room to discuss what has taken place. Ray displays a slide that has the word "You" in the center of a rectangle. He explains that this is an aerial view. On the slide are a number of cloud-like images with the word "Stuff" on the inside of each one. Basically, we're surrounded by organizational "stuff." Stuff happens.

Jim explains that we react to stuff and then we lose focus. We not only lose focus, we lose the relationship. "Remember, stuff is not personal." Jim explains that the experience at each level of the hierarchy is quite different. Tops are bombarded with complexity and responsibility. Middles are torn between service to those above and to those below. Bottoms feel vulnerable and customers feel neglected.

Ray asks people in each group to describe their experience. "How does it make you *feel?*" he asks again and again. "Tell it like it is without blame." From our discussion, the resulting message is, "Ignore the stuff and your reaction to it. Keep the relationship going."

We walk back to the Hope environment and the horn sounds. As I wait for a product, I see that middle managers and Bottoms are much busier now with the workload of customers. I watch Beth deal with Bottoms. There is some kind of problem related to their shoes. Is a strike brewing? I wait the full day, but Beth never contacts me. I experience what *Seeing Systems* indicated. Oshry is right. A typical emotion for a customer is one of feeling summarily neglected.

Day 4 starts with an apology from Beth. She knew she promised to meet yesterday and didn't. I thank her for that acknowledgement and feel the consolation of working with a person who owns up. She introduces me to Tom, a Middle. He explains that the Bottoms are working at a solution and will make a presentation today. He's more knowledgeable about what's being accomplished than Beth is. He introduces me to Bob from the Bottom group. Bob says it won't be long. Day 4 ends.

In the journal I record continued feelings of neglect, but I also record the brief feeling of optimism at having met people closer to production. I jot down that Tops are too involved with others to take care of me and I sense their company is in turmoil. Beth has good communication skills and a good attitude, but her performance and that of her company is less than what I want. I

Chapter 13

record that the performance of Tops is related more to the system that they are in rather than to their skill or attitude.

Mid-way in Day 5 Beth convenes the presentation and I listen to Bob describe the creative work they've done. He goes through factors the team considered. In particular, they've considered the risk of brand new programming. Their recommendation is a heavy daily schedule of The Howard Stern Show. "His show's very popular and you'll be pleased if you choose Howard Stern." I stifle a chuckle. I had expected a show created from their imagination and, to me, Howard Stern is not a match for my Midwest proprieties. But Bob, like all others in the company, is sincere and fully engaged and probably had too little time to be creative, so I thank him for the team's effort.

Bob heads back to his area after our handshake. Beth has too much on her plate and she starts scanning the room for brush fires, forgetting to close the deal with me. I get her attention and suggest we discuss financial arrangements. As I hand her a small amount of cash, the horn sounds. We move back to the other room to sort it all out.

While the main emphasis has been on relationships, Ray and Jim help us see what happened financially. Each customer had a certain amount of cash available to pay for services. Eventually we uncover that the company captured 18% of the available customer money. Salaries and taxes exceed the meager revenue. Ray points out that the Tops didn't pay themselves and the company is in the red. The mood grows somber and the stillness stretches uncomfortably as the people ponder their part in the company's demise. Finally, a Bottom breaks the tense silence—"At least we got a sock."

At break, I confirm the time for tomorrow's debriefing and head back to Pendle Hill.

What Will Work Back Home?

Concentrating on the unfamiliar highway does not block out the concepts that are bouncing inside my head: maintain relationships, ignore the "stuff," ache for community, invest in it through hard work, let go.

Wherever you are, make the pot...

Chapter 14 – But Seek the Welfare of the City

It is necessary to have a community to embody a new pattern of living. A single person cannot live a new social pattern alone.[1]

Sandra Cronk, *Gospel Order*

During the evening meal the discussion is varied, but serious. I remain amazed at the concern Quakers have about the state of the nation and world affairs, especially world peace. Word of my mission is out and those around the table appear anxious to share their insights. They mention specific community experiments that either succeeded or failed. Book titles and community names abound—*A Place called Community, God's Government Begun, Bowling Alone, Transcendental Wild Oats,* Harmony Farms, Strawberry Creek and Monteverde in Costa Rica.

Contributors offer tidbits of humor. A woman named Rachel smiles and tells of one community in conflict. The community has split in two and the parties at odds are affectionately named the "tardyites" and the "tightites." I turn the conversation sober when I ask the all-too-simplistic question, "What is the one thing that would make community work?" There's a long pause and then June Etta offers two words—Gospel Order. Slowly, people ponder this response and then begin to nod. June Etta sees my furrowed brow and explains that Gospel Order is a Quaker concept that says we are all related to each other through God. A force outside ourselves, a force much greater than ourselves, calls us to gather and live in peace. June Etta's careful description turns intense, "If people could live with the full meaning of Gospel Order, community would work anywhere, everywhere." I do like all others at the table and attend to the food on my plate, letting this profound vision sink in.

Chapter 14

Our silence is interrupted by the announcement that there's a birthday today! (Dessert is served only on birthdays.) A late night labor of love, the honoree and a friend have prepared a very tall stack of crepes. Everyone stands and we form a large circle around the honoree, clapping and singing a special happy birthday song indigenous to Pendle Hill.

Back at Waysmeet I review some of the impressions of the day. The people of Pendle Hill and Avalone have been genuinely warm. Karen Oshry and Bobbi Kelly have helped orchestrate my stay and I feel indebted and grateful. The day had started with a remarkable experience at morning meeting and the interviews with Bobbi and Tom were fruitful. The simulation with Avalone helped me better understand the work of Barry Oshry and his simulation that raises awareness of emotional reactions to systemic workplace forces. I've come to see a deep sense of responsibility that Quakers place upon themselves for their own actions. Collectively, they have come to say, "If not here, then where?"

This form of responsibility is a missing piece back home. It's not that my fellow workers have any less heart or potential. Somehow, they've become convinced that they are separate from the system and their bosses the sole and rightful caretakers. My belief is very different—*we* are the system. Our actions sustain or change the container surrounding us. We should be saying, "If not us, who?"

Cornflakes and Community

At breakfast a woman approaches and asks if she can talk with me about her favorite subject—community. I guess that she is about my age and notice her high energy level. I feel comfortable in her presence. Donna McDaniel is from Southborough, Massachusetts, which has too quickly doubled in size from 4,500 to 9,000. She reminds me that Massachusetts' communities have town meetings where, "anyone can vote on anything!" She writes a biweekly newspaper column on community for a Southborough newspaper. McDaniel is here at Pendle Hill on a research scholarship to write a book on the relationships among Quakers and African Americans.

She came here to study and "because of the intrigue of living in community. I love being in this community. I don't know how I can leave when the time comes." She tells me that Pendle Hill is a special place to her because it is a community of shared spiritual values. "It has a long history of amazing Friends who have come here and contributed enormously to the lives of other Friends. Here, there are people to eat with. To be with. Really interesting people."

I ask, "From your experience, what guidelines would help a community be successful?"

She beams. "Communicate, communicate, communicate." She fires off her sentences in rapid succession. "Tell the truth. Let us know who you really are. What are your passions? Who are your heroes? Don't talk about each other. If you have a complaint, bring it to the person responsible." She moves beyond the question to say that the difficulty of sustaining a community can only be met through a deep commitment. "Members have to be willing to give and endure whatever it takes to be in community. They understand it's difficult so they are prepared to go the distance. Most are mature enough to be open and accepting of others, including their perceived faults."

I ask her about creating space, a trusting environment where people can speak and listen to each other. She says that the space where community resides appears when commitment is present and there's a willingness to tell one's truth. "Telling the truth is a great space creator." Sooner or later, different expectations eventually surface in the community and collide. The tension begs for good communication. "Talk, don't assume." Untested assumptions hurt a community more than frank dialog.

Donna lists the positive aspects of community and moves to the tougher side. "Sometimes you're with people who seem to make it harder and you figure they're NOT the people you want to be with. Of course, that means they are the perfect ones. It's hard. It takes doing. It's not easy." She too quotes Parker Palmer: "Our companions are given to us by grace." The ones who most shake up our view of the world and our own self-concept are the bearer of gifts.

Donna has stressed "truth telling" as one key element of community and I ask for details. She replies, "I spoke about a specific spiritual need I have and was quite stunned, bowled over, by the high level of response, the connections it created and continues to create." On another occasion she expressed a concern that too much was being left unsaid and invited anyone interested to a community sharing session. She expected a handful of people, but twenty-two came. Truth telling encourages a response from others. These experiences bear out the fruits of honestly expressing what one is thinking and feeling.

Donna especially likes the opportunities to rapidly switch from being alone to being with people. Emerging from the solitude of reading, researching and writing, people are close at hand to her. The immersion in her solitary work and the ability to quickly balance that with community life is particularly satisfying. She says that today is community workday and she tells about a work song that's often sung at Pendle Hill. "As you sing the word 'community' seven times, you start to notice yourself singing 'Come unity. Come unity.'"

Our time together concludes with final thoughts. Besides the softer issues, sustainability boils down to being economically viable and sharing the work. Both of those are another side of commitment, the same core value that says, "If we can't do it here, then where?" The same question begs asking, whether it's spoken in an intentional community or a town. Donna recalls the words of essayist Scott Russell Sanders, "Taking part in the common life means dwelling in a web of relationships, the many threads tugging at you while also holding you upright."

"Now that I've lived here, I can't imagine returning to the same life I led before." Like Donna, I realize, with each new encounter, that I will forever be changed by my visit.

Switching Worlds

I walk across the compound from Main House to the van. The debriefing with Avalone is next.

The traffic is light and the way to the conference center is familiar. There must be fewer sessions scheduled today because I easily find an empty parking space.

Jim begins the debriefing session with a slide showing three column headings—Predictable Condition, Predictable Response

Disregarded

and Familiar Experience. I recognize this as one of Oshry's concepts. Our experiences in systems have a strong emotional aspect. The slide shows that Tops are likely to feel overloaded. That's the predictable condition. The predictable response is to do more and more—sucking up the responsibility. The familiar experience is to feel burdened. Jim stresses that being burdened perpetuates itself. When a Top tries to do more and more, the feeling of being overloaded only gets worse. Tops get caught in a reinforcing loop. I no longer wonder where the image comes from of the boss blowing off steam. The incessant and increasing overload causes a pipe to rupture.

As we move down the slide, I see how Bottoms are a perfect match for Tops. The predictable condition for Bottoms is to feel disregarded. I think about how often I have felt left out of major discussions whose results eventually affect me and how few times my opinion has been sought. The predictable response from a Bottom who feels disregarded is to hold "Them" responsible for the work situation. Even though Bottoms help create a "Them," they feel oppressed. Having given up their power by naming a "Them" who supposedly has all the power, Bottoms are less likely to be proactive. Eventually Tops feel the ball being dropped and do more and more. It's a perfect fit, except for two things—it's dysfunctional and everyone's miserable. I'm convinced that's what's happening back home. Our leaders suck up too much authority when the workers don't act in a situation defined as "out of their hands."

Ray takes over and asks about our feelings during the simulation. "Tops, what did you feel? Did you feel burdened? Was that a familiar feeling? Did your experience fit the predictable condition?" And Ray probes with three others. "What does the predictable response cost you in terms of your health? Your relationships? Your effectiveness?" He smiles, but gently challenges further. "Is it always going to be like this? Can this be changed? Can YOU change?" He slowly looks at each one of us.

We're engaged. We want something better. The tension is surprisingly high. A participant named Ron tries to shift the energy, "Is it typical that Tops don't give themselves money?" Before Ray can respond, a voice offers, "Only in a simulation!" Everyone

Chapter 14

laughs and the pressure eases. And over the subsiding chuckles I hear, "The shoe stops with the CEO."

Ray offers one solution. "Back at the office, stop. Step back. Remove yourself from the situation. Think about what you're experiencing and relate it to predictable conditions and predictable responses." Questions ensue. "Can a Top temporarily be a Middle?" "Could I sometimes be a Bottom?"

It appears that some haven't quite internalized one point. You determine what relationship you have by how you *feel*. That's how you know what role you're in. If you feel like you're being pulled in opposite directions, you are probably a Middle in that situation. It's understandable that this point has not yet sunk in. How often are feelings given a place in corporate life?

Actualized, Ray's suggestion—Stop, step back—would be a new behavior back home. What most of us do is get caught up in our emotions and resort to blaming, weaving a story that names a scapegoat. We can suppress the knee jerk reaction. We can realize that there are predictable responses that can be avoided, if we know they exist. Partnership remains a real possibility.

Jim takes over and says that we have choices. We can get hooked on "stuff" or move beyond it. We can take "stuff" personally or decide it's systemic. We can make up a story about the people in the situation or *ask* those people about their world.

He moves through the advice for Tops and Middles, reaching the Bottoms. What would healthy choices for Bottoms look like? Bottoms can refrain from giving up their power. Instead of seeing themselves as victims, they can see themselves as co-creators. Famous for complaining, Bottoms can reframe a complaint into a potential project. Bottoms need a vision as much as anyone else. They need to network, as well. Healthy choices exist. Bottoms can move past the "stuff" to create an environment of greater satisfaction and productivity.

We take a break and Ray indicates that the group will be moving away from the Oshry material. It's my cue to leave and I thank Ray and Jim for their hospitality. As I leave the conference room, the poster by the door displays a Marcel Proust quote, "The real voyage of discovery is not in seeking new landscapes but in having new eyes." I can't help but wonder what the workplace would

Disregarded

be like if we all could "see" that systems produce "stuff," and that we weaken relationships by wrongfully attributing "stuff" to the people around us.

The traffic on I-476 is light. As I drive south I marvel at how dissimilar the trappings are between the corporation and Pendle Hill, like the shock of sauna to spring-fed lake. But underneath the surface is a comforting realization, a wonderful and rich shared theme—keep the relationships going, no matter what. Stay connected with those around you, for somewhere in the relationship is your salvation.

Back at Pendle Hill

I use the rest of the morning to organize—a fill-up and a car wash. Tomorrow morning I'll leave for home. I walk to the center's bookstore and return with a half dozen of Pendle Hill's special form of communication—the Pendle Hill pamphlet. I've used the advice of those I've met to make my selections and I find the rationale for the pamphlets on a back cover:

> At the heart of every new movement and institution is an idea. The idea may not at first be clearly defined, but the idea is there, seeking embodiment, first in the spoken or written word and finally in the lives and actions of men. Part of the idea motivating the experiment of Pendle Hill was publishing. The pamphlets aim to be tracts for our times, speaking to the condition of the people of our generation. Like the early Christian or Quaker tracts the pamphlets present a variety of points of view, but all, in some way, are derived from the fundamental Pendle Hill idea. Variety is evidence of life; cold uniformity presages death.[2]

I like the image of words burrowing into the hearts of men until action results. I like the implied openness, the willingness to speak and to listen. And I love the words that support honoring diversity: "Variety is evidence of life."

Chapter 14

Kate Garland: a Union of Personal and Institutional Mission

Because Bobbi and Tom covered so much territory, I wonder if the final two interviews will yield much that's new, but I'll find out soon enough. I'm scheduled to interview a woman named Kate Garland. Back at Main House, we meet. With attractive short hair and glasses, she's dressed in jeans, tennis shoes and a sweatshirt with the word "Maine" on it.

Kate suggests we grab a cup of coffee and we head for the southern most public space in Main House. It's a large room but its distance from the bustle of the dining area creates a private atmosphere. I explain that I'm attempting to learn what the workplace can adopt from studying community. She responds quickly, "The workplace *is* a community! I believe a community is a people gathered for a common purpose. Purpose shapes the gathering, giving it form." I note that Kate, like many residents, uses the words *gather* and *gathering* in a most careful way. Almost imperceptible is a change in tone, saying to me that "gathering" strikes an emotional chord.

Kate observes that we tend to separate the sacred and the secular, but that in a faith community the two are integrated. Some questions that faith communities ask: "To what degree have we integrated the sacred and the secular?" "How do we work here?" She suggests that there is a kind of monastic element at Pendle Hill that acknowledges that Spirit is present while washing dishes, cutting vegetables, making beds—any task.

As Kate describes a few of her earlier life experiences, she communicates a relaxed spontaneity that washes away any feeling of "stranger" or "visitor" that I hold. I have the same feeling of ease when talking to my closest friends. Kate has been at Pendle Hill for a year, but I can sense that long ago she put a pot on the stove, set the burner to simmer and climbed in.

Kate graduated from seminary but did not feel led to be ordained. At least two things held her back—church politics and a feeling her calling was elsewhere. So far in the interviews I have been careful not to comment on the remarks made by my subjects, but this time I cannot resist. I respond that she demonstrated great courage, that it would be so easy to just accept the fruits of her labor and take the well-beaten path. She replies that others

Disregarded

have made that observation. She came to Pendle Hill, "because it has a reputation for engaging in peace and justice activity. I'd been riding the fence and knew I needed to become clear about what I believe. I felt I was being called and needed clarity on that as well."

For seven years she had traveled back and forth to Scotland, doing volunteer work in various religious retreat centers. Gradually she realized her calling was to be hospitable to others. This realization became especially keen at Pendle Hill. Kate repeats a Celtic rune that touches her. "Put food in the eating place. Softly, softly, softly goes the Christ in the stranger's guise."

She believes that life is an ongoing process of discernment. "I can assign much to God that isn't of God and I must work at discerning what comes from my true, authentic self. The silence of the Quakers helps. Here, I can be open to The Spirit, the Presence of God within me. In my heart I'm a Quaker."

She echoes Bobbi and Tom when she declares that it is still "real life" here with chores and aggravations. But underneath it all is the Pendle Hill mission. She points out the unusual nature of this place, "Elsewhere it's hard to find the director of an organization mopping floors and cleaning toilets."

I ask about space. A recent course she took offered the term "relational space." That space contains a respectful awareness of others, but also a respect for one's own boundaries and needs, "else we are a doormat." When problematic differences occur we use a grievance process, which is part of Gospel Order.

"To be ready for this place, you have to expect change. You share toilets, washers and dryers and have to ask permission for food between meals because you don't know if the cook has plans for it. You make adjustments. But, for me, it is also a place where I receive a sense of safety, security, companionship, friendship, support and a call for everyone to be accountable. We must be able to say, 'Oops, I goofed.' This place has given me a depth to my faith and I'm inspired by the spontaneous witness I see." I can't help but wonder if there is irony in Kate's discovery of deepened faith in an egalitarian environment, with its belief in direct access to God, over years in the seminary. Or is it more a matter of ongoing discernment and maturity?

Chapter 14

   I'm in agreement with Kate as she describes the importance of identifying and honoring each person's gifts. Something important happens when we place people in positions where they can use their gifts. "When someone notices a person is drained and sagging, a job switch often brings life and vitality. Sometimes the one switch is doubly good because the person who fills the vacancy may now be in a more suitable job as well." I note that all three interviewees have remarked about how comfortable they are here. It seems to me that part of a good "fit" is not only being in a good place, but also finding the niche within that place.

   I ask Kate about stories that are a part of Quaker tradition. The first to surface for her relates to their consensus model. "Trying to reach a decision is like herding cats." And she describes what it's like to be a Quaker, "Ask ten people that question and get twelve answers." And, still smiling, she offers another, "In times of silent worship, will what I say improve on the silence?" But, my favorite turns out to be a story she tells that pokes a little fun at the serious dedication of Quakers to peace. Such dedication can become a personal challenge in times of stress. "There's a story about a farmer who keeps getting kicked by the cow he's milking. Finally, he's so fed up that he looks at the cow square in the eye and says, 'I won't kick you but, if you don't stop, I'll sell you to the farmer down the road and *he* will!'"

   I ask Kate what the workplace might use from the experience of community. She suggests that a faith community can offer the workplace the practice of finding the place where the worker works best. Too often we try to cram a person into a slot instead of creating a slot that is designed to express a person's gifts. Kate believes that successful organizations are concerned about fit. Also, corporations are very shortsighted in getting rid of older employees. These people not only have valuable skills, but they also have irreplaceable experience and maturity. Be honest about reality, as well. Keep checking on what needs to change. Keep asking if the organization is on target with what people deeply care about and need.

   We're reaching the end of our time together and Kate says the metaphor for her life at Pendle Hill is probably "restless seeker." I challenge her by noting earlier comments about finding her vocation and her faith. She looks back with a relaxed smile and says, "Yes, but that is the paradox. The faith journey is unpredictable. I'm always asking for help in being open. It's a walk into the unknown. Out of darkness comes movement. Thank goodness God is patient and respectful," and with a broader smile yet adds, "although a gentle whack to get my attention is a possibility!"

I thank Kate for her time and great help and she is generous in her good wishes for me.

I've just enough time to make my final appointment. I'm to meet Nancy Morgan in the library and that is housed, along with an expansive art studio, in a large three-story building to the south. I find the library easily and guess that the sole person in the area is Nancy, and it is. She's at a very large table and is using a laptop. She moves away from the laptop and we find seats at the corner of the table.

Nancy Morgan: a Powerful Vision

Nancy was formerly a cook at Pendle Hill while her husband "stayed home" with their children. Now they've reversed roles. Steve works as registrar at Pendle Hill and Nancy stays with the children. However, Nancy is also pursuing a master's degree.

Nancy probes for what exactly it is that I'm here for. It's apparent that she will keep my needs in mind as we talk. *Relationship* is the first keyword as we begin the interview. Nancy's take on community is that communities form automatically as relationships develop. There are two kinds of communities—intentional and unintentional. The first forms when community is part of the collective goal. Pendle Hill's community was intentional in its inception, but is sustained unintentionally. She is exact in her characterization of current day Pendle Hill; "There is community here unintentionally since the institutional goals are coordinated with exclusive small groups that separate themselves from the community as a whole. Those who currently define institutional goals perceive the community in the subservient position of existing to support the institution, instead of the institution and community existing in partnership with one another."

"Shared" is the second keyword. In response to words that come to mind related to community, Nancy fires off, "shared

Chapter 14

experience, shared relationships, sharing in their lives, collective intent, collective goals. You sustain a community by sustaining the relationships of its members." Another keyword comes to mind—clarity. "Clarity of vision, goals, interests and resources is vital. I'm big on being clear." I realize that Nancy's "being clear" and Donna's "Talk, don't assume," are closely related.

The high level of confidence embedded in her responses surprises me. She's energized. It is evident that community, as a concept and a reality, is important to her. She continues. "Your job is also your life at Pendle Hill. If you leave, you would leave everything. The risk is high. For those that want help in deciding to come here, I would inquire about the work they want to do." I see, again, the concern over "fit" much like that of Kate. I think about the way too many of us go about finding a job. While job-hunting, our apprehension is so high that satisfying our panic can be about landing a job—any job. The main issue is security or maybe status. Our concern is much less about finding the position that is a match for our talents. And have we done the work that has helped us determine our gifts and our call? Bobbi, Tom and Kate demonstrate to me the fruits of having done the soul work. The universe reacts favorably to the use of their gifts and, while they probably haven't sought it, personal happiness results as well. Here, people are helping each other find their gifts and their place in the community.

Nancy addresses space. "There are pockets of safety here. There is not a whole group effort at community, but many have found safe places to process their pain and their struggles. If you build walls, you'll create problems for yourself." Nancy gives me the impression that she holds herself and Pendle Hill to the highest of standards. Gradually, I'm seeing a vision being painted that demands more than what most communities have been able to create. I probe some, "You said that there is not a whole group effort at community. Is a whole group effort too much to ask?" "No!" she exclaims. "I believe it can be done. You can process in large groups. If you can't, you've lost a great deal. If you can't process in large groups, you are reduced to leadership by a small group and you've lost the wisdom available in the whole group."

Nancy stands and there's a flurry of movement. She's combing

Disregarded

the shelves for written reinforcement. She finds and then begins to stack books next to me—*Sitting in the Fire, Beyond Consensus* and *The Walking People*. She sits down and continues in earnest, "The more you want to be a part of the 'inner circle,' the more careful you have to be."

"Is a world with no inner circles Utopia?" I ask.

Nancy lowers her head, looks intently at me with her dark eyes. "The problems of the world have become so big that they must be solved by large groups."

She points to her favorite book on the table, *The Walking People,* and says that it's the oral history of forerunners of the Iroquois now recorded in print by Paula Underhill. The history stretches back to the tribe's crossing the land bridge between Asia and North America. The account demonstrates that the Iroquois valued whole group wisdom over small group leadership. Every member was respected. The tribe survived because they maintained their discipline to honor each person. Sooner or later each member gave a vital contribution that insured the tribe's survival through its greatest trials.

I think about home. We seem to be surprisingly fragile. There, a person's gifts are a threat to others. If I am proactive on an issue, the boss seems to react from one of two positions: my actions require even more of him or the boss thinks that he should have been doing something about the issue all along. The boss is living under the terrible burden of having to be everything to all people and I get the sense that an expression of gifts is most unwelcome. I'm also a threat to my colleagues. We hunger for recognition and whomever steps forward to do a task threatens to capture what little recognition is available. This systemic rivalry ends up feeling so very personal. Nancy provides an inspiring rationale for respecting each other.

I ask about advice for the workplace. She suggests that "People are people everywhere. Your group will not be any better or worse than any other. They will be both open and rigid, petty and wise. What happens depends on the level of maturity and ideals they bring. Recognize the inevitability of conflict and the gift within it. Conflict is an opportunity to deepen. Facilitating its resolution is teachable and accessible. Jack, some people here

Chapter 14

have driven me crazy, but sooner or later they have given me something that blew me away. I wouldn't have gotten that gift from them without maintaining my relationship with them."

I think about work and how we are straining to be pleasant to each other. I'm sure we all feel off balance. I guess with all my heart that we all want something more. Nancy and the others are really saying that we are blocking the exchange of gifts.

I ask her to describe what she wants to accomplish through her studies and discover she would like to learn how to deconstruct oppressive institutional structures. I share my own hope for American business that, to be competitive, many will recognize that democratic means are not only a powerful strategy, but also a vital value. She disagrees. "Capitalism is oppressive because it thrives on cheap labor. The experience of African Americans and Latin Americans in the U.S. alone proves it." She resumes the description of her dream. A doctorate will follow that will have helped her develop ways to construct new communal forms.

I'm blown away. I wasn't ready to receive the wealth of information Nancy offered. The depth, the framework, the historical roots, the concepts and the future plan—it's all there. What I've been learning is being driven home even harder.

And, finally, I ask if Nancy has a story, saying or poem that's important to her and speaks to community. She goes still and reverently says that her favorite is from Jeremiah:

> But seek the welfare of the city
> Where I have sent you into exile,
> And pray to the Lord on its behalf,
> For in its welfare you will find your welfare.[3]

"Nancy, if community is where you feel at home, how does the word 'exile' fit?" I ask. She looks back intently, "We have a responsibility to be open. You have to be ready for people to throw you off balance, to take you to unfamiliar ground."

We part and, again, it was so easy for me to express my thanks and gratitude. I realize how thoughtful Bobbi has been to pick such great people for me to meet.

Disregarded

Preparing to Leave

I'm back from dinner, having posted a short thank you note on the message board on my way out. I've been blessed with the hospitality of these people and felt fully supported in my work. My last bit of research is to study the art studio. It's open 24/7 and I make my way there.

During discussion over dinner I learned that art is stressed at Pendle Hill, not solely for the product, but, rather, what the process can uncover about The Spirit, the artist and the dance between the two. Upon entering the studio, I see that all sorts of projects can be created here.

The quotes posted on cupboard door fronts, shelving and posts attract me. "Ecstasy, then the laundry" is one such quote and I think how this matches what I see in Bobbi—an ingrained, matter-of-fact, everyday approach to community. I think of Kate as I read a quote of Abraham Joshua Heschel: "Above all remember that you must build your life as if it were a work of art." That Tom Jenik overcame bad advice when he chose to listen to his own soul is in harmony with M. C. Richards: "We have to realize that a creative being lives within ourselves whether we like it or not, and we must get out of its way, for it will give us no peace until we do." And I sense that Nancy holds herself and this community to the highest ideals—"The important thing to remember is this: to be ready at any moment to give up what you are for what you might become, W.E.B. DuBois."

I begin to think that one idea remains obscured, that I hadn't uncovered something that all of these people could have spoken to. I had kept my interviewees pointed toward human efforts to create and sustain community, but at no time did I ask them about its spiritual elements. I assumed that these people of faith know that, at least for them, "The Light" is an essential ingredient. I had guided them into talking about the secular, while sensing all along that they listen for a voice inside not all their own.

As I walk back to Waysmeet I know there's too much to process right now and I decide to be content with sorting it out when I get home. I ready everything for an early departure and sleep comes swiftly.

Chapter 14

Toward Home

It's 6:00 am and I turn left out of the Pendle Hill compound. The weather will be good and I pray for an uneventful journey. My return trip looms less ominous in this direction because I've proven to myself that it's doable in a day. The light traffic on I-476 poses no problem and I'm soon on the Pennsylvania toll road. Like last night, I decide to make sense of my notes later on, but the experience is too strong. Bits and pieces keep floating to the surface. Images of morning meeting appear. Themes of openness, diversity, responsibility, gifts, fit, and caring relationships swirl about. The faces of these sincere people emerge. Maybe the most radical view that all shared was their willingness to respect those thought to be irritating. Didn't they all expect of themselves the discipline to weather through conflicts? Weren't they all open to be changed through their relationships? Doesn't their commitment to each other produce the bonds of community that I saw?

The hills begin to sharpen and the lanes thicken with trucks. I use the radio occasionally for company and to stay awake, but the stations fade rapidly. I press the scan button and the radio races through the entire range of frequencies without landing on a station. Finally, I locate one. The DJ is bold, irreverent and I try to tune him out. Drivers jockey for position as a tunnel looms. A car pulls alongside and two small faces press against the glass and stare my way. Suddenly it's dark and the ricocheting tire sounds compete with the DJ.

"The Howard Stern Show will be right back!" breaks through, then fades in a static cloud. I'm curious if the children are still watching, wondering why the man beside them is howling with uncontrollable laughter.

Chapter 15 – Deep Respect and Courage

Every government degenerates when trusted to the rulers of the people alone. Thomas Jefferson

Over the last few days my thoughts have drifted back to Pendle Hill. What's my concept of community now? Upon studying my notes, I end up sensing both the simplicity and challenge of what I've heard. The essence of community is easy to describe, but difficult to do.

Deep respect. Courage. And a fence to put around them. That's the short version. That's what it boils down to. Deep respect. Courage. I realize that irony is embedded in my discovery. I've applied my best intellectual skills during my quest, considering countless "heady" topics, only to end up with matters of the heart. Hmm.

It seems to me that both respect and courage must be present in order for community to have a chance. Those at Pendle Hill demonstrated reverence, openness and tolerance toward others. Those traits formed the deep respect that I observed. But openness puts one at risk, thereby asserting the need for courage. I heard people speak about their life philosophy in inspiring ways: Bobbi Kelly had said, "Something will always shake you. I value that." Kate Garland remained open, even knowing a "whack" was a possibility. Nancy Morgan shared, "You have to be ready for people to throw you off balance, to take you to unfamiliar ground." Even the ones that had tried her patience had, "given me something that blew me away." Shaken. Whacked. Blown away. These are people who, through their courage, dare to practice deep respect toward others as a way of life.

Chapter 15

I now more clearly see the rightness of the word courage in the Courage to Teach program title. Courage to be one's self. Courage to engage with others. Courage to stay in relationship with challenging people. Courage to embrace the unfamiliar, to learn and grow.

In *Productive Workplaces* author Marvin Weisbord writes that, in general, all workers seek the same things – dignity, meaning and community.[1] We will find dignity only by offering our respect to each other. In other words, we will have to live what we seek. Our practices must demonstrate that everyone has value. We must be able to feel that there is room for our contributions. And we must make room for the ideas and work of others. Those different from us offer something unique to the community that we cannot provide.

For us to find meaning, we will have to courageously circulate and speak in a charged environment that honors multiple perspectives. We will learn which values we share with others and which ones are uniquely our own. Using a systems perspective, we will value the complex mix of individual meanings as "differentiation" – a system's ability to contain countless ways to adapt in order to survive. We may come to realize that redefining our jobs and the missions of our institutions is required in order to recapture meaning.

And community? We are disconnected from each other. And the condition is a widespread reality. At Goddard College in Vermont I had heard the term "lone cowboys" used by a Scandinavian man to describe the culture in his organization. To my surprise, at the future search conference training in New York, a German participant referred to the employees of his corporation as "lone cowboys." Astonished by the distant geography and identical descriptors, I could only conclude disconnection was worldwide. We'll have to understand and acknowledge how difficult it is to create strong bonds, in order to garner the courage and resolve to do so. We have cause to remain hopeful as we attempt to improve the culture of our workplaces. Community is not out of reach. We are always living in community; it is our level of consciousness and associated behaviors that thwart its full expression. To risk by loving others is to invite community.

Up, Up

The atmosphere is much more relaxed as school resumes in late August. Hopefully, we're renewed from summer vacation. I chuckle to myself, "All our cans are full." I recall that Roberta Kraft had recently explained to her students that she had a brimming can of patience for them. She would use the patience as necessary and – be forewarned – "when the patience is gone, it's gone."

I'm caught off guard with what happens next. The faculty lunchroom acts as an informal confessional:

"The last few years have been stressful."

"I was tired of living under a rock."

"School should be a place for laughter."

"Maybe I can stop looking over my shoulder."

"Some nights I couldn't sleep."

These confessions are not offered eye to eye, however. They're tossed out casually while walking to the sink for a paper towel, setting a plate of spaghetti on the table or waiting by the microwave. I'm surprised that even the people least caught up in the conflict are letting out a big sigh of relief.

Danzle's gone.

Over the summer, Danzle, his wife and daughter moved out-of-state. No one seems to know why. Did he need a new challenge? Did somebody realize how much some of us were suffering? Had the split become troublesome to someone higher up? I don't have a clue. All I know for sure is that the silent ones have now begun to speak.

I'll always associate Danzle with our split. While the Insiders pinned down the Outsiders, the largest staff group—The Fence Riders—remained silent. With their power of numbers they could have told the warring players, "Stop that. We don't do that here." The absence of their leadership allowed the violence to continue and the split to widen. I interpreted their silence as evidence of our self-reliant culture. It said, "Save yourself. We aren't related. That's not my problem, that's your problem." But, it's as likely that my colleagues were afraid. Any action on their part would have made them visible and increased the likelihood of becoming a target. Their heartfelt confessions suggest this to be true.

Chapter 15

I probably underestimated the amount of chaos they had experienced in their own lives. Some of that turmoil was internal as I came to discover. In what I hope was done with love, I had asked a respected colleague from this group if he realized he was "on the fence." He smiled and replied, "Yes, I know. I'm trying to remain naïve and trick myself into believing I don't have to act. I'm desperately fighting the urge to grow up."

I know that we have to be more courageous than we have been in the past. We have to speak frankly to colleagues and to those in power out of respect and sheer practicality. Employees deserve to have frequent opportunities to discuss what matters most. They also need to understand and confirm agreements in order to commit themselves fully. Managers deserve to know where employees really stand on issues. They must know if workers are engaged, ambivalent or strongly opposed. Is an employee's "Yes" backed by conviction or just an empty gesture to placate? Leading the charge, managers need to know if followers are right behind them or letting them move ahead alone.

Governance

The silence I've noticed here may also reflect another serious condition of the workplace. In *Stewardship* Peter Block makes an astute observation. If we think democracy is good for us, why don't we believe it's good for the workplace?[2] (I remember that power arrangements were important themes for Weisbord and the Pendle Hill Quakers as well. Egalitarian forms of governance encouraged communal strength.) A workplace isn't democratic if workers are too afraid to speak. What fundamental free speech violations are being committed in workplaces where people are sanctioned for expressing their opinion? Often, subtle threats and punitive measures are the glue that holds hierarchies together. Shouldn't the glue of organizations be the values and vision of its people instead of their fears? Sadly, coercive actions can be injustices that target courageous and caring people. It is important for us to underscore the existence of wrongful sanctions as evidence of power gone amuck and claim it as an opportunity to transform relationships.

What name do we give a fear-driven government? It is an

"ism" that discourages individuality—totalitarianism—an apolitical organizational philosophy and set of practices that diminish the freedoms of members.[3] Maybe the most profound characteristic of totalitarianism is that it is undetectable. All around us, only a few sense and understand the spell it casts. The longer it can remain hidden, the more powerful its influence grows. Its concentrated power at the top is the antithesis of freedom and democracy. Its reach results in "fear, isolation, loss of internal space, and ultimately, the disappearance of self."[4] Due to the pervasiveness and stealth nature of totalitarianism, many of us would be shocked to learn that we are "the oppressed." Educator and activist Paulo Freire states the challenge for those caught in its grasp – "The central problem is this: How can the oppressed, as divided, unauthentic beings participate in developing the pedagogy of their liberation?"[5]

I know that one can't preach to the oppressed that they are oppressed and deserve freedom. That realization will most readily come from extensive dialog and reflection amongst themselves. Discussion and time are the key ingredients for a shift in consciousness. Activists believe that human rights must be recaptured by each generation. Complacency is the food that feeds the voracious appetite of totalitarianism.

Our current workplace culture often mimics a kind of parent/child relationship between managers and workers. I understood this clearly one day when my son phoned. At age 25, he had been appointed factory manager and he was calling to vent over his earliest impressions of his employees. "Dad, they act like children!" Absent, from his perspective, were responsibility, initiative, problem solving and creativity. The conclusion reached by many employees of a patriarchy—"If somebody else is in charge, I'm not responsible."

This same mentality was evident during a conversation with one of my students. I had approached Juan and told him that I hadn't received any homework from him. His instant response was "That's not my problem, that's your problem."

But workers are as frustrated as managers. My guess is that the employees who were working with my son were muttering to themselves that someone wet behind the ears was bossing them. In the absence of employee responsibility and initiative, the urge that surfaces within leaders to exercise more control is difficult to resist. Taking more control provides a sense of safety for a supervisor, yet the move doesn't translate into organizational effectiveness. Workers also seek safety—through anonymity. In a crowd, no one's at fault. While frustrated with each other, in the end both parties still choose to satisfy their unexamined need for safety through counterproductive roles.

Maintaining this unhealthy parent/child relationship causes organizational malaise. Maybe that is why the Grail myths, with their ailing kings, have such barren kingdoms. Like the instructive myths, we have placed the responsibility of entire kingdoms on the shoulders of a paltry few, giving them jobs too large to do. Under the stress and impossible expectations, many become infirm. The afflictions of the kings eventually spread throughout their kingdoms.

I believe that the alternative to all of this is a movement[6] by a majority of workers to recapture dignity, meaning and community for themselves and vitality for their organizations. Employees have to bring their organizations back into balance, for it is not the ailing king who eventually restores the kingdom. Like the kings of myth, modern leaders are often unable to transform their kingdoms. Heavily managed, even if from afar, they must heavily manage. And when leaders experience the relentless pull of multiple responsibilities from above and below, a paralysis of sorts can result. I remember how my boss had straddled the doorway, trying to decide whether to join our team or continue on his way. Caught in a straightjacket of their own, the elite cannot liberate themselves or the oppressed, as Gandhi has said. Freire clearly implies the same thing – "This is the great humanistic and historical task of the oppressed: to liberate themselves and their oppressors as well."[7]

A successful movement that addresses parity will create healthier partnerships between employees and management. Partnerships have vastly different power arrangements than hierarchies. No patriarch, no supreme authority or manna god exists

Disregarded

in a partnership. Power and responsibility are shared. Cooperation replaces compliance.

Two stories demonstrate to me that a transformation of relationships is not only necessary, but desirable as well.

Getulio Vargas was Brazil's dictator from 1930-1945. He returned as elected President in 1950, with his country's people clearly suffering. Vargas' approach in 1950 was the antithesis of a dictator's. He realized that only the unification and empowerment of his people could help the situation. Addressing his fellow citizens of Brazil, he said, "I need your unity...I need for you to form a strong and cohesive bond."[8]

The other story is close to home. My son relocated to become plant manager of a factory bursting at the seams. Corporate purchased an empty factory building and invested millions in outfitting it. After the move to the new facility, no combination of thought, action and will resulted in more than dismal profitability; often, "the numbers" were in the red. All felt the increasing pressure to perform; everything fell under scrutiny, including everyone's job. It was finally decided to reorganize into teams. Teams would be given the power to order raw material, schedule the work, make the products, arrange for shipping and communicate with suppliers and customers. After some intense months of "learning by fire" the factory's profitability quadrupled. The redistribution of power was responsible for the change. Solidarity and empowerment are not evils or conditions to be feared; they can be the solutions to pressing problems.

When my thoughts drift back to the present situation, I wonder if our new principal, Danzle's former assistant, will see some of us through distorted lenses. The road could remain steep and treacherous. But I also consider that better times are ahead. Right now it's too early to tell, too soon to drop one's guard.

Up, Up and Away

Thankfully, the first nine weeks goes well. I can feel the tone change with each passing faculty meeting. It turns out that our new principal has a sense of humor and a light touch. Colleagues

Chapter 15

greet each other in the hallway with decidedly higher spirits and renewed sincerity—we're making efforts to mend.

In late October I get an email from Sue Hardy. She's pulled a rabbit out of the hat and will make it to retirement. She writes that she'll be leaving at the end of the semester. I believe that the miracle of her survival obscures the likelihood that she has nothing left to give, that the marathon she's run has left her completely spent. Her heroism has been purchased with every ounce of her life energy.

After Christmas break, as I work on entering semester grades, a student hurriedly enters my room and shyly says, "Mrs. Lowell says to look out your window." Curiosity builds with each step toward the window. From my vantage point on the third floor, I can see that the front lawn is swarming with middle school students carrying balloons. Suddenly they're aloft, filling the air with color. I whisper to myself, "So this is Sue's distinctive sendoff; more like a guilt offering, if you ask me."

The balloons quickly shrink to tiny specks, an apt metaphor of Sue's departure. Today's bitterness disappears with them when I reconsider that the sendoff could be genuine. I know in my heart that I've got to let go of the cynicism that's lurking inside. This is but a small piece of the work ahead.

Workplace Stress...

The air is crisp today, but the interior of the van is warm from the sun that's penetrating the clear sky. I sit like a statue, as a light breeze rocks the van, and stare at the speedometer. Zero. The cars on the highway west of the parking lot hum high in my left ear and then lower in my right as they head north.

I swallow hard. In every way—I'm alone.

What had I been thinking? When referred to a hematologist had I expected the diagnosis of a cold? Cancer is what he said.

The consult, which ended moments ago, was a roller coaster. "You are younger than the typical patient... We should be optimistic... There is no cure at this time... New therapies are being tested... It's too early to know what's ahead."

As I try to make sense of the diagnosis, the past warning

signs finally become real. I follow them to this moment like breadcrumbs along a path. I also acknowledge and link today's news with the recent diagnosis of Crohn's disease. The stress at work has definitely taken its toll.

I drop into a dark and bottomless place, then anger explodes. I realize that cancer isn't the source of this eruption. I'm enraged at my own carelessness—I've lost hope. It only takes a moment for me to learn that one cannot live without it. It's the life force of every day, but today it's especially critical. No wonder hope is called a holy virtue. I scold myself, promising never to be so reckless again. Coaxing it out of hiding, I begin to feel better.

As I drive home and consider how I'll tell my family, two thoughts surface. Sometimes we have to learn something over and over until we truly "get it." I begin to wonder if my work with winter and death hasn't really sunk in like I thought it had. Just how many layers must be penetrated? It appears that I've been offered another chance to learn.

I'm mortal. Every day is a gift.

The other thought seems a little strange—I'm going to love those cells. The errant cells are part of me and I decide to see them that way. I refuse to divide myself in two, already knowing what splits feel like, already knowing the power of wholeness.

Down, Down

Three months between diagnosis and school's end begin to dissolve like a puddle on a sunny day. I receive another rejection of a retirement proposal I've submitted. To grant my request "would not be in the best interests of the district." My calculations say that it would. I wonder if my math is correct, then wonder if the decision is personal or policy.

Still feeling defensive, I decide to check my personnel file, something I've never done. Has someone been filling it full of nonsense? I greet our main office secretary and tell her that I would like to see my file. Her face registers shock and that raises my concern.

I open my file and anxiously flip through the pages of courses taken and certificates issued. I realize I've been holding my breath all the while. I relax more with each page. Unlike Sue Hardy's ponderous file, nothing's been placed into mine in years.

When I reach the last two sheets, I slow down. One is a hand-written letter by a parent. Her claim was that I pressured her daughter to sell grapefruit during a band fundraiser. It's been sixteen years since I left music and I can't recall anything about the situation.

The other page is a written reprimand which resurrects a bitter memory. It was the time of budget cuts and my band director partner had been laid off. I was attempting to do the job of two. There was a purchase freeze on. One beginning band student had her new clarinet, but didn't have a book. I had called central office a number of times to get permission to purchase the $2.50 book, but the acting superintendent hadn't been available. Between bites of a sandwich and other pressing work, I told the secretary to let the superintendent know that I would be calling him to explain later, but I was taking the initiative to order the book. The reprimand was issued the next day.

I close my personnel file. So that's what twenty-five years of service looks like on paper. Jeez. In my opinion, it points to a culture short on celebration, a place quick to condemn and control the god to be worshipped. It's evidence enough for me that our current organizational culture rarely honors or leverages human potential. I had to travel outside my organization for someone to ask me about my identity, purpose and trajectory. The Courage to Teach Program was a curriculum of questions aimed at helping me uncover my true identity. Before that experience, I was very much like Vivienne in David Huddle's novel *La Tour Dreams of the Wolf Girl* who says, "Until you began to ask me about my life, I never saw it, because to me it was invisible."[9]

Caring for Spirit

Beyond "staying in business" and "serving the customer," I believe that some key purposes of organizations are to help people uncover meaning, personal identity and encourage the expression of who they are. But that belief is not widely held even by workers. While I helped my son's employees identify shared values, a senior member of the group talked to me over the din of conversation. He confessed, "I've learned to leave myself at home when going to work. When I go home, I become myself again." What struck me was the pride with which he spoke. In his mind, he had beaten the system. He didn't seem to grasp the price he was paying during most of his waking hours. But maybe he sensed he was a machine at work, an instrument in an even bigger machine. Better to leave one's soul at home than to have it abused.

A workplace that encourages its members to leave their true selves at home goes against what Joseph Campbell says "is the great Western truth:

> that each of us is a completely unique creature and that, if we are ever to give any gift to the world, it will have to come out of our own experience and fulfillment of our own potentialities, not someone else's."[10]

Arthur Miller and Ralph Mattson write about what they've observed in the workplace in *The Truth About You*. Their workplace observations collide with Campbell's statement. Together, the two statements suggest how misguided our organizations can be:

> You enter the world of work…over a period of 40 to 45 years, we are given assignments, coached, appraised, trained, developed, promoted, transferred, given results/objectives to fulfill, put in work groups, exhorted to make a commitment, expected to align with group goals…without anybody at any time during nearly half a century spending a few hours to find out what we are good at and motivated to do.[11]

Disregarded, our experience yields pain, frustration and disappointment as reflected in the opening of Studs Terkel's book *Working*:

> … work, is, by its very nature, about violence—to the spirit as well as to the body. It is about ulcers as well as accidents, about shouting matches as

Chapter 15

well as fistfights, about nervous breakdowns as well as kicking the dog around. It is, above all (or beneath all), about daily humiliations. To survive the day is triumph enough for the walking wounded among the great many of us.[12]

Disregarded, we want to kick more than the dog. We respond in kind by disregarding those around us, above us and below us. Everyone becomes disregarded.

If we ignore the gifts and motivations of each other, loss of spirit is nearly assured. I recall watching two girls in my eighth grade computer class ignore assignments from the beginning of our time together. All that seemed to matter to them was their tight friendship. I often encouraged them, saying, "I see a lot of potential in you two." Before the class ended they became productive. I approached them at semester's end and asked why they had decided to engage in their schoolwork. One of them looked at the other for confirmation while saying, "Well, Mr. Bender, I think we had lost hope." This certainly was an astute observation for a middle school student to make. Stuffing them full of knowledge and over controlling them, we had beaten down their spirit. At least, temporarily, they had rediscovered their own flames.

I head into summer with thoughts of traveling up the Lake Michigan coast. We had a very good reason to name our 28' sloop "Present Moment." While sailing, my focus centers on the wind and waves. Trimming the sails and listening to the water stroke the hull further capture my attention. Living fully in the present, I rob the past of its negative power.

Chapter 16 – Come Unity

In the end... it is the reality of personal relationships that saves everything.[1]

Thomas Merton

It's taken a very long time for me to fully understand my excitement about community. Early on I must have made a subconscious connection between community and effective schools research. That connection has important implications for not only schools, but other organizations as well. One approachable and useful piece of research is Susan Rosenholtz's *Teacher's Workplace*. In it she reveals that strong social bonds comprise the crucial ingredient for organizational effectiveness. In short, employee collegiality is the most significant factor related to school success. Strongly collegial organizations can accomplish their missions. I see that "collegiality" has two key elements. First, it represents a group composed of members who individually feel a strong sense of responsibility to the accomplishment of organizational goals. Second, each member is committed to extensive listening and sharing as critical, enabling behaviors of success.

Rosenholtz approaches organizational effectiveness from the employee's perspective. "To understand schools, we must understand them as teachers do."[2] We could gain powerful insights if we were to take that stance elsewhere. To better understand workplaces, we must understand them as employees do.

The cohesiveness and communication of a collegial group depends on how its members define their work. The definition is derived through daily discussions that continually tweak and reaffirm what the work is and how it is to be done. If employees describe their work as difficult, non-routine and technical, they

Chapter 16

create an environment that calls for collaborative action. So challenging to do well, it is work that can't be done alone. Individual and group learning is mandatory if individuals and their organizations are to succeed.

A major difference between healthy and unhealthy organizations can be heard in the stories members tell about reality. Those in healthy organizations do more truth telling. Decisions are more effective and such honesty builds trust, drawing members toward each other. Those working in environments plagued by especially weak social fabrics can't resist the urge to become self-reliant. Unaligned, alone, employees experience deepening isolation and cynicism and resort to rationalization about their performance.

A new hire who joins an effective work community will be carefully introduced to the vision, mission and shared goals of the organization. That person is likely to acquire a vocabulary used by existing members that helps classify and give meaning to the processes applied to work. Because communication is effective, the clarity of important matters helps the new hire learn appropriate behaviors. Meanings are altered and reinforced with everyday interactions that stay focused on core issues of the organization.

Here, I get the feeling that no one feels empowered enough to seriously mentor new teachers. I was always pleased to see a new teacher outside of my area approach with questions, diligently trying to make sense of his environment. He displayed a lot of spunk. But I also knew that his approach signaled that no one in his area was helping him. When new hires join an ineffective work community, the lack of clarity in the organization works against the formation of successful behaviors. How to practice one's craft is unclear. Current workers are distant from each other or low levels of collegiality are present, so new hires sink or swim on their own. It soon becomes obvious to the new employee that work is a solitary activity.

If the work is difficult and there is little help, performance outcomes are unpredictable. The non-technical culture of ineffective workplaces plants feelings of uncertainty into the souls of workers. The lack of control and the powerlessness experienced encourages new hires to create protective strategies—it's somebody else's fault, being invisible is wise, excelling at non-core subjects can save face, etc. In vibrant workplaces conversation centers around craft, but in unhealthy ones, rationalized storytelling, cover-ups and gossip command much of the time.

I think I see why collegiality is so challenging to develop. A well-intentioned push to share in strong cultures usually succeeds and reduces uncertainty, but in weak cultures it backfires. Starting with so few resources and social capital before the push, the pressure to share in weak cultures only ends up confirming that the ambiguity of work is real and all are powerless to do anything about it. Potential efforts at collaboration will cause employees to wonder about the consequences of seeking aid. Employees avoid asking for help in order to protect themselves from experiencing more uncertainty or embarrassment.

Countless times I've heard a phrase from colleagues spoken in frustration—"At least I can shut my door and teach." I don't know how much the phrase speaks to the well-documented need of teachers to do what they think best in their classrooms or a sign that isolation has its own rewards. To me, the phrase implies an abdication of responsibility to the entire organization. Conditions outside the classroom affect what goes on inside it. I believe that the welfare of the system beyond my immediate control is part of my responsibility. In my case, it reaches to the state and federal levels. In the corporate world, it can extend to a different country and an unfamiliar culture. I have a responsibility to communicate upward as well as sideways. It was at Pendle Hill that I was introduced to the fitting verse from Jeremiah: "But seek the welfare of the city...for in its welfare you will find your welfare."[3] If we truly care about our work, we must actualize that care by nurturing and transforming the wider landscape that cannot but influence "my work."

Rosenholtz challenges the "great person theory."[4] One leader does not an effective organization make. Governance matters and it should be skewed toward generous participation by employees, especially in the area of professional practice. Assuming that collegiality and community are present, the best course of action is to display respect for workers by empowering and trusting them. Micromanagement or over-management is counterproductive.

Chapter 16

There is a direct correlation between powerful bureaucratic control and the failure to reach goals.

So my excitement comes from seeing how a deep respect for others creates the openness to learn from them. Because asking for help, and even offering help, places one in a vulnerable position, courage is also a vital trait that must be present if collegiality is to take place. Again, the respect and courage displayed at the community of Pendle Hill plays a predominant place in my thinking about successful organizations.

Thinking Backward

Recurring thoughts of cancer help me realize that I must retire at the end of the school year, regardless of the financial consequences. As I consider leaving, I can't help but reflect on the last handful of years. The Courage to Teach Program and my experiences at work ran parallel to each other and were so profoundly different that, when joined, acted like rocket fuel. The gap between the two demanded an explanation. All of the people here at Crawford are capable of communal life appropriate for the workplace, yet we had split. The ache inside me was like no other. At Pendle Hill I discovered a phrase to describe my condition. I was "pained by the potential of the place." I became a seeker. I was hell-bent to find out why groups split apart and how they hold together.

I was also sought. In the Courage to Teach Program, I was taught how to listen. On retreat, one is encouraged to become still and quiet—to be open to whomever or whatever desires a relationship. The most profound learnings *came* to me.

I've forgotten some of the details of my time at the Fetzer Institute retreats, but a great deal remains alive. The most powerful influences that survive are an appreciation of fear and paradox. I trust it was Palmer's Quaker economy that got to these issues early. I now realize that the retreats provided antidotes for my needs of safety and simplicity.

My appreciation of the influence of fear on our lives eventually yielded an entirely different tone to my own. I hear my wife in the next room preparing for a performance. She's practicing Mendelssohn's oratorio *Elijah* and the vocal parts overlap dozens of times with their entreaties to "Be not afraid." Interspersed repeatedly is "Though thousands languish." Though others are caught up in debilitating fear, we can choose to "be not afraid" and live courageously. We're made of better stuff than we think we are. Finding courage might be as simple as sharing our fears with others, bringing them out of the closet and, in so doing, uncover the shared need to overcome them. Safety is an illusion as well as a goal that can only render life lifeless.

Understanding paradox destroyed the foundations of my simple either/or thinking. Paradox continues to help me honor the ideas and experiences of others. It provides relief from exhausting win/lose battles, joining halves into wholes. It's the key to being real about the world and self. Simplicity is also an illusion and a goal that, if obtained, robs life of its richness and myriad possibilities.

I also recall two other retreat themes—abundance and gratitude. When I'm able to appreciate the abundance around me, my anxiety is reduced and my confidence in the future increases. I sincerely know there's enough of what I need, even if it isn't immediately evident. Belief in abundance unleashes creativity. If one resource isn't forthcoming, all other possibilities remain open for exploration.

Being grateful comes from my awareness of abundance. Gratitude encourages my acknowledgement of the countless, unearned blessings I have. It pushes my vision outward, reducing my excessive self-reliance. I cannot help but become humble. With new eyes, I look to others and the universe as resources and partners. As I become more appreciative of the abundance around me, I end up being surprisingly content.

The four personal transformations framework has survived as well. I can choose to 1) reexamine my motives, 2) discover my gifts, 3) strengthen relationships and 4) balance the dance between means and ends. In addition to seeking transformation, I need to remember that inner work includes uncovering what already exists. My path must include remembering and recapturing true self as much as becoming. Sister Sue Tracy had described the intent of her community as one of uncovering what lay in hiding. Without a doubt, part of Palmer's intent was to do likewise.

Chapter 16

Time to Go

The rumor mill spreads news that a retirement incentive will be offered at the end of the year. When the details appear, I realize that I qualify.

After submitting my paperwork, I start thinking about what I've contributed to my community through my teaching. The music contributions are the most tangible. Helping band students progress from Mary Had a Little Lamb to an honest performance of a symphonic work was very satisfying. And I always believed that I taught much more than notes. Many life skills can be modeled while making music. Relationships with former students remain so very special to me.

I started the middle school computer program with six computers and twenty-four students to a class; the curriculum evolved from basic literacy to programming to applications. It was a captivating challenge to continually rethink course offerings and methods.

Work on the school improvement team was particularly energizing and rewarding, even when undermined. I learned that the work excited something deep inside. I found my service as association representative and negotiator rewarding as well. Something in me values working with and being an advocate for folks at the bottom of the organizational chart. It was the relationship with my struggling peers that salvaged light from all the darkness.

I believe that the initiatives I was involved in—the team schedule, the future search and the offer to partner, to name a few, stirred up too much anxiety and frustration. Each initiative must have challenged managers already stretched to the limit. To me, the initiatives were much needed medicine, but they must have looked like poison to my bosses.

After each thwarted initiative, I would assume I was powerless and needed power, but I was wrong. Meeting force with force invites escalation. The power of our convictions is enough. The missing key ingredient in each case was a critical mass of colleagues. More colleagues would have had to join our little group for us to be taken seriously. It was easy for those above to dismiss or negate my work or the work of our small school improvement team. As it was, I think we were seen as meddling, taking on roles reserved in the past for only managers. But I know better. It would be a grave disservice to an institution if its rank and file perceived management as the sole engine of change, source of power and architect of relationships.

Followers lead.

When I would think about what our fundamental "problem" was, many images surfaced. When I sought their root, I was left with a simple explanation—we had known no other way to be. This realization did not indict anyone. When talking to fellow retreatants, it was clear that all were discovering the benefits of intentional space for the first time. While on retreat, we learned new ways to live with others. While respect and courage were in very short supply on the surface at Crawford, I believed that each staff member was readily capable of demonstrating both. A carefully shaped container, to include a variety of communal practices and ways to deal with conflict, would have brought out the best in each one of us.

I do not look at these initiatives as "failures." They've been learning opportunities and honest efforts to improve. There is much to be said for mistakes. As in writing computer code, one learns more from mistakes than from code that works the first time. As Mother Teresa instructed, "We are called not to be successful but to be faithful." Dealing with the fickle muse of change, sometimes our intentions may be all that survive.

Change

I suspect that many of us are fed up with change, but what we've experienced so far is our collective ineptness. Our ignorance of the change process has brought about a great deal of suffering. We don't understand optimal time frames, new leadership and followership roles, communication skills and psychological needs surrounding the subject of change. In the sweep of history, we may be the ones that learn the most about change and its rapidly increasing pace.

Trouble is, if an initiative offering substantial benefits were to be introduced, we'd opt for rejection. In a mock apology letter from management to employees, appearing in *Training* magazine over a decade ago, Bob Filipczak conceded countless programs "du jour," sticking with nothing, implementing poorly, losing patience, creating an illusion of change and failing to clarify goals—realizing that employees had gone from "skepticism to cynicism to downright intransigence...Now we've got a lot of burned-out workers...For our complicity in this dismal state of affairs, we are sincerely sorry."[5] A similar letter of apology from employees to management could certainly be composed.

In order to grow more successfully, we'll have to acknowledge that change is difficult and painful. The pain of loss accompanies real growth, for we must give up something in order to gain something else. And suffering seems to be the enabler of change. We have to be experiencing some form of pain in order to consider that change might be necessary.

Once an initiative is underway, we have to curb our impatience and be willing to live in a milieu that may have elements of unfamiliarity for long periods of time. We have to reframe change as an adventure. We have to be delighted upon being surprised instead of petrified.

But most importantly, we have to be compassionate toward each other. Even the smallest change invokes feelings deep inside that range from "uncomfortable" to "terrified." In *The Ordeal of Change* author Eric Hoffer writes that he had worked as a laborer, picking peas for about six months, until that season came to a close. After traveling to an area where he could continue picking vegetables, only beans this time, he sensed the impending change. "And I still remember how hesitant I was that first morning as I was about to address myself to the string bean vines. Would I be able to pick string beans? Even the change from peas to string beans had in it elements of fear."[6]

Leaders and followers must dance a new dance. For me to risk another initiative, some leader would have to understand this place from my perspective. Some leader would have to see the barriers, disregard, mistrust and humiliations flung at employees below. As Darcy said at the chili committee meeting, "Leaders trivialize our lives." Some leader would have to recognize that my work and my contact with our customers are as important as any political or financial reality. My recommendations ignored and my abilities underutilized, some leader would have to begin to grasp

Disregarded

how organizational structures and attitudes stifle my contributions. Some leader would have to understand that the relationship between us must be transformed. That new relationship would also help me see things that I minimally do now—the pressures, responsibilities, complexities and perspectives of leaders.

What could start such a transformation? As I try to picture that, I remember a line someone used at a chili committee meeting—"Please help me understand." In that plea rests humbleness, openness, respect and a willingness to grow. Of course, there's so much more to it than that. There is the inner journey that greatly influences our readiness and resolve. Something inside must call us to act; it includes a change of heart that colors all that we are. There is the outer journey that requires strong connections be made among organizational members as well as the establishment of policies and practices that support working together.

Looking back, I see that the state legislature had it right, if only for a brief period of time. The passage of PA 25, with its provision for local control of each building, was on the mark. No one could have guessed that the complexity of our task would require a deep understanding of power, psychology, years of patience and support. How many legislators knew about the glorious spark they had created, but also the daunting struggle we faced? Now, faith rests with the carrot and stick of testing—high stakes manipulation, a failure to trust, an abdication of support and an almost impossible challenge to find meaning.

Gift and Shadow

I've been thinking of how work eventually uncovered some of my strengths and weaknesses—that through work I discovered more and more of myself. I'd thought that my gift was objectivity. I'd thought that sharing leading-edge concepts or best practices with colleagues and the administration was my contribution. I now believe that my gift is faithfulness. I've been faithful to those who needed my support, those who fell under attack—and to this place—until I could no longer tolerate the resistance. At this point, I don't believe that saying, "Enough. No more initiatives." is being unfaithful. It is faithfulness with no way to turn.

I came back to my alma mater, expecting to contribute and

Chapter 16

holding myself to that standard. It appears that my expectation has remained different than what this place wants from its people. What is often asked of organizational members parallels the character Procrutes of Greek mythology who would ambush travelers and take pleasure in stretching or cutting off the legs of his victims to fit an iron bed. A giant, he found no compelling reason to respect others. To be Procrustean is to exhibit a detached disregard for individuality. We've had it backwards. It is not a rightful charge for the individual to conform to the arbitrary demands of power. It is the distorted institution that must renew—for its health, growth and survival.

As a change agent, I tried to improve this place, only to learn that I have changed. The joke's on me. I set a trap and fell in. On the other hand, since I've changed, the world has changed—whether through my new perceptions or some small impact from my being or doing. Because I feel a growing readiness to befriend all that comes with change, I can't help but tie together individual growth and organizational improvement.

My vision of workplace transformation is based on people committing themselves to personal renewal and formation that will increase their capacity to change, hence that of the organization's ability to change. Those with greater self-knowledge can more readily participate in and weather system-wide change initiatives. I believe that we'll have limited success in improving our organizations until we intentionally support and honor personal growth and identity. Quaker Tom Jenik said it well, "Change is hard to come by...I do know that you can't change without knowing who you are." Both human systems and psychological frameworks support his belief.

The personal change process can't be coerced. It must come from invitational, open-ended programs that are void of hidden agendas and underlying goals to manipulate. Our organizations already impact employees in life-changing ways. The unemployed from closings and takeovers know this. Those with ravaged pensions know. Countless others who have lost heart do as well.

I have found things to be out of order in this place. That problems exist is undeniable. But part of the problem is that I have been out of order. I have often used the dark side of my gift, being too proactive or spreading myself thin to the point of obscuring my identity and focus. I see that it's likely that Danzle and I may even have had the same Achilles heel. My guess is that we wrongfully, unknowingly thought that the state of the workplace was exclusively our responsibility.

With my shadow as a strong reality, I realize that my story about this place contains no antagonists, only people like me holding the promise of connection. While on my quest, the wisest of those I met advised me to acknowledge and embrace my shadow. Early on, I hoped my struggle with Danzle would look like a classic western. Observers could easily tell that I was the one wearing the white hat. But my journey looks more like an episode of Star Wars.[7] At the surface level, it too looks like a struggle between good and evil, but further down, it points to the complex array of shadows and light in each one of us.

Luke Skywalker's maturation is almost complete when Yoda instructs, "One thing remains. Vader. You must confront Vader."[8] Confronting shadow is the missing link to wholeness. When Skywalker and Vader duel, the seemingly simple struggle between good and evil is undone. What Luke Skywalker thought was alien and terrible is so close as to be of his own blood. At its deepest level, Vader and Skywalker comprise a single character, framed as two separate entities for our examination and reflection.

At his impending death, Lord Darth Vader asks for what is most important—"Help me take this mask off. Just for once, let me look on you with my own eyes."[9] All the while Luke Skywalker stares down at a paradox—foreboding but non-threatening, hideous but loving. At the most critical moment of his life, Vader knows that seeing clearly is closure and salvation.

We need not fear our shadow. Hidden within it is a gift—the increased capacity for compassion and community. As the all-powerful Death Star explodes and cheers go up, we can falsely believe that good has conquered an external evil instead of understanding that the ultimate victory comes from discovering and embracing the shadow within. If we are to be responsible for ourselves, we will not perpetuate the ruse that labels self as pure and the other as evil. Without an appreciation of the damage

Chapter 16

each of us can do to others, we will be the cause of much suffering. In the end, self-knowledge potently benefits everyone.

Board Meeting

After the notification of my retirement is accepted, I decide to attend all related events. Sue Hardy often advised, "Celebrate or lose it." The two formal events that pertain to my retirement are a school board meeting and our end-of-year building party.

The room is full of retirees and their families as the board meeting begins. When my name is called, I walk to the front to receive my certificate and then get caught off guard. I'm invited to address the crowd. Having no inkling that I'd be asked to speak, I sense my eyes move toward the ceiling in hopes of pulling words out of thin air and, in fact, a few do come. "I guess that my hope is, if someone watched me carefully, that person would realize that what I've tried to do came out of love."

I surprise myself. Where did *that* come from? But, as I think about it, I really know. Sometimes fear and my own needs motivated me, but much of what I did did originate from love. One can't live in an organization for forty years and not grow to deeply care about it, warts and all.

Building Party

On my final day I am prepared to tell some stories to colleagues. I remember the time my partner and I had congratulated our marching band students for a great performance at the marching band festival. We dismissed them so they could get refreshments and relax. Shortly, we saw them filing into the bleachers, at attention, single file. From the other side of the field we could see their pride and unity. My partner and I looked at each other in bewilderment, not knowing how to handle the unexpected. How many students had their legs crossed, praying for a bathroom break? The memory is strong because of seeing students display motivation and discipline from within—what we hope for all of our students.

When I first started the computer program, I had to kick out a group of five boys every night around 5:30 p.m., over two

Disregarded

hours past the end bell. Those boys were on fire. My role? Keep the door unlocked and engage only when asked a question. I talk about the young lady who would eventually become valedictorian who called me at home, asking if I could unlock my room at Sunday noon so that she could make a fancy cover page and charts for her report.

Yet another time, having spent the day in a bookstore in Ann Arbor, I was about to head home. The attendant of the parking ramp exclaimed, "Mr. Bender! It's great to see you. I really felt you treated me with respect. Parking is free for you." Maybe more than anything else, I'd like to think that most of my students could say the same.

What did I learn from tough times? I struggled mightily as the sole band director while under budget cuts and with my partner on lay off. Upon walking into the band room office, I discovered that maintenance personnel were pulling out my phone. After muttering, "Cost savings," they apologized but left with phone in hand. To a band director, a phone is oxygen, the lifeline to the instrument repair shop, music store and parents. Already spent, I stood frozen, with no energy left to help me keep from sinking into despair. The silence was broken by an administrator who popped in, saying, "We need someone for the dunk tank on Saturday morning. Are you willing?" I learned that things can get so dark that the only choice left is laughter.

Near the Door

I've tried to see our superintendent twice today and have missed him both times. The second time to central office I tell my need to the Universe. I can't leave without shaking his hand. He's the gatekeeper and I'm the change agent. Our worlds set off sparks when they touch. But, I know there are strong similarities between us in demeanor, discipline and dedication. His car and mine are the two in the parking lot on Sundays.

As I head for the exit the last time, we meet on the stairs. "I understand you've been looking for me," he says. I get to say what I'd hoped to, "I really respect the amount of time and effort you've put into this place. I wish you well in the future." He does the same over a handshake and there's nothing left to do but head home. As I exit for the last time, a line from Gung Ho surfaces—"We were this close."[10]

It's over for me. Whatever is done is done. Whatever is not done must remain so. But it's not over for those that remain. Community is possible here. So is a shared vision. Here, all manner of things can grow anew. It's left for me to wonder who will step forward out of love and if others will respond in kind.

Out the Door

The door swings wide and the muggy air declares that spring can no longer hold back summer. The custodians are already throwing into the dumpster large trash bags of ancient spelling lists and battered leaf reports. Teachers and aides call to each other across the parking lot in giddy tones.

As the engine turns over, an unfamiliar feeling sweeps over me. I'm in no man's land, uncharted territory. While backing out of my spot, "No more roadblocks!" creeps into consciousness and then evaporates in the afternoon sunshine.

I turn right out of the lot, then stop at the stop sign at Rose. On Patterson the crossing guard signals for me to stop, and eventually waves me on. The light turns red on Beatrice and also on Brody.

And then I begin to laugh.

Come,
let us help
each other grow
toward beings
of inner beauty,
and in so doing
more easily weave
the vibrant quilt
of unity.

Notes

Front Epigraph
1. His Holiness the Dalai Lama, in the Foreward to *Peace is Every Step: The Path of Mindfulness in Everyday Life* by Thich Nhat Hanh (New York: Bantam, 1992), p. vii.

Introduction
1. For information about the Center for Courage and Renewal (formerly the Center for Teacher Formation), call 1-888-849-4889 or see www.couragerenewal.org.

Chapter 1 – The Journey Begins
(Pages 1-16)

1. John Jay Bonstingl, *Schools of Quality: An Introduction to Total Quality Management in Education* (Thousand Oaks, CA: Corwin Press, 2001), p. 28. www.Bonstingl.com. Reprinted by permission of the author.
2. Mary Walton, *The Deming Management Method* (New York: Perigree Books, 1986), p. 148. Reprinted by permission of the author.
3. Thomas S. Kuhn, *The Structure of Scientific Revolutions* (Chicago: University of Chicago Press, 1996), p. 122.
4. Joel Arthur Barker, *Future Edge: Discovering the New Paradigms of Success* (New York: William Morrow and Company, 1992), p. 69.
5. Peter M. Senge, *The Fifth Discipline: The Art and Practice of the Learning Organization* (New York: Doubleday, 1990), p. 221.

Chapter 2 – On Retreat
(Pages 17-33)

1. Thomas Merton, "The Woodcarver," in *The Way of Chuang Tzu* (New York: New Directions Publishing Corp., 1969), pp. 110-111. Copyright ©1965 by The Abbey of

Gethsemani. Reprinted by permission of New Directions Publishing Corp.
2. Robert M. Persig, *Zen and the Art of Motorcycle Maintenance: An Inquiry into Values* (New York: Quill/William Morrow, 1979), p.34.
3. Persig, *Zen and the Art of Motorcycle Maintenance,* p. 34.

Chapter 3 – Staying in Touch
(Pages 34-44)

1. Miguel de Cervantes, *Don Quixote* (http://en.wikisource/wiki/Don_Quixote/ Volume_2/Chapter_XXIII)
2. Brenda Ueland, *If You Want to Write: A Book about Art, Independence and Spirit* (Saint Paul, MN: Graywolf Press, 1987), p. 29.
3. Mel Brooks and Carl Reiner, *The 2000 Year Old Man in the Year 2000.* (Rhino Records, 1997).
4. Anne Lamott, *Bird by Bird: Some Instructions on Writing and Life* (New York: Anchor Books, 1995), p. 86.
5. E. F. Schumacher, *A Guide for the Perplexed* (New York: Harper and Row, 1977), p. 39.
6. Rainer Maria Rilke, *Letters to a Young Poet,* M. D. Herter Norton (trans.) (New York: W. W. Norton & Company, Inc., 1954), p. 59. Reprinted by permission of the publisher.
7. Martin Buber, *I and Thou,* Ronald Gregor Smith (trans.) (New York: Scribner, 1987), p. ix.
8. Roland Barth, *Improving Schools from Within: Teachers, Parents and Principals Can Make the Difference* (San Francisco: Jossey-Bass, 1990), p. 16.

Chapter 4 – Winter, Death, Dormancy, Renewal
(Pages 45-57)

1. Annie Lennox, "Cold" on *Diva* compact disc (New York: Arista Records, Inc., 1992).
2. May Sarton, "On a Winter Night," in *Selected Poems of May Sarton* (New York: W. W. Norton & Company, 1978), p. 96.

Chapter 5 – Ambushed
(Pages 58-76)

1. Donna Schaper, *A Book of Common Power: Narratives Against the Current* (San Diego, CA: LuraMedia, 1989), p. 154. Reprinted by permission of the author.
2. Rainer Maria Rilke, Stephen Mitchell (trans. & ed.), *The Selected Poetry of Rainer Maria Rilke* (New York: Vintage Books, 1989), p. 245.
3. Rilke, *The Selected Poetry of Rainer Maria Rilke*, p. 245.
4. Julia Cameron, *The Artist's Way: A Spiritual Path to Higher Creativity* (New York: Putnam's Sons, 1992), p. 44.
5. Mary Oliver, "On Winter's Margin," in *New and Selected Poems* (Boston: Beacon Press, 1992), p. 255.
6. Rilke, *The Selected Poetry of Rainer Maria Rilke*, p. 245.

Chapter 6 – Spanning the Chasm
(Pages 77-94)

1. Jelaluddin Rumi, Coleman Barks (trans.), *The Essential Rumi* (San Francisco: Harper SanFrancisco, 1995), p. 36. Reprinted by permission.
2. Book by Joseph Stein based on the stories of Sholom Aleichem, libretto and music by Jerry Bock, lyrics by Sheldon Harnick, *Fiddler on the Roof* (New York: Proscenium Publishers, 1964), p. 27.
3. Lynn Minton, "Fresh Voices" column in *PARADE Magazine*, July 24, 1994 (New York: PARADE Publications, Inc.). Reprinted by permission of the publisher.
4. Martin Buber, David Antin and Jerome Rothenberg (trans.), "The Angel and the World's Dominion" in *Tales of Angels, Spirits and Demons* (New York: Hawk's Well Press, 1958), p. 9-11.
5. Rainer Maria Rilke, *Letters to a Young Poet*, M. D. Herter Norton (trans.) (New York: W. W. Norton & Company, Inc., 1954), p. 35. Reprinted by permission of the publisher.
6. Rilke, *Letters to a Young Poet*, p. 35.
7. Parker J. Palmer, *The Promise of Paradox: A celebration of contradictions in the Christian life* (Washington, D.C.: The

Servant Leadership School, 1993), p. 39. Reprinted by permission of the author.
8. Palmer, *The Promise of Paradox: A celebration of contradictions in the Christian life*, p. 39.
9. Palmer, *The Promise of Paradox: A celebration of contradictions in the Christian life*, p. 54.
10. Palmer, *The Promise of Paradox: A celebration of contradictions in the Christian life*, p. 90.
11. Robert Frost, E. C. Lathem (ed.), *The Poetry of Robert Frost* (New York: Holt, Rinehart and Winston, 1969), p. 277.
12. Charles Dickens, *A Tale of Two Cities* (New York: Dodd, Mead & Company, Inc., 1942), p. 3.
13. Lao Tsu, Gia-Fu Feng & Jane English (trans.), *Tao Te Ching* (New York: Vintage, 1989), p. 66.
14. Rilke, *Letters to a Young Poet*, p. 35.

Chapter 7 – Know Thyself
(Pages 95-109)

1. Jelaluddin Rumi, Coleman Barks (trans.), *The Essential Rumi* (San Francisco: Harper SanFrancisco, 1995), p. 36. Reprinted by permission.
2. Joseph Campbell, Diane K. Osbon (ed.), *A Joseph Campbell Companion: Reflections on the Art of Living* (New York: HarperPerennial, 1995), p. 96.
3. Gordon Lawrence, *People Types and Tiger Stripes* (Gainesville, FL: Center for Applications in Psychological Type, Inc., 1993), p. 14.
4. Don Richard Riso, *Discovering Your Personality Type: The New Enneagram Questionnaire* (New York: Houghton Mifflin, 1995), p. 78.
5. Lawrence, *People Types and Tiger Stripes*, p. A-16.
6. Paul D. Tieger and Barbara Barron-Tieger, *Do What You Are: Discover the Perfect Career for You Through the Secrets of Personality Type* (Boston, MA: Little & Brown and Co., 1995), pp. 184-186.
7. Tieger and Barron-Tieger, *Do What You Are: Discover the Perfect Career for You Through the Secrets of Personality Type*, pp. 183-184.

8. Arthur F. Miller and Ralph T. Mattson, *The Truth About You* (Berkeley, CA: Ten Speed Press, 1989), pp. 29-33.
9. Parker J. Palmer, *Let Your Life Speak* (San Francisco: Jossey-Bass, 2000), p. 21. Reprinted by permission of the publisher.
10. Palmer, *Let Your Life Speak*, p. 25.
11. Palmer, *Let Your Life Speak*, p. 74.
12. Palmer, *Let Your Life Speak*, p. 76.
13. Palmer, *Let Your Life Speak,* p. 78.
14. Palmer, *Let Your Life Speak,* p. 84.
15. Joseph Campbell, *The Hero with a Thousand Faces* (Princeton, NJ: Princeton University Press, 1949), p. 337.
16. John L. Brown and Cerylle A. Moffet, *The Hero's Journey: How Educators Can Transform Schools and Improve Learning* (Alexandria, VA: Association for Supervision and Curriculum Development, July 1999), p. 92. Reprinted by permission of the publisher.
17. Brown and Moffet, *The Hero's Journey: How Educators Can Transform Schools and Improve Learning*, p. 92.

Chapter 8 – From Scarcity to Abundance
(Pages 110-128)

1. Thich Nhat Hahn, *Living Buddha, Living Christ* (New York: Riverhead Books, 1995), p. 86.
2. Marge Piercy, "The Low Road," in *The Moon is Always Female* (New York: Knopf, 1980), p. 44.

Chapter 9 – Chili, Served Hot
(Pages 129-150)

1. Mahatma Gandhi, *Non-Violence in Peace and War, Vol. II* (Ahmedabad, India: Navajivan Publishing House, 1948).
2. Parker J. Palmer, *A Movement Approach to Social Change: The Model* (An unpublished outline for the Fetzer Institute, dated 11/12/92). Five attributes out of eight are reprinted from the movement model's "Stage I. Divided No

More" and "Stage II. Communities of Support." For a readily available resource, see Palmer's *The Courage to Teach: Exploring the Inner Landscape of a Teacher's Life* (San Francisco: Jossey-Bass Publishers, 1998), pp. 163-183.
3. Jennifer James from my notes of a keynote address to Michigan Association of Computer Users in Learning (MACUL) annual conference. Date unknown.
4. Saul D. Alinsky, *Rules for Radicals: A Pragmatic Primer for Realistic Radicals* (New York: Vintage Books, 1989), p. 42.
5. Nelson Mandela, South Africa presidential inaugural address, May 9, 1994.
6. Mahatma Gandhi, Thomas Merton (ed.), *Gandhi on Non-Violence* (New York: New Directions, 1965), p. 7.
7. Matthew 12:25, *The Open Bible*, The New King James Version, expanded edition (New York: Thomas Nelson Publishers, 1983), p. 985.
8. Ernest Hemingway, *A Moveable Feast* (New York: Scribner, 1964), p. 12.
9. Jerry B. Harvey, *The Abilene Paradox and Other Meditations on Management* (New York: Lexington Books, 1988), pp. 13-36.
10. E. F. Schumacher, *A Guide for the Perplexed* (New York: Harper and Row, 1977), p. 84.
11. Seymour Sarason, *The Predictable Failure of Educational Reform: Can We Change Course Before It's Too Late?* (San Francisco: Jossey-Bass, 1990), p. 78. Reprinted by permission of the publisher.
12. Pages 29-30. Reprinted by permission of the publisher. From *Stewardship: Choosing Service Over Self-Interest,* copyright ©1996 by Peter Block, Berrett-Koehler Publishers, Inc., San Francisco, CA. All rights reserved. www.bkconnection.com.
13. Robert Kelley, *The Power of Followership: How to Create Leaders People Want to Follow and Followers Who Lead Themselves* (New York: Currency Books, 1992), p. 175.
14. Peter Senge, et al, *The Fifth Discipline Fieldbook: Strategies and Tools for Building a Learning Organization* (New York: Currency Books, 1994), pp. 14-15.
15. Lowell Ganz and Babaloo Mandel (screenplay), Ron Howard (director) *Gung Ho* (TM & Copyright © 1986 Paramount Pictures), http://homevideo.paramount.com.

16. Jerry B. Harvey, *The Abilene Paradox* training film is based on the first chapter in Harvey's book *The Abilene Paradox and Other Meditations on Management* (Carlsbad, CA: CRM Learning) http://www.crmlearning.com.
17. Ganz and Mandel, *Gung Ho*.
18. Ganz and Mandel, *Gung Ho*.
19. Ganz and Mandel, *Gung Ho*.
20. Ganz and Mandel, *Gung Ho*.

Chapter 10 – Hanging by a Thread
(Pages 151-168)

1. John Donne, "Meditation XVII," *Devotions Upon Emergent Occasions*.
2. Rainer Maria Rilke, Stephen Mitchell (trans. & ed.), *The Selected Poetry of Rainer Maria Rilke* (New York: Vintage Books, 1989), p. 245.
3. Albert Brooks (writer and director), *Defending Your Life* (Warner Bros. Pictures, Inc., 1991), http://www2.warnerbros.com.
4. Parker J. Palmer, *A Movement Approach to Social Change: The Model* (An unpublished outline for the Fetzer Institute, dated 11/12/92). Two attributes out of four are reprinted from the movement model's "Stage II. Communities of Support." For a readily available resource, see Palmer's *The Courage to Teach: Exploring the Inner Landscape of a Teacher's Life* (San Francisco: Jossey-Bass Publishers, 1998), pp. 163-183.
5. Bruce Wayne Tuckman. "Developmental sequence in small groups," *Psychological Bulletin,* (Washington, DC: American Psychological Association, 1965), Vol. 63, pp. 384-399.
6. James Autry, *Love and Profit: The Art of Caring Leadership* (New York: Avon Books, 1994), p. 29.
7. Autry, *Love and Profit: The Art of Caring Leadership,* p. 31.
8. Jelaluddin Rumi, Coleman Barks (trans.), *The Essential Rumi* (San Francisco: Harper SanFrancisco, 1995), p. 111. Reprinted by permission.

Chapter 11 – The Last Straw
(Pages 169-185)

1. Margaret J. Wheatley, *Leadership and the New Science: Learning About Organization from an Orderly Universe* (San Francisco: Berrett-Koehler, 1994), p. 54.
2. To learn more about this group of dedicated facilitators and their organization, go to http://www.futuresearch.net/network/whatis/index.cfm
3. Kurt Lewin, Gertrude W. Lewin (ed.), *Resolving Social Conflicts; Selected Papers on Group Dynamics* (New York: Harper & Row, 1948), p 82.
4. Robert Fritz, *The Path of Least Resistance: Learning to Become the Creative Force in Your Own Life* (New York: Fawcett Columbine, 1989), p. 31.
5. See Claes Janssen's site, http://www.claesjanssen.com/four-rooms/about-the-four-rooms-of-change/index.shtml
6. Mary Oliver, "The Summer Day," in *New and Selected Poems* (Boston: Beacon Press, 1992), p. 94.
7. Marge Piercy, "Councils," from *Circles on the Water: Selected Poems of Marge Piercy* (New York: Knopf, 1982) p. 116.
8. Marge Piercy, "The seven of pentacles" (a poem within the suite of 11 poems based on cards of the Tarot deck), from *Circles on the Water: Selected Poems of Marge Piercy* (New York: Knopf, 1982) p. 128.

Chapter 12 – Minuteman
(Pages 186-202)

1. Sigmund Freud, *Civilization and its Discontents* (London: Hogarth Press, 1939).
2. Ernest Becker, *Escape from Evil* (New York: The Free Press, 1975), p. 11.
3. Carl Jung, "After Catastrophe," in *Collected Works,* Vol. 10 (Princeton, NJ: Bollingen, 1970), p. 203.
4. Becker, *Escape from Evil,* p. 95.
5. Becker, *Escape from Evil,* p. 35.

6. Becker, *Escape from Evil,* p. 35.
7. Diane Ackerman, *A Natural History of the Senses* (New York: Vintage Books, 1995), p. 229.
8. Parker J. Palmer. "Reflections on a Program for 'The Formation of Teachers,'" an occasional paper of the Fetzer Institute, also found on The Center for Courage & Renewal website, http://www.couragerenewal.org/?q=resources/writings/reflection.
9. St. John of the Cross, Mirabai Starr (trans.) *Dark Night Of The Soul* (New York: Riverhead Books, 2002), p. 159.
10. Jean Vanier, *From Brokenness to Community* (New York: Paulist Press, 1992), p. 6.
11. Vanier, *From Brokenness to Community,* p. 23.
12. Vanier, *From Brokenness to Community,* pp. 26-28.
13. retold from Kosho Uchiyama, *Opening the Hand of Thought* (New York: Penguin, 1993). Also see Jean Smith (ed.) *365 Zen: Daily Readings* (San Francisco: HarperSanFrancisco, 1999), p. 33.

Chapter 13 – Pendle Hill: An Experiment Living in Community
(Pages 203-219)

1. Friends Worship, I have been unable to find the source of this work.
2. I am indebted to Bobbi Kelly of Pendle Hill for arranging the interviews with community members.

Chapter 14 – But Seek the Welfare of the City
(Pages 220-235)

1. Sandra Cronk, *Gospel Order: A Quaker Understanding of Faithful Church Community (Pamphlet 297)* (Wallingford, PA: Pendle Hill Publications, 1991), p. 8. Reprinted by permission of Pendle Hill Publications, Wallingford, PA.
2. Severyn T. Bruyn, *Quaker Testamonies & Economic Alternatives (Pamphlet 231)* (Wallingford, PA: Pendle Hill Publications, 1980), back cover. Reprinted by permission of Pendle Hill Publications, Wallingford, PA.
3. Jeremiah 29:7, *The Holy Bible* (NRSV).

Chapter 15 – Deep Respect and Courage
(Pages 236-247)

1. Marvin Weisbord, Productive *Workplaces: Organizing and Managing for Dignity, Meaning and Community* (San Francisco: Jossey-Bass, 1987). As the subtitle implies, as well as the first eight chapters of the book, Weisbord's study of five workplace innovators has reinforced his belief that we all seek dignity, meaning and community.
2. Pages 238-241. Reprinted by permission of the publisher. From *Stewardship: Choosing Service Over Self-Interest,* copyright ©1996 by Peter Block, Berrett-Koehler Publishers, Inc., San Francisco, CA. All rights reserved. www.bkconnection.com.
3. For an in-depth look at totalitarianism, see Earl Shorris, *The Oppressed Middle: Politics of Middle Management, Scenes from Corporate Life* (Garden City, New York: Anchor/Doubleday, 1981).
4. Shorris, *The Oppressed Middle*, p. 11.
5. Paulo Freire, *Pedagogy of the Oppressed* (New York: Continuum, 1998), p. 30.
6. For an explanation of movements, see Parker J. Palmer, *The Courage to Teach: Exploring the Inner Landscape of a Teacher's Life* (San Francisco: Jossey-Bass, 1998), pp. 163-183.
7. Freire, *Pedagogy of the Oppressed,* p. 26.
8. Freire, *Pedagogy of the Oppressed,* p. 132.
9. David Huddle, *La Tour Dreams of the Wolf Girl* (Boston, MA: Houghton Mifflin, 2002), pp. 61-62.
10. Joseph Campbell with Bill Moyers, *The Power of Myth* (New York: Anchor Books, 1988), p. 186.
11. Arthur F. Miller and Ralph T. Mattson, *The Truth About You* (Berkeley, CA: Ten Speed Press, 1989), p. xii.
12. Studs Terkel, *Working: People Talk About What They Do All Day and How They Feel About What They Do* (New York: Ballantine, 1974), p. xiii.

Chapter 16 – Come Unity
(Pages 248-261)

1. *The Hidden Ground of Love: The Letters of Thomas Merton on Religious and Social Concerns* by Thomas Merton, edited by

William Shannon (New York: Farrar, Straus and Giroux, Copyright 1985 by the Merton Legacy Trust), p. 294.
2. Susan J. Rosenholtz, *Teacher's Workplace: The Social Organization of Schools* (White Plains, New York: Longman, 1989), p. 3.
3. Jeremiah 29:7, *The Holy Bible* (NRSV).
4. Rosenholtz, *Teacher's Workplace: The Social Organization of Schools,* p. 219.
5. Bob Filipczak, "Weathering Change: Enough Already!" *Training,* September 1994, p. 23.
6. Eric Hoffer, *The Ordeal of Change* (New York: Harper & Row, 1967), p. 3.
7. George Lucas (story), Leigh Brackett and Lawrence Kasdan (screenplay), Irvin Kershner (director) *Star Wars: Episode V – The Empire Strikes Back* (© Lucasfilm Ltd. & ™.) Used under authorization.
8. Lucas, Brackett and Kasdan, *Star Wars: Episode V – The Empire Strikes Back.*
9. Lucas, Brackett and Kasdan, *Star Wars: Episode V – The Empire Strikes Back.*
10. Lowell Ganz and Babaloo Mandel (screenplay), Ron Howard (director) *Gung Ho* (™ & Copyright © 1986 Paramount Pictures), http://homevideo.paramount.com.

Bibliography

Ackerman, Diane. *A Natural History of the Senses.* New York: Vintage Books, 1995.

Ackerman, Laurence D. *Identity is Destiny: Leadership and the Roots of Value Creation.* San Francisco: Berrett-Koehler, 2000.

Alcott, Louisa May. *Transcendental Wild Oats and Excerpts from the Fruitland Diaries.* Harvard, MA: Harvard Common Press, 1975.

Alinsky, Saul D. *Rules for Radicals: A Pragmatic Primer for Realistic Radicals.* New York: Vintage Books, 1989.

Argyris, Chris. *Overcoming Organizational Defenses: Facilitating Organizational Learning.* Boston, MA: Allyn and Bacon, 1990.

Autry, James A. *Life & Work: A Manager's Search for Meaning.* New York: Avon Books, 1994.

Autry, James A. *Love and Profit: The Art of Caring Leadership.* New York: Avon Books, 1991.

Badaracco, Joseph L., Jr. *Defining Moments: When Managers Must Choose between Right and Right.* Boston, MA: Harvard Business School Press, 1997.

Baldwin, Christina. *Calling the Circle: The First and Future Culture.* Newberg, OR: Swan Raven and Company, 1994.

Barker, Joel Arthur. *Future Edge: Discovering the New Paradigms of Success.* New York: William Morrow and Company, Inc., 1992.

Barth, Roland. *Improving Schools from Within: Teachers, Parents and Principals Can Make the Difference.* San Francisco, Jossey-Bass, 1990.

Becker, Ernest. *Escape from Evil.* New York: The Free Press, 1975.

Becker, Ernest. *The Denial of Death.* New York: The Free Press, 1973.

Bellah, Robert N., et al. *Habits of the Heart.* Berkeley, CA: University of California Press, 1996.

Block, Peter. *Stewardship: Choosing Service Over Self-Interest.* San Francisco: Berrett-Koehler, 1996.

Block, Peter. *The Answer to How is Yes: Acting on What Matters.* San Francisco: Berrett-Koehler, 2002.

Block, Peter. *The Empowered Manager: Positive Political Skills at Work.* San Francisco: Jossey-Bass, 1987.

Bly, Robert. *A Little Book on the Human Shadow.* San Francisco: HarperSanFrancisco, 1988.

Bohm, David. *On Dialogue.* New York: Routledge, 1996.

Bolles, Richard N. *How to Find Your Mission in Life.* Berkeley, CA: Ten Speed Press, 1991.

Bolman, Lee G., Terrence E. Deal. *Leading with Soul: An Uncommon Journey of Spirit.* San Francisco: Jossey-Bass, 1995.

Bonhoeffer, Dietrich. *Life Together.* San Francisco: HarperSanFrancisco, 1954.

Bonstingl, John Jay. *Schools of Quality: An Introduction to Total Quality Management in Education.* Thousand Oaks, CA: Corwin Press, 2001.

Boyett, Joseph, Jimmie Boyett. *The Guru Guide: The Best Ideas of the Top Management Thinkers.* New York: John Wiley & Sons, 1998.

Bridges, William. *Making Sense of Transitions: Strategies for Coping with the Difficult, Painful, and Confusing Times in Your Life.* Reading, MA: Perseus Books, 1980.

Bridges, William. *Managing Transitions: Making the Most of Change.* Reading, MA: Addison-Wesley, 1991.

Brooks, Albert (writer and director). *Defending Your Life.* Warner Bros. Pictures, Inc., 1991.

Brooks, Mel, Carl Reiner. *The 2000 Year Old Man in the Year 2000.* Rhino Records. 1997.

Brown, John L., Cerylle A. Moffett. *The Hero's Journey: How Educators Can Transform Schools and Improve Learning.* Alexandria, VA: Association for Supervision and Curriculum Development, 1999.

Buber, Martin, Ronald Gregor Smith, trans. *I and Thou.* New York: Scribner, 1987.

Buber, Martin, David Antin & Jerome Rothenberg, trans. *Tales of Angels, Spirits, and Demons.* New York: Hawk's Well Press, 1958.

Bruyn, Severyn T. *Quaker Testamonies & Economic Alternatives.* Pendle Hill Pamphlet #231. Wallingford: PA. Pendle Hill Publications, 1980.

Burns, James MacGregor. *Leadership.* Harper & Row, 1978.

Cameron, Julia. *The Artist's Way: A Spiritual Path to Higher Creativity.* New York: Putnam's Sons, 1992.

Campbell, Joseph, Diane K. Osbon, ed. *A Joseph Campbell Companion: Reflections on the Art of Living.* New York: HarperPerennial, 1995.

Campbell, Joseph. *The Hero with a Thousand Faces.* Princeton, NJ: Princeton University Press, 1949.

Campbell, Joseph, Bill Moyers. *The Power of Myth*. New York: Anchor Books, 1988.

Cervantes, Miguel de, *Don Quixote*. (http://en.wikisource/wiki/Don_Quixote/

Chaleff, Ira. *The Courageous Follower: Standing Up To and For Our Leaders*. San Francisco: Berrett-Koehler, 1998.

Chappell, Tom. *The Soul of a Business: Managing for Profit and the Common Good*. New York: Bantam, 1994.

Ciulla, Joanne B. *The Working Life: The Promise and Betrayal of Modern Work*. New York: Three Rivers Press, 2000.

Cohen, Don, Laurence Prusack. *In Good Company: How Social Capital Makes Organizations Work*. Boston, MA: Harvard Business School Press, 2001.

Collins, James C., Jerry I. Porras. *Built to Last: Successful Habits of Visionary Companies*. New York: HarperBusiness, 1997.

Collins, Jim. *Good to Great: Why Some Companies Make the Leap...and Others Don't*. New York: HarperBusiness, 2001.

Cooper, David A. *Silence, Simplicity, and Solitude: a Guide for Spiritual Retreat*. New York: Bell Tower, 1992.

Cronk, Sandra L. *Gospel Order: A Quaker Understanding of Faithful Church Community*. Pendle Hill Pamphlet #297. Wallingford, PA: Pendle Hill Publications, 1991.

Cuban, Larry. *The Managerial Imperative and the Practice of Leadership in Schools*. Albany, NY: State University of New York Press, 1988.

Cudney, Milton R., Ph.D., Robert E. Hardy, Ed.D. *Self-Defeating Behaviors: Free Yourself from the Habits, Compulsions, Feelings, and Attitudes That Hold You Back*. San Francisco: HarperSanFrancisco, 1991.

de Bono, Edward. *Six Action Shoes*. New York: HarperBusiness, 1991.

de Bono, Edward. *Six Thinking Hats*. Boston, MA: Little, Brown and Co., 1985.

De Geus, Arie. *The Living Company: Habits for survival in a turbulent business environment*. Boston, MA: Harvard Business School Press, 1997.

Dickens, Charles. *A Tale of Two Cities*. New York: Dodd, Mead & Company, Inc., 1942.

DePree, Max. *Leadership is an Art*. New York: Dell, 1989.

Dillard, Annie. *Teaching A Stone To Talk: Expeditions And Encounters*. New York: Harper & Row, 1982.

Dolan, W. Patrick. *Restructuring Our School: A Primer on Systemic Change*. Leawood, Kansas: Systems & Organization, 1994.

Donne, John. *Devotions Upon Emergent Occasions*. http://www.anglicanlibrary.org/donne/devotions/devotions17.htm

Doyle, Michael, David Straus. *How to Make Meetings Work*. New York: Jove, 1982.

Erikson, Erik H. *The Life Cycle Completed*. New York: W. W. Norton, 1985.

Evans, Robert. *The Human Side of School Change: Reform, Resistance, and the Real-Life Problems of Innovation*. San Francisco: Jossey-Bass, 2001.

Ferguson, Marilyn. *The Aquarian Conspiracy: Personal and Social Transformation in Our Time*. Los Angeles, CA: Jeremy Tarcher, 1987.

Filipczak, Bob. "Weathering change: enough already!" *Training*, September 1994.

Fisher, Roger, William Ury. *Getting to Yes: Negotiating Agreement Without Giving In*. New York: Penguin, 1983.

Fletcher, Jerry, Kelle Olwyler. *Paradoxical Thinking: How to Profit from your Contradictions*. San Francisco: Berrett-Koehler, 1997.

Foster, Jack. *How to Get Ideas*. San Francisco: Berrett-Koehler, 1996.

Freire, Paulo. *Pedagogy of the Oppressed*. New York: Continuum, 1998.

Freud, Sigmund. *Civilization and its Discontents*. London: Hogarth Press, 1939.

Fritz, Robert. *The Path of Least Resistance: Learning to Become the Creative Force in Your Own Life*. New York: Fawcett Columbine, 1989.

Frost, Rober, E. C. Lathem, edit. *The Poetry of Robert Frost*. New York: Holt, Rinehart and Winston, 1969.

Gandhi, Mahatma, *Non-Violence in Peace and War*. Ahmedabad: Navajivan Publishing House, 1948.

Gandhi, Mahatma, Thomas Merton ed. *Gandhi on Non-Violence*. New York: New Directions, 1965.

Ganz, Lowell and Babaloo Mandel (screenplay), Ron Howard (director). *Gung Ho*. TM & Copyright © 1986 Paramount Pictures.

Gilbert, Roberta M. M.D. *Extraordinary Relationships: A New Way of Thinking About Human Interactions*. New York: John Wiley & Sons, 1992.

Golding, William. *Lord of the Flies.* New York: Capricorn Books, 1959.

Grant, Jim, Char Forsten. *If You're Riding a Horse and It Dies, Get Off.* Peterborough, NH: Crystal Springs Books, 1999.

Greenleaf, Robert K. *Servant Leadership: A Journey into the Nature of Legitimate Power and Greatness.* Mahwah, NJ: Paulist Press, 1991.

Hamm, Thomas. *God's Government Begun: The Society for Universal Inquiry and Reform, 1842-1846.* Bloomington, IN: Indiana University Press, 1995.

Handy, Charles. *The Age of Paradox.* Boston, MA: Harvard Business School Press, 1995.

Handy, Charles. *The Age of Unreason.* Boston, MA: Harvard Business School Press, 1990.

Harvey, Jerry B. *How Come Every Time I Get Stabbed in the Back My Fingerprints Are on the Knife? And Other Meditations on Management.* San Francisco: Jossey-Bass, 1999.

Harvey, Jerry B. *The Abilene Paradox and Other Meditations on Management.* New York: Lexington Books, 1988.

Harvey, Jerry B. *The Abilene Paradox* (film). Carlsbad, CA: CRM Learning.

Hawken, Paul. *Growing a Business.* New York: Fireside Books, 1987.

Hemingway, Ernest. *A Moveable Feast.* New York: Scribner, 1964.

Henderson, Anne T., et al. *Beyond the Bake Sale: An Educator's Guide to Working with Parents.* Washington, D.C.: National Committee for Citizens in Education, 1991.

Hesse, Hermann. *The Journey to the East.* New York: The Noonday Press, 1968.

Hock, Dee. *Birth of the Chaordic Age.* San Francisco: Berrett-Koehler, 1999.

Hoffer, Eric. *The Ordeal of Change.* New York: Harper & Row, 1967.

Homer. *The Odyssey.* New York: Bantam Books, 1962.

Huddle, David. *La Tour Dreams of the Wolf Girl.* Boston, MA: Houghton Mifflin, 2002.

Hyde, Lewis. *The Gift: Imagination and the Erotic Life of Property.* New York: Vintage Books, 1983.

Johnson, Barry, Ph.D. *Polarity Management: Identifying and Managing Unsolvable Problems.* Amherst, MA: HRD Press, 1996.

Joyce, Bruce, James Wolf, Emily Calhoun. *The Self-Renewing School.* Alexandria, VA: Association for Supervision and Curriculum Development, 1993.

Jung, Carl. *Collected Works, Vol. 10,* Princeton, NJ: Bollingen, 1970.

Kauffman, Draper L., Jr. *Systems One: An Introduction to Systems Thinking.* Minneapolis, MN: S.A. Carlton, 1980.

Kelley, Robert. *The Power of Followership: How to Create Leaders People Want to Follow and Followers Who Lead Themselves.* New York: Currency Books, 1992.

Kidder, Tracy. *The Soul of a New Machine.* New York: Avon, 1981.

Kim, Daniel H. *Systems Archetypes 1.* Waltham, MA: Pegasus Communications, Inc., 1994.

Koestenbaum, Peter, Peter Block. *Freedom and Accountability at Work: Applying Philosophic Insight to the Real World.* San Francisco: Jossey-Bass, 2001.

Koestenbaum, Peter. *Leadership: The Inner Side of Greatness, a Philosophy for Leaders.* San Francisco, Jossey-Bass, 2002.

Kotter, John P. *Leading Change.* Boston, MA: Harvard Business School Press, 1996.

Kubler-Ross, Elisabeth, M.D. *On Death and Dying: What the dying have to teach doctors, nurses, clergy, and their own families.* New York: Touchstone, 1997.

Kuhn, Thomas S. *The Structure of Scientific Revolutions.* Chicago: University of Chicago Press, 1996.

Kurtz, Ernest, Katherine Ketcham. *The Spirituality of Imperfection: Storytelling and the Journey to Wholeness.* New York: Bantam Books, 1994.

Lamott, Anne. *Bird by Bird: Some Instructions on Writing and Life.* New York: Anchor Books, 1995.

Land, George, Beth Jarman. *Breakpoint and Beyond: Mastering the Future Today.* New York: Leadership 2000 Press, 1992.

Lawrence, Brother. *The Practice of the Presence of God.* Brewster, MA: Paraclete Press, 1985.

Lawrence, Gordon. *People Types and Tiger Stripes.* Gainesville, FL: Center for Applications in Psychological Type, Inc., 1993.

Lazear, David. *Seven Ways of Knowing: Understanding Multiple Intelligences.* Palantine, IL: Skylight Publishing, 1991.

Leman, Dr. Kevin. *The New Birth Order Book: Why You Are the Way You Are.* Grand Rapids, MI: Fleming H. Revell, 1998.

Levinson, Daniel J. et al. *The Seasons of a Man's Life.* New York: Ballantine, 1978.

Lewin, Kurt, Gertrude W. Lewin, ed. *Resolving Social Conflicts; Selected Papers on Group Dynamics.* New York: Harper & Row, 1948.

Lipsitz, Joan. *Successful Schools for Young Adolescents*. New Brunswick, NJ: Transaction Books, 1984.

Lucas, George (story), Leigh Brackett and Lawrence Kasdan (screenplay), Irvin Kershner (director). *Star Wars: Episode V – The Empire Strikes Back*. © Lucasfilm Ltd. & ™.

Lulic, Margaret A. *Who We Could Be at Work*. Boston, MA: Butterworth-Heinemann, 1996.

Machiavelli, Niccolo. *The Prince*. New York: Bantam Books, 1981.

Marcic, Dorothy. *Managing with the Wisdom of Love: Uncovering Virtue in People and Organizations*. San Francisco: Jossey-Bass, 1997.

McCullough, Donald. *Say Please, Say Thank You: The Respect We Owe One Another*. New York: Perigree, 1998.

Meadows, Donella H. *Global Citizen*. Washington, D.C.: Island Press, 1991.

Merton, Thomas, William Shannon, ed. *The Hidden Ground of Love: The Letters of Thomas Merton on Religious and Social Concerns*. New York: Farrar, Straus and Giroux, 1985.

Merton, Thomas. *The Way of Chuang Tzu*. New York: New Directions, 1969.

Miller, Arthur F., Ralph T. Mattson. *The Truth About You*. Berkeley, CA: Ten Speed Press, 1989.

Mindell, Arnold. *Sitting in the Fire: Large Group Transformation Using Conflict and Diversity*. Portland, OR: Lao Tse Press, 1995.

Minton, Lynn. "Fresh Voices," *PARADE Magazine*, New York: PARADE Publications, Inc., July 24, 1994.

Mitroff, Ian I., Elizabeth A. Denton. *A Spiritual Audit of Corporate America: A Hard Look at Spirituality, Religion, and Values in the Workplace*. San Francisco: Jossey-Bass, 1999.

Morely, Barry. *Beyond Consensus: Salvaging Sense of the Meeting*. Wallingford, PA: Pendle Hill Pamphlet #307, Pendle Hill Publications, 1993.

Naisbitt, John. *Global Paradox*. New York: Avon Books, 1994.

Nhat Hanh, Thich. *Being Peace*. Berkeley, CA: Parallax Press, 2005.

Nhat Hanh, Thich. *Peace is Every Step: The Path of Mindfulness in Everyday Life*. New York: Bantam Books, 1992.

Nhat Hanh, Thich. *Living Buddha, Living Christ*. New York: Riverhead Books, 1995.

Noddings, Nel. *The Challenge to Care in Schools: An Alternative Approach to Education*. New York: Teachers College Press, 1992.

Nouwen, Henri. *In the Name of Jesus – Reflections on Christian Leadership*. NY: Crossroad, 1996.
Nuland, Sherwin B. *How We Die: Reflections on Life's Final Chapter*. New York: Vintage Books, 1995.
O'Connor, Elizabeth. *Cry Pain, Cry Hope: A Guide to the Dimensions of Call*. Washington, D.C.: The Servant Leadership School, 1987.
O'Connor, Elizabeth. *Eighth Day of Creation: Discovering Your Gifts*. Washington, D.C.: The Servant Leadership School, 1971.
O'Connor, Elizabeth. *Journey Inward, Journey Outward*. New York HarperCollins, 1975.
O'Connor, Elizabeth. *Servant Leaders, Servant Structures*. Washington, D.C.: The Servant Leadership School, 1991.
Oliver, Mary. *New and Selected Poems*. Boston: Beacon Press, 1992.
Oshry, Barry. *Leading Systems: Lessons from the Power Lab*. San Francisco: Berrett-Koehler, 1999.
Oshry, Barry. *Seeing Systems: Unlocking the Mysteries of Organizational Life*. San Francisco: Berrett-Koehler, 1996.
Owen, Harrison. *Open Space Technology: A User's Guide*. San Francisco: Berrett-Koehler, 2000.
Owen, Harrison. *The Power of Spirit: How Organizations Transform*. San Francisco: Berrett-Koehler, 2000.
Palmer, Parker J. *A Movement Approach to Social Change: The Model*. Unpublished outline for the Fetzer Institute, 11/12/92.
Palmer, Parker J. *A Place Called Community*. Wallingford, PA: Pendle Hill Publications, 1977.
Palmer, Parker J. *Leading From Within: Reflections on Spirituality and Leadership*. Washington, D.C.: The Servant Leadership School, 1990.
Palmer, Parker J. *Let Your Life Speak: Listening to the Voice of Vocation*. San Francisco: Jossey-Bass, 2000.
Palmer, Parker J. "Reflections on a Program for 'The Formation of Teachers,'" http://www.couragerenewal.org/?=resources/writings/reflection
Palmer, Parker J. *The Active Life: Wisdom for Work, Creativity and Caring*. New York: HarperCollins, 1990.
Palmer, Parker J. *The Courage to Teach: Exploring the Inner Landscape of a Teacher's Life*. San Francisco: Jossey-Bass, 1998.
Palmer, Parker J. *The Promise of Paradox: A celebration of contradictions in the Christian life*. Washington, D.C.: The Servant Leadership School, 1993.

Palmer, Parker J. *To Know As We Are Known: Education as a Spiritual Journey*. San Francisco: HarperCollins, 1993.
Parker, Marjorie. *Creating Shared Vision*. Clarendon Hills, IL: Dialog International, Ltd., 1990.
Pearson, Carol S. *Awakening the Heroes Within: Twelve Archetypes to Help Us Find Ourselves and Transform Our World*. San Francisco: HarperSanFrancisco, 1991.
Persig, Robert M. *Zen and the Art of Motorcycle Maintenance: An Inquiry into Values*. New York: Quill/William Morrow, 1979.
Peters, Thomas J., Robert H. Waterman, Jr. *In Search of Excellence: Lessons from America's Best-Run Companies*. New York: Warner Books, 1982.
Piercy, Marge. *Circles on the Water: Selected Poems of Marge Piercy*. New York: Knopf, 1982.
Piercy, Marge. *The Moon is Always Female*. New York: Knopf, 1980.
Putnam, Robert D. *Bowling Alone: The Collapse and Revival of American Community*. New York: Touchstone, 2000.
Putnam, Robert D., et al. *Better Together: Restoring the American Community*. New York: Simon and Schuster, 2003.
Quinn, Daniel. *Ishmael: An Adventure of the Mind and Spirit*. New York: Bantam Books, 1995.
Raffel, Burton, trans. *Beowulf*. New York: Mentor, 1963.
Richards, Dick. *Artful Work: Awakening Joy, Meaning, and Commitment in the Workplace*. New York: Berkley Books, 1997.
Richards, M.C. *Centering: In Pottery, Poetry, and the Person*. Hanover, NH: Wesleyan University Press, 1989.
Rilke, Rainer Maria, Stephen Mitchell ed. *The Selected Poetry of Rainer Maria Rilke*. New York: Vintage Books, 1989.
Rilke, Rainer Maria, M. D. Herter Norton, trans. *Letters to a Young Poet*. New York: Norton, 1954.
Riso, Don Richard, Russ Hudson. *Personality Types: Using the Enneagram for Self-Discovery*. New York: Houghton Mifflin, 1996.
Riso, Don Richard. *Discovering Your Personality Type: The New Enneagram Questionnaire*. New York: Houghton Mifflin, 1995.
Rogers, Everett M. *Diffusion of Innovations*. New York: The Free Press, 1983.
Rogers, Mary Beth. *Cold Anger: A Story of Faith and Power Politics*. Denton, TX: University of North Texas Press, 1990.
Rosenbluth, Hal F., Diane McFerrin Peters. *The Customer Comes Second and Other Secrets of Exceptional Service*. New York: William Morrow and Company, 1992.

Rosenholtz, Susan J. *Teacher's Workplace: The Social Organization of Schools.* White Plains, New York: Longman, 1989.

Rumi, Jelaluddin, Coleman Barks, trans. *The Essential Rumi,* San Francisco: Harper SanFrancisco, 1995.

Sarason, Seymour B. *The Predictable Failure of Educational Reform: Can We Change Course Before It's Too Late?* San Francisco: Jossey-Bass, 1990.

Sarton, May. *Selected Poems of May Sarton.* New York: W. W. Norton & Company, 1978.

Schaper, Donna. *A Book of Common Power: Narratives Against the Current.* San Diego, CA: LuraMedia, 1989.

Schumacher, E. F. *A Guide for the Perplexed.* New York: Harper and Row, 1977.

Schwartz, Peter. *The Art of the Long View.* New York: Currency Books, 1996.

Senge, Peter M. *The Fifth Discipline: The Art and Practice of the Learning Organization.* New York: Doubleday, 1990.

Senge, Peter, et al. *Schools That Learn: A Fifth Discipline Fieldbook for Educators, Parents, and Everyone Who Care About Education.* New York: Currency Books, 2000.

Senge, Peter, et al. *The Fifth Discipline Fieldbook: Strategies and Tools for Building a Learning Organization.* New York: Currency Books, 1994.

Shorris, Earl. *The Oppressed Middle: The Politics of Middle Management, Scenes from Corporate Life.* Garden City, New York: Anchor Press/Doubleday, 1981.

Sinetar, Marsha. *Do What You Love, The Money Will Follow: Discovering Your Right Livelihood.* New York: Dell, 1989.

Sinetar, Marsha. *To Build the Life You Want, Create the Work You Love: The Spiritual Dimension of Entrepreneuring.* New York: St. Martin's Press, 1995.

Sizer, Theodore R. *Horace's Compromise: The Dilemma of the American High School.* Boston, MA: Houghton Mifflin, 1985.

Smith, Jean, ed. *365 Zen: Daily Readings.* San Francisco: HarperSanFrancisco, 1999.

St. John of the Cross, Mirabai Starr, trans. *Dark Night Of The Soul.* New York: Riverhead Books, 2002.

Stein, Joseph (author), Jerry Bock (music), Sheldon Harnick (lyrics). *Fiddler on the Roof.* New York: Proscenium Publishers, 1964.

Sweeney, Linda Booth. *When a Butterfly Sneezes: A Guide for Helping Kids Explore Interconnections in Our World Through Favorite Stories.* Waltham, MA: Pegasus Communications, Inc., 2001.

Terkel, Studs. *Working: People Talk About What They Do All Day and How They Feel About What They Do.* New York: Ballantine, 1974.

Thompson, C. Michael. *The Congruent Life: Following the Inward Path to Fulfilling Work and Inspired Leadership.* San Francisco: Jossey-Bass, 2000.

Tieger, Paul D., Barbara Barron-Tieger. *Do What You Are: Discover The Perfect Career For You Through The Secrets Of Personality Type.* Boston, MA: Little & Brown and Co., 1995.

Tillick, Paul. *The Courage to Be.* New Haven, CN: Yale University Press, 1980.

Tuckman, Bruce. "Developmental sequence in small groups," *Psychological Bulletin,* 63, 384-399 (1965).

Tsu, Lao, Gia-Fu Feng & Jane English, trans. *Tao Te Ching.* New York: Vintage, 1989.

Uchiyama, Kosho. *Opening the Hand of Thought.* New York: Penguin, 1993.

Ueland, Brenda. *If You Want to Write: A Book about Art, Independence and Spirit.* Saint Paul, MN: Graywolf Press, 1987.

Underwood, Paula. *The Walking People: A Native American Oral History.* Bayfield, CO: Tribe of Two Press, 1994.

Vanier, Jean. *Community and Growth.* Mahwah, N.J.: Paulist Press, 1989.

Vanier, Jean. *From Brokenness to Community.* New York: Paulist Press, 1992.

Walton, Mary. *The Deming Management Method.* New York: Perigree Books, 1986.

Watkins, Jane Magruder, Bernard J. Mohr. *Appreciative Inquiry: Change at the Speed of Imagination.* San Francisco: Jossey-Bass, 2001.

Watzlawick, Paul, Ph.D., et al. *Change: Principles of Problem Formation and Problem Resolution.* New York: W.W. Norton, 1974.

Weisbord, Marvin R. *Productive Workplaces: Organizing and Managing for Dignity, Meaning and Community.* San Francisco: Jossey-Bass, 1987.

Weisbord, Marvin R., et al. *Discovering Common Ground: How Future Search Conferences Bring People Together to Achieve Breakthrough Innovation, Empowerment, Shared Vision, and Collaborative Action.* San Francisco: Berrett-Koehler, 1992.

Weisbord, Marvin R., Sandra Janoff. *Future Search: An Action Guide to Finding Common Ground in Organizations & Communities.* San Francisco: Berrett-Koehler, 1995.

Wheatley, Margaret J. *Leadership and the New Science: Learning About Organization from an Orderly Universe.* San Francisco: Berrett-Koehler, 1994.

Wheatley, Margaret J. *Turning to One Another: Simple Conversations to Restore Hope to the Future.* San Francisco: Berrett-Koehler, 1994.

Wheatley, Margaret J., Myron Kellner-Rogers. *A Simpler Way.* San Francisco: Berrett-Koehler, 1996.

Yalom, Irvin D. *The Theory and Practice of Group Psychotherapy.* New York: Basic Books, 1995.

About the Author

If vocation is about doing what you "can't not do," then Jack Bender's vocation is thinking, speaking, and writing about the workplace. This involves addressing the subjects of power, relationships and personal growth, among many others.

His formal workplace experiences include positions of US Army officer, prison music teacher, cashier, laborer, salesperson, DJ, computer programmer, musician, heavy equipment operator and public school teacher.

Bender currently speaks, writes and facilitates large group work as well as mediating a variety of conflict resolution cases. He holds a BME from Central Michigan University and a Specialist in Educational Leadership from Western Michigan University.

He has created award-winning educational software, written music lyrics and band arrangements, and published newspaper, journal and website articles on a wide variety of topics encompassing future search conferences, land use, computer technology, music, community, personal growth and motorcycling.

Bender has received the Army Commendation Medal, numerous concert and marching band awards, selected for the pilot program of The Courage to Teach and chosen as a competing finalist for the Christa McAuliffe Fellowship.

He resides with his wife Cindy in Zeeland, Michigan.

This page and page 289 are a continuation of the copyright page.

Excerpt from SCHOOLS OF QUALITY: AN INTRODUCTION TO TOTAL QUALITY MANAGEMENT IN EDUCATION by John Jay Bonstingl reprinted by permission of the author (www.Bonstingl.com). Published by Corwin Press, Thousand Oaks, California. Copyright ©2001.

Excerpt from THE DEMING MANAGEMENT METHOD by Mary Walton reprinted by permission of the author. Published by Perigree Books, New York. Copyright ©1986.

"The Woodcarver" by Thomas Merton, from THE WAY OF CHUANG TZU, copyright ©1965 by The Abbey of Gethsemani. Reprinted by permission of New Directions Publishing Corp.

Excerpts from LETTERS TO A YOUNG POET by Maria Rainer Rilke, Herter Norton translator. Copyright ©1954. Reprinted by permission of W. W. Norton & Company, Inc., New York.

Excerpt from A BOOK OF COMMON POWER: NARRATIVES AGAINST THE CURRENT by Donna Schaper reprinted by permission of the author. Published by LuraMedia, San Diego, CA. Copyright ©1989.

Excerpts from THE ESSENTIAL RUMI by Jelaluddin Rumi, Coleman Barks translator, reprinted by permission of Coleman Barks. Copyright ©1995. Published by Harper SanFrancisco, San Francisco, CA.

Excerpt from "Fresh Voices" by Lynn Minton, PARADE Magazine (July 24, 1994 edition) reprinted by permission of Parade Publications, New York. Copyright ©1994 Parade Publications. All rights reserved.

Excerpts from THE PROMISE OF PARADOX: A CELEBRATION OF CONTRADICTIONS IN THE CHRISTIAN LIFE by Parker J. Palmer reprinted by permission of the author. Originally published by The Servant Leadership School, Washington, D.C. Copyright ©1993.

Excerpts from LET YOUR LIFE SPEAK: LISTENING TO THE VOICE OF VOCATION by Parker J. Palmer. Copyright ©2000. Reprinted by permission of Jossey-Bass, Inc.

Excerpts from THE HERO'S JOURNEY: HOW EDUCATORS CAN TRANSFORM SCHOOLS AND IMPROVE LEARNING by John L. Brown and Cerylle A. Moffett, a July 1999 member book. Copyright ©1999 by the Association of Supervision and Curriculum Development. All rights reserved. Reprinted by Permission. The Association for Supervision and Curriculum Development is a worldwide community of educators advocating sound policies and sharing best practices to achieve the success of each learner. To learn more, visit ASCD at www.ascd.org.

Excerpt from THE PREDICTABLE FAILURE OF EDUCATIONAL REFORM: CAN WE CHANGE COURSE BEFORE IT'S TOO LATE? by Seymour B. Sarason. Copyright ©1990. Reprinted by permission of Jossey-Bass, Inc.

Excerpt from STEWARDSHIP: CHOOSING SERVICE OVER SELF-INTEREST by Peter Block. Copyright ©1996. Reprinted with permission of Berrett-Koehler Publishers, Inc., San Francisco, CA. All rights reserved. www.bkconnection.com.

Excerpt from GOSPEL ORDER: A QUAKER UNDERSTANDING OF FAITHFUL CHURCH COMMUNITY Pendle Hill Pamphlet #297 by Sandra L. Cronk. Copyright ©1991. Reprinted by permission of Pendle Hill Publications, Wallingford, PA.

Excerpt from QUAKER TESTAMONIES & ECONOMIC ALTERNATIVES Pendle Hill Pamphlet #231 by Severyn T. Bruyn. Copyright ©1980. Reprinted by permission of Pendle Hill Publications, Wallingford, PA.

Excerpts from STAR WARS: EPISODE V – THE EMPIRE STRIKES BACK © Lucasfilm Ltd. & ™. All rights reserved. Used under authorization.

To order *Disregarded*...

Best way – Submit your order at www.Inner–Work.com

Phone orders – 1-888-523-6337 Please have your credit card available.

Postal orders - InnerWork, 9182 Bluff Lake St., Zeeland, MI 49464

(Your contact information will not be shared.)

Name: _____

Address1: _____

Address2: _____

City: _____

State: _____ Zip Code: _____

Telephone: _____

Email address: _____

Please specify shipping choice (Single copy rate provided here):

_____ USPS Priority Mail (2-3 day delivery) $3.95

_____ USPS Media Mail (3-10 days, depending on distance) $1.95

Credit card company: _____

Card number: _____

Name on card: _____

Expiration date: _____

Security code: _____